© Jane Magellanic

THOMAS FRANK is the author of *The Wrecking Crew*, *What's the Matter with Kansas?*, and *One Market Under God*. A former opinion columnist for *The Wall Street Journal*, Frank is the founding editor of *The Baffler* and a monthly columnist for *Harper's*. He lives outside Washington, DC.

Also by Thomas Frank

The Wrecking Crew

What's the Matter with Kansas?

One Market Under God

The Conquest of Cool

Additional Praise for *Pity the Billionaire*

"No one fools Thomas Frank, who is the sharpest, funniest, most intellectually voracious political commentator on the scene. In *Pity the Billionaire* he has written a brilliant exposé of the most breathtaking ruse in American political history: how the Right turned the biggest capitalist breakdown since 1929 into an opportunity for themselves."
—Barbara Ehrenreich

"The question Frank goes on the road to investigate this time is: What the f**k is wrong with America? Short-sighted fiscal policies have tanked the economy Great Depression–style, millions are jobless, foreclosures are at record highs, and pizza has been declared a vegetable. Why aren't the adorable heads of the conservative-right wingdings behind much of the mess stuffed on pikes outside the White House? Is a good portion of the country suffering from Stockholm syndrome? Did somebody put something in our *tea*? What, pray tell, are the victims of these catastrophic policies thinking as they stand outside Arby's banging out 'She's a Grand Old Flag' on their tin cups? Read the book. Tom Frank, as ever, makes some wickedly clever observations and produces some surprising answers."   —Elissa Schappell, *Vanity Fair*

"*Pity the Billionaire* deserves to be read by Right and Left alike. . . . The thesis is provocative, and the book is witty and highly readable. It is also backed up by some revealing ethnography that Frank has collected after months of tracking the 'resurgent Right' across America. . . . A timely reminder that it is not just personalities that matter in the Republican contest; there are also some bigger shifts under way in America's social fabric."   —*Financial Times* (London)

"A road map for everyone who wonders, while watching the hodgepodge of Republican presidential candidates: How the heck did all this happen?" —*Fortune*

"A sobering account of how the architects of the economic downturn convinced a plurality of Americans that austerity, draconian budget cuts, zero regulation, refusing to tax the rich, and the withering away of the state is the answer to hard times." —*Pittsburgh Post-Gazette*

"Concisely detailed . . . Well researched . . . A must-read for the historians who will one day attempt to explain just what happened to the United States during the Great Recession. Step by painful step, Frank recounts the process by which the economy was subverted for private gain as the defense stood by watching. . . . Highly recommended." —*Seattle Post-Intelligencer*

"Depression-era populists invoked the Boston Tea Party as a rallying cry against corporate greed. Here, Thomas Frank lays out with biting wit how today's conservatives co-opted that symbol and forged a pseudopopulist front to defend the enablers of market failure. The enemy of the 99 percent, he contends, is more the intellectual than the robber baron. . . . A guide to help real populists elude their saboteurs." —*Mother Jones*

"An insightful, bitingly humorous book." —*Kirkus Reviews*

Pity
the
Billionaire

The Hard-Times Swindle
and the Unlikely Comeback
of the Right

Fully Updated and Expanded Edition

Thomas Frank

Picador

A Metropolitan Book
Henry Holt and Company
New York

www.picadorusa.com
www.twitter.com/picadorusa • www.facebook.com/picadorusa
picadorbookroom.tumblr.com

Picador® is a U.S. registered trademark and is used by Henry Holt and Company under license from Pan Books Limited.

For book club information, please visit www.facebook.com/picadorbookclub or e-mail marketing@picadorusa.com.

"Brother, Can You Spare a Dime?" by E. Y. "Yip" Harburg and Jay Gorney Published by Glocca Morra Music (ASCAP) and Gorney Music (ASCAP) Administered by Next Decade Entertainment, Inc. All Rights Reserved. Used by Permission.

Designed by Meryl Sussman Levavi

ISBN 978-1-250-02035-2

First published in the United States by Metropolitan Books, a division of Henry Holt and Company

First Picador Edition: October 2012

10 9 8 7 6 5 4 3 2 1

Images of small men usually arise and persist widely only because big men find good use for them.

—C. WRIGHT MILLS, *White Collar*

Contents

Introduction: Signs and Wonders   1

1. End Times   13

2. 1929: The Sequel   26

3. Hold the Note and Change the Key   44

4. Nervous System   61

5. Making a Business of It   77

6. A Mask for Privilege   91

7. Mimesis   116

8. Say, Don't You Remember   132

9. He Whom a Dream Hath Possessed
Knoweth No More of Doubting   155

10. The Silence of the Technocrats   169

    Conclusion: Trample the Weak   187

    Notes   195

    Acknowledgments   217

    Index   219

Introduction:
Signs and Wonders

This book is a chronicle of a confused time, a period when Americans rose up against imaginary threats and rallied to economic theories they understood only in the gauziest terms. It is about a country where fears of a radical takeover became epidemic even though radicals themselves had long since ceased to play any role in the national life; a land where ideological nightmares conjured by TV entertainers came to seem more vivid and compelling than the contents of the news pages.

Seen from another perspective, this is a chronicle of a miraculous time, of another "Great Awakening," of a revival crusade preaching the old-time religion of the free market.[1] It's the story of a grassroots rebellion and the incredible recovery of the conservative movement from the gloomy depths of defeat. Inevitably the words "populist" and "revolt" are applied to it, or the all-out phrase chosen by Dick Armey, the Washington magnifico who heads one of the main insurgent organizations: a "true bottom-up revolution."[2]

Let us confess that there is indeed something miraculous, something astonishing, about all this. Consider the barest facts: this is the *fourth* successful conservative uprising to happen in the last half century,* each one more a-puff with populist bluster than the last, each one standing slightly more rightward, and each one helping to compose a more spell-binding chapter in the historical epoch that I call "the Great Backlash," and that others call the "Age of Reagan" (the historian Sean Wilentz), the "Age of Greed" (the journalist Jeff Madrick), the "Conservative Ascendancy" (the journalist Godfrey Hodgson), or the "Washington Consensus" (various economists).

Think about it this way. It has now been more than thirty years since the supply-side revolution conquered Washington, since laissez-faire became the dogma of the nation's ruling class, shared by large numbers of Democrats as well as Republicans. We have lived through decades of deregulation, deunionization, privatization, and free-trade agreements; the neoliberal ideal has been projected into every corner of the nation's life. Universities try to put themselves on a market-based footing these days; so do hospitals, electric utilities, churches, and museums; so does the Post Office, the CIA, and the U.S. Army.

And now, after all this has been going on for decades, we have a people's uprising demanding that we bow down before the altar of the free market. And this only a short while after the high priests of that very cosmology led the world into the greatest economic catastrophe in memory. "Amazing" is right. "Unlikely" would also be right. "Preposterous" would be even righter.

---

* 1. The original backlash of the Vietnam War era, culminating in the election of Richard Nixon. 2. The tax revolts and culture wars of the seventies, climaxing with the Reagan Revolution of 1980. 3. The "Contract with America" and the Gingrich Revolution of 1994.

In 2008, the country's financial system suffered an epic breakdown, largely the result—as nearly every credible observer agrees—of the decades-long effort to roll back bank supervision and encourage financial experimentation. The banks' stumble quickly plunged the nation and the world into the worst recession since the thirties. This was no ordinary business-cycle downturn. Millions of Americans, and a large number of their banks, became insolvent in a matter of weeks. Sixteen trillion dollars in household wealth was incinerated on the pyre Wall Street had kindled. And yet, as I write this, the main political response to these events has been a campaign to roll back regulation, to strip government employees of the right to collectively bargain, and to clamp down on federal spending.

So let us give the rebels their due. Let us acknowledge that the conservative comeback of the last few years is indeed something unique in the history of American social movements: a mass conversion to free-market theory as a response to hard times. Before the present economic slump, I had never heard of a recession's victims developing a wholesale taste for neoclassical economics or a spontaneous hostility to the works of Franklin Roosevelt. Before this recession, people who had been cheated by bankers almost never took that occasion to demand that bankers be freed from "red tape" and the scrutiny of the law. Before 2009, the man in the bread line did not ordinarily weep for the man lounging on his yacht.

The Consensus Speaks

The achievement of the thing is even more remarkable when we remember the prevailing opinion climate of 2008. After the disasters of the George W. Bush presidency had culminated in the catastrophe on Wall Street, the leading lights of the Beltway consensus had deemed that the nation was traveling in a new direction. They had seen this movie before, and they knew how it was supposed to go. The plates were shifting. Conservatism's decades-long reign was at an end. An era of liberal ascendancy was at hand. This was the unambiguous mandate of history, as unmistakable as the gigantic crowds that gathered to hear Barack Obama speak as he traveled the campaign trail. You could no more defy this plotline than you could write checks on an empty bank account.

And so *The Strange Death of Republican America*, by the veteran journalist Sidney Blumenthal, appeared in April of 2008—even before the Wall Street crash—and announced that the "radical conservative" George W. Bush had made the GOP "into a minority party."[3] In November, Sean Wilentz, the erstwhile historian of the "Age of Reagan," took to the pages of *U.S. News & World Report* to herald that age's "collapse." The conservative intellectual Francis Fukuyama had said pretty much the same thing in *Newsweek* the month before. That chronicler of the DC consensus, *Politico*, got specific and noted the demise of the word "deregulator," a proud Reagan-era term that had been mortally wounded by the collapse of (much-deregulated) Wall Street.[4]

The thinking behind all this was straight cause-and-effect stuff. The 2008 financial crisis had clearly discredited the conservative movement's signature free-market ideas; political scandal and incompetence in the Republican Party had rendered its moral posturing absurd; and conservatism's taste for strident rhetoric was supposedly repugnant to a new generation of postpartisan, postracial voters. Besides, there was the obvious historical analogy that one encountered everywhere in 2008: we had just been through an uncanny replay of the financial disaster of 1929–31, and now, murmured the pundits, the automatic left turn of 1932 was at hand, with the part of Franklin Roosevelt played by the newly elected Barack Obama.

For the Republican Party, the pundit-approved script went as follows: it had to moderate itself or face a long period of irrelevance. And as it failed to take the prescribed steps, the wise men prepared to cluck it off the stage. When the radio talker Rush Limbaugh made headlines in early 2009 by wishing that the incoming President Obama would "fail," the former Bush speechwriter David Frum slapped him down in a much-discussed cover story for *Newsweek*. Judged by the standards of what would come later, of course, Limbaugh's wish sounds quaint, even civil; at the time, however, it seemed so shocking that Frum depicted such rhetoric as "kryptonite, weakening the GOP nationally." Venomous talk might entertain the party's bitter-enders, Frum acknowledged, but the price of going in that direction was the loss of the "educated and affluent," who increasingly found "that the GOP had become too extreme."

The GOP's strange drive toward self-destruction was a favorite pundit theme. When former vice president Dick Cheney announced that he preferred Limbaugh's way to the route of moderation, the *New York Times* columnist Charles Blow laughed that Cheney was "on a political suicide mission. And if his own party is collateral damage, so be it." When certain conservatives proposed a test to detect and punish heresy among Republican politicians, the *Washington Post* columnist Kathleen Parker called it a "suicide pact." The respected political forecaster Stu Rothenberg concluded in April 2009 that "the chance of Republicans winning control of either chamber in the 2010 midterm elections is zero. Not 'close to zero.' Not 'slight' or 'small.' Zero."[5]

Dustbin? No Thanks

What the polite-thinking world expected from the leaders of the American Right was repentance. They assumed that conservative leaders would be humbled by the disasters that had befallen their champion, George W. Bush; that Republicans would confess their errors and make haste for the political center. The world expected contrition.

What it got was the opposite, delivered on the point of a bayonet. Instead of complying with the new speed limit, the strategists of the Right hit the gas. Instead of tacking for the center, they sailed hard to starboard. Instead of seeking accommodation, they went on a quest for ideological purity. Instead of elevating their remaining centrists to positions of power, they purged them.

Now, the idea that the disasters of the Bush years spelled the end for conservatism was reasonable enough if you accepted assumptions that were thought to be obvious in those days: When a political group screwed up, people didn't vote for it any longer. When elected officials wandered too far into the fields of ideology, some mysterious force of political gravity always pulled them back to the "center." And so it was simple. The Right, under its beloved leader, George W. Bush, had disgraced itself; now it was the other team's turn at bat. Political epochs were supposed to run in thirty-year cycles or something, and the GOP's thirty years were up.

That Republicans might seek a way out of their predicament by turning their back on the center and peddling an even more concentrated version of their creed was not, by the conventional thinking of those innocent days, a viable option. And there were famous examples to tell us why, too. Back in 1983, to name the closest analogy, the British Labour Party had reacted to the rise of Margaret Thatcher by convincing itself that what the public really wanted from it was a puri-fied and even more left-wing alternative; the strategy fetched them a painful electoral thumping.

What all these formal, geometric calculations did not take into consideration were the contents of the politics themselves. Conservatives had been repudiated before, they had bounced back before, and they knew that voters don't judge an idea by placing it on some bell-curve chart and measuring the degree to which it deviates from the range of accepted Beltway opin-ion. Whether Republicans chose to move "left" or "right" was less important than how they addressed the economic catastrophes facing the nation. And their conservative wing had a coherent theory to tell the world. Everywhere you looked, they declared, you saw a colossal struggle between average people and the "elites" who would strip away the people's freedoms. The huge bailouts that followed the finan-cial crisis, they said, were evidence of a design on our savings by both government and Wall Street. Regulation, too, was merely a conspiracy of the big guys against the little. So while one side sat back and waited for the mystic tides of history to sort things out, conservatives acted. They reached deep into their own tradition and came up with a way to grab the opportunities that hard times presented.

Rather than acknowledge that they had enjoyed thirty years behind the wheel, they declared that they had never really got their turn in the first place. The true believers had never actually been in charge, the "Conservative Ascendancy" never really existed—and therefore, the disastrous events of recent years cast no discredit on conservative ideas them-selves. The solution was not to reconsider conservative dogma; it was to double down, to work even more energetically for the laissez-faire utopia.

Pure idealism of this sort is unusual in American politics,

however, and the jaded men of the commentariat sat back and waited for the system to punish the wayward ones, for the magnetic pull of the "center" to work its corrective magic. But this time the gods didn't intervene in the usual way. In 2010, a radicalized GOP scored its greatest victory in congressional elections in many decades.

Little Man, What Now?

How did this happen? Well, the simplest explanation for the conservative comeback is that hard times cause people to lash out at whoever is in power. In 2010, that happened to be Democrats. Ergo, their rivals staged a comeback. But surely the two parties are not simply interchangeable, like Coke and Pepsi. They are able to control their own fate to some degree, to differentiate themselves from each other. Besides, history provides enough examples of public sentiment moving consistently in a particular direction to show that it need not always flop aimlessly back and forth.

Another widely held view attributes the conservative resurgence to white racism, which is supposed to have been whipped into flames by the election of a black president. Indeed, one may point to some spectacular flare-ups of bigotry directed against the president and his party. But individual prejudice and a handful of name-calling incidents should not be enough to indict an entire movement, no matter how repugnant we find that prejudice and those names to be. Regardless of the racial fears some partisans hold in their heart of hearts, the new conservatism does not systematically generate racist statements or policies, and its leaders take pains to converse in the polite language of diversity.[6]

Yet other commentators seek to explain the Right's revival

by pointing to the ways it has "leveraged" the Internet, just as Barack Obama once did. Conservatives are using the web to recruit followers; they are blogging like mad; they're all atwitter with rageful tweets. In this view, the message is nothing and the medium is everything, and you could probably get King George III himself elected if you built an awesome-looking website and got all clickety-click interactive.

Old ways of thinking about conservatism have proved equally unsatisfactory in the new situation. For years, it was possible to understand the laissez-faire revival of recent decades by noting the various forms of mystification in which the debate was always cloaked—namely, the culture wars. From the seventies to the years of George W. Bush, the great economic issues weren't settled by open argument or election-year slogans; they were resolved by a consensus of political insiders in Washington while the public fought over abortion and the theory of evolution.

But the conservative flowering of 2009–2011 was different. For the first time in decades, the Right wanted to have the grand economic debate out in the open. The fog of the culture wars temporarily receded. Should you sign up for the online discussion forum maintained by the Tea Party Patriots, one of the leading organizations of the revived Right, you will see a warning that "no discussions on social issues are allowed"; that participants are to restrict themselves to the subjects of "limited government, fiscal responsibility, [and] free markets." The conservative movement's manifesto for 2010, the "Contract from America," mentioned not a single one of the preceding decades' culture-war issues. When the *Washington Post* conducted a poll of nearly every Tea Party group in the nation, it discovered that "social issues, such as same-sex marriage and abortion rights, did not register as concerns."[7] And although I attended a number of Tea Party rallies over the last few years, I never once saw an antiabortion appeal on a protester's sign or heard one from the podium.*

This is not to say that the Right proceeds about its work while renouncing confusion or mystification. Just the opposite: in defending "capitalism," the leaders of the latest conservative uprising don't really bother with the actually existing capitalism of the last few years, even though capitalism's particulars have made for scary headlines on the front pages of every newspaper in the land. They generally do not discuss credit default swaps or the deregulatory triumphs that made them so destructive. They do not have much to say about the massive oil spill in the Gulf of Mexico—the news story that shared the front pages with conservative primary victories all through the summer of 2010—nor about "foreclosuregate," the revelation a few months later that banks had cut all sorts of legal corners in order to hustle borrowers in default out of their houses as quickly as possible.

Instead, the battle is joined at the level of pure abstraction. Economics have become the latest front in the culture wars. The issue, the newest Right tells us, is freedom itself, not the doings of the subprime lenders or the ways the bond-rating agencies were compromised over the course of the last decade. Details like that may have crashed the economy, but to the renascent Right they are almost completely irrelevant. What matters is a given politician's disposition toward free

---

* Of the hundreds of Tea Party protest signs photographed, selected, and printed by conservatives themselves for the 2010 Tea Party coffee-table book *Don't Tread on Us*, only two are concerned with abortion. By contrast, there are easily a hundred suggesting that President Obama or other Democrats are communists or socialists. See Mark Karis, ed., *Don't Tread on Us: Signs of a 21st Century Political Awakening* (Los Angeles: WND Books, 2010).

markets and, by extension, toward the common people of the land, whose faithful vicar the market is.

Now, there is nothing really novel about the idea that free markets are the very essence of freedom. What is new is the glorification of this idea at the precise moment when free-market theory has proven itself to be a philosophy of ruination and fraud. The revival of the Right is as extraordinary as it would be if the public had demanded dozens of new nuclear power plants in the days after the Three Mile Island disaster; if we had reacted to Watergate by making Richard Nixon a national hero.

So disjunctive does this spectacle appear that onlookers naturally assume the newest Right's motivations must lie elsewhere, as we have noted. The movement's positions bear so little relation to lived reality that observers sometimes feel they need pay its actual statements no mind at all.

But this is a mistake. If we wish to understand this latest right-wing triumph, we must begin by taking seriously what the Right actually says at its rallies, and prints on its signs, and shouts from its podiums. We must pick our way through the tangle of conspiracy dreams and libertarian fancies that make up the right-wing renaissance. And by all means, we must read the conservative texts themselves—the words of the politicized TV newsmen, the orotund phrases of the radio talkers, the end-of-the-world rhetoric that one noticed at the Tea Parties.

This is a book that seeks to explain hard-times conservatism, to understand the enthusiasm for an anything-goes economic arrangement that persists in spite of all the failures and bank-breaking catastrophes that our previous efforts to achieve such an arrangement have inflicted upon us.

Free-market capitalism is not the sort of system for which people rally in the streets, even in prosperous times. That they would do so in the months after the freest part of the market deposited so many of their fellow citizens onto the scrap heaps of unemployment and bankruptcy tells us much about the genuine disgust abroad in the land, about the raw need to raise one's voice.

It also tells us much about the way the resurgent Right has capitalized on the nation's anguish to create a protest movement that virtually promises to make the anguish worse. This is the story of a swindle that will have terrible consequences down the road. And though it sounds curious to say so, the newest Right has met its goals not by deception alone—although there has been a great deal of this—but by offering an idealism so powerful that it clouds its partisans' perceptions of reality.

Now, constructing an alternative reality would normally put a worldly political movement at a profound disadvantage. But this case is different. The reborn Right has succeeded *because* of its idealism, not in spite of it; because idealism in the grand sense is precisely what our fallen economic world calls for.

CHAPTER 1

End Times

For the people of the most prosperous nation in the world, recessions are often existential crises, times when everything we believe is called into question. In fat years we think of our economic life in almost magical terms—the visionary wisdom of the stock-picking crowds, the brand spirit that is supposed to inhabit our sneakers—but in hard times the fantasies lie in shards on the ground, and the awful reality is that much harder for the shimmering dreams that preceded it.

In 2008 and 2009, the middle-class world came apart. Every time we checked, the value of our retirement fund had fallen by another third; friends lost their jobs; industries like construction and auto manufacturing came to a standstill; and we discovered, with a sickening feeling, that we owed far more on our mortgage than our house was worth. The landmark institutions of middle-class life were crumbling around us. General Motors and Chrysler declared bankruptcy; Merrill Lynch, broker to the common man, desperately sold itself one weekend in 2008; IndyMac, Wachovia, Washington Mutual, Bear Stearns, and Lehman Brothers disappeared.

It looked like society itself was disintegrating, and for the first time in our comfortable suburban lives, we felt the atavistic touch of panic.

For our parents and grandparents, however, these events may have seemed a little more familiar. The country went down virtually the same road in the years 1929–33, with stock markets crashing, banks failing, factories closing, and foreclosures mounting. So similar were the two disasters that comparisons to the Great Depression became a media commonplace in 2008, the inevitable model to consider when looking to make sense of the current debacle.

The literary critic Edmund Wilson called his book of Depression essays *The American Earthquake*, and though I've read it several times over the course of my life it wasn't until 2009 that I really understood what he meant by that phrase. Had you been one of the many who put your savings in stocks in the twenties, you would have watched your investments lose half their value, then lose half of what remained, then half again. Had you bought your stocks on margin, you would have lost it all at the very beginning.

Had you been one of the responsible ones who kept your savings in the bank, you may well have lost it anyway. Financial institutions were exposed to the disaster by definition, and when your local bank failed—as almost half of American banks did in the years after the 1929 crash[1]—it was a pretty sure bet that no nice man from the FDIC would show up to make it all better. You simply lost most of your savings. And when your town bank went down, your town went down, too.

In 1933, the fear among bank depositors grew so contagious that state governors tried to stop the runs on the banks by forcing them to close, or take a "bank holiday"—a move that brought economic activity to a stop in the United States.

Manufacturing and construction were moribund by that time anyway, and the economy had already shrugged off about a third of the labor force. A huge part of the population now had no way of earning a living no matter how hard they tried; and, as the once-famous labor historian Irving Bernstein pointed out in a once-famous history of the period, "no one knows what proportion of the others were on part time." We do know that people stopped leaving jobs voluntarily, regardless of how badly their boss treated them—times were too desperate for gestures like that. We know that marriages declined, as did the birthrate; that the suicide rate rose, and that newspapers published sensational stories on starvation in America.[2]

Unemployment relief, back then, was an entirely local matter, and after the first year or so of the downturn it essentially no longer existed. There was "organized looting of food" in the big cities, Bernstein tells us, and in a number of places unemployed people set up economies based on barter rather than on dollars—even though the dollars of the day were fully backed by gold and no one feared inflation. Per capita income fell so far that by 1933 it was lower than it had been in 1900.[3] What's more, there was no guarantee that things would ever return to "normal." Economists of the time were enchanted by the idea of "equilibrium"—of the coming day when the free fall would stop and supply and demand resume their happy orbits—but it slowly dawned on them that economies could find a kind of equilibrium with 33 percent unemployment just as naturally as they could with 3 percent unemployment.[4]

And so the catastrophe of 1929–33 did to the certainties of laissez-faire economics what science did to nineteenth-century religion and what the slaughter of World War I did to old-fashioned patriotism: it knocked out the props. "Everything nailed down is coming loose," people used to say back then: The Depression made business leaders into laughingstocks and transformed economic orthodoxy into so many fairy tales.[5] It flattened a century of bankerly wisdom and shook to pieces the country's consensus knowledge, the sacred principles upon which everyone from postman to president had once agreed. "Like the forces of war," wrote Peter Drucker in his 1939 classic, *The End of Economic Man*, "depression shows man as a senseless cog in a senselessly whirling machine which is beyond human understanding and has ceased to serve any purpose but its own."[6]

When we recall that Drucker was an eminent management theorist, his statement can be read as a fairly harsh indictment of classical economic arrangements. But it was scarcely the harshest. That was supplied by the headlines of the day: Bankers who contrived to reward their friends and rescue themselves as the floor caved in. Wall Street heroes who went to prison. Men of substance whose reassuring predictions were almost immediately contradicted by events.

Disintegration was the great literary theme of those days, and writers returned again and again to imagery of desolation and hopelessness: Express trains making their runs with just one or two passengers while armies of tramps traveled in boxcars. Fruit rotting on the ground in the countryside while people starved in the cities. Settlements built of trash down at the city dump. The economist John Maynard Keynes famously compared the collapse to the Dark Ages. The editor of *Nation's Business* saw "fear, bordering on panic, loss of faith in everything, our fellowman, our institutions, private and government."[7] Even Calvin Coolidge, the figurehead of the business civilization, gave up. Once he had been so confident in the old system that he had declared, "The man who builds a factory builds a temple." Four days before he

died in 1933, Coolidge pondered the panorama of waste surrounding him and told a friend, "In other periods of depression it has always been possible to see some things which
were solid and upon which you could base hope, but as I
look about, I now see nothing to give ground for hope—
nothing of man."[8]

The Hard-Times Scenario

The social patterns of hard times are supposed to be a simple
thing, as impersonal and as mechanical as the forces that
shutter our factories and bid down the price of our stocks.
Markets disintegrate, layoffs mount, foreclosures begin, and
before you know it, the people are in the streets, yelling for
blood. We grow desperate, anxious, rebellious. The idols of
our past become targets of derision. We demand that the government do something about it—punish the perps, rescue the
victims. We look for insurance against further catastrophe,
and stricter supervision of the economy, to make sure it doesn't
happen again.

Or so it was in the thirties. And once the crisis was past,
Americans came to believe that the course they had followed
in the Depression was a universal pattern, a template for how
people behave in hard times. Like the economists' "automatic
stabilizers"—the government spending that kicks in when
unemployment crosses a certain line—the public's reaction to
severe recessions is supposed to be predictable, automatic. The
economy stumbles, the people scream, and the politicians of
both parties rush to rescue us from the disaster: one leads to
the other by a process as natural and as reliable as gravity.

When the catastrophe comes, the thirties taught us, certain
legislative deeds will follow swiftly. Unemployment insurance
will be extended, and extended again. There will be massive

investment in public works. Commissions will be named to investigate the causes of the crisis. Agencies will be set up to keep people from losing their houses to foreclosure.

Those hurt by the downturn will start to take action themselves. Union organizing and a wave of strikes will sweep the country in response to the complete breakdown of capitalism's promise. The people will protest, of course, voicing their discontent in public places and maybe descending on Washington like the "Bonus Army" of unemployed World War I vets who took to the road in 1932.

In the larger culture, fundamental matters of subsistence will take precedence over noble principles. That was true in the thirties, anyway, as economic calamity induced Americans to abandon Prohibition, their great national experiment in federal uplift. They turned away from the preceding decade's strange fads in art and religion. Dabblers in Dada came home from Paris to write "reportage" about coal miners in Kentucky.

As the economy falls apart, the assumption goes, we will also rediscover a certain neighborliness, a sense of community and even collectivism that comes from shared privation. "The 1930s," writes the historian Warren Susman, "was *the* decade of participation and belonging." The "rugged individualism" extolled by Herbert Hoover gave way to the generosity and social solidarity documented by Studs Terkel in his oral history *Hard Times*. Writers and intellectuals grew anxious to be part of a larger group, to escape the economy's sense of futility with collective action. Being a "good neighbor" became one of the great themes of the Roosevelt presidency. According to Robert McElvaine, an eminent historian of the Depression, all of these developments expressed a larger shift in values, "a search for a life of community and sharing, as opposed to the acquisitive individualism of modern industrial capitalism."[9]

In politics, class issues will become paramount. When Huey Long won his first race for the governorship of Louisiana in 1928,* notes the historian Alan Brinkley, the politics of the state were completely reconfigured. Suddenly, traditional cultural divides ceased to count. "It no longer seemed to matter whether the parish was Protestant or Catholic, northern or southern," Brinkley writes in a history of thirties protest movements. "What mattered was its wealth, or lack of it."[10]

This new mood will naturally make pariahs of the business class. Let the unemployment rate hit 10 percent, let our pension funds lose their value, and suddenly we no longer thrill to hear about the fabulous lifestyles of the wealthy, the amazing earnings of the investment bankers, or the wonderful cars and homes and private planes that fill the hearts of tycoons with joy. In the thirties, the public even resisted recovery measures when they seemed to benefit the politicians' business-class cronies more than the common people.

Above all, there will be a grand shifting of the philosophical plates. The economic collapse of the thirties cleared the way for economic ideas that had been marginalized before. "The decadent international but individualistic capitalism, in the hands of which we found ourselves after the war, is not a success," wrote the British economist Keynes, a leader of the new school, in the awful year 1933. "It is not intelligent, it is not beautiful, it is not just, it is not virtuous—and it doesn't deliver the goods. In short, we dislike it, and we are beginning to despise it."[11] Americans, for their part, were willing to try almost anything. Economists entertained new schools

---

* Of course, 1928 was not a Depression year. But Louisiana was so poor even before the crash, and Huey Long would soon become such an archetypal Depression figure, that we include this episode as an honorary example.

of thought. The Keynesian doctrine of countercyclical deficit spending began to overtake laissez-faire orthodoxy, and an amazing assortment of less memorable ideas enjoyed their brief moments of glory.

If the hard-times pattern is fixed, so are the moves it supposedly forbids. Here the lessons come not from the successful Roosevelt presidency but from the disastrous administration of his predecessor, Herbert Hoover. Never again, it has always been thought, would a hard-times president pine for balanced budgets in the Hoover manner or chase the illusion of stability represented by the gold standard. Nor would there be any audience for views like those of Treasury Secretary Andrew Mellon, who famously advised Hoover to "liquidate labor, liquidate stocks, liquidate the farmers, liquidate real estate." Such actions, according to Mellon, "will purge the rottenness out of the system. High costs of living and high living will come down. People will work harder, live a more moral life. Values will be adjusted and enterprising people will pick up the wrecks from less competent people."[12] Mellon's advice reflected the orthodoxy of the day: let the downturn take its course, let the failures fail, let the weak be purged, and have confidence that the strong will emerge stronger than ever.

Mellon's idea was disastrous where it was tried[13] and politically poisonous where it was spoken. It rightly followed Mellon into political oblivion. From the enlightened heights of 1954, it was possible for the economist John Kenneth Galbraith, in a passage about Mellon's famous advice, to declare that "a developing depression would not now be met with a fixed determination to make it worse."*

---

* A curious echo of Mellon's dictum about hard times forcing people to "live a more moral life" occurs in Robert Bork's mournful meditation, *Slouching Towards Gomorrah*, in which he briefly considers "a deep economic depres-

The Millionaire's Union

The recurrence of the hard-times scenario isn't really a matter of political opinion; both liberals and conservatives expect economic downturns to bring specific, predictable consequences.

For those on the left, of course, hard times have always served as the great moment of vindication, the period when it becomes impossible for anyone to deny the old order's viciousness. When the system ruins investors and tells workers to hit the bricks, those investors and workers begin to question said system. That's why economic crisis automatically gives rise to a "legitimacy crisis" in which the established order of things is shaken to the foundations. This effect is thought to be almost mechanical in its certainty. After all, as the old saying goes, when corn is two dollars a bushel, the farmer is a conservative; when it's one dollar a bushel, the farmer is a radical.

Radicalism of the dollar-a-bushel kind was everywhere in the "Red Decade," and leftists have always assumed that a second collapse of the business civilization would bring a second dose of the same. "If another Depression came, we'd have a revolution," the crusading Texas congressman Wright Patman assured Studs Terkel in 1970. "People wouldn't take it any more. They have more knowledge." *

---

sion" as one way of bringing about "moral regeneration." The idea is immediately discarded for "lacking broad public support." See *Slouching Towards Gomorrah: Modern Liberalism and American Decline* (New York: HarperCollins, 2003), p. 336. The Galbraith quote appears in *The Great Crash: 1929* (Boston: Houghton Mifflin, 1955), p. 199.

* Then again, maybe they would take it. Patman was a fiery left-wing populist during the Depression, but today his congressional district is represented by Louie Gohmert, a Tea Party favorite who has become famous for proposing a zero percent corporate tax rate and for his trademark fear: that terrorists are

For conservatives, the scenario is equally inevitable, but it comes laden with dread rather than vindication. It was the economic collapse of the early thirties, after all, that ended capitalism's golden age, that destroyed the credibility of laissez-faire orthodoxy, and that transformed business leaders from heroes into goats. The decade that followed was, for them, an unequaled disaster. It saddled bankers and merchants with taxes of every description, it launched an invasive regulatory regime, and, of course, it ushered in the prickly presence of organized labor.

Conservative panic ran riot in those days. Establishment types famously feared revolution in the early thirties; they saw communist influence behind every squeak of protest. "More communistic than the communists" was the verdict pronounced in 1934 by the newspaper baron William Randolph Hearst on the Roosevelt administration, and in that same year a group of superwealthy industrialists came together to form the American Liberty League, which denounced the deeds of FDR as so many assaults on the Constitution. "The New Deal represents the attempt in America to set up a totalitarian government," blustered the league's president in a typical 1936 radio speech, "one which recognizes no sphere of individual or business life as immune from governmental authority and which submerges the welfare of the individual to that of the government."[14]

But the Right just couldn't catch a break. Not even totalitarian-baiting could turn the tide of the awful thirties; the public was far more interested in mocking the "Millionaire's Union," as the league was lampooned, than in rallying around its spectacular fears of the Constitution laid waste.[15]

---

planning to have jihadist babies born in the United States. The Patman quotation comes from Terkel, *Hard Times: An Oral History of the Great Depression* (New York: Pantheon, 1970), p. 285.

So Franklin Roosevelt built his great coalition of blue-collar workers and other traditional outsiders, winning electoral triumphs by popular-vote majorities of a kind rarely seen since; in the House of Representatives his Democrats held, as of 1937, more than three-quarters of the seats. So lasting was the thirties realignment that Democrats retained that majority, with two brief intermissions, until the Gingrich Revolution of 1994.

Spirits of '76

Here is an example of the hard-times scenario, drawn from a chapter of the history of the Midwest.

The state of Iowa boomed along with farm prices in the years just after World War I; the nation convinced itself that farms were the thing to own; everything was mortgaged and mortgaged again; it was a scene of unrivaled prosperity. Ten years later, in the pit of the Depression, the price of farm products had fallen to a sliver of former values. Now no amount of hard work sufficed to keep up the farmer's mortgage payments, and the farm foreclosures began. By 1933, a third of the cases in Iowa courts were foreclosures.[16]

As conditions soured and no relief came from the Hoover administration, Iowa farmers began to organize themselves into a "Farmers' Holiday Association," the name being a dark joke on the euphemistic "bank holidays." The idea was for farmers to withhold their products from the market until prices rose and the politicians did something to help them bear their crushing burden of debt.

But this was the thirties, people were desperate, and matters quickly got out of hand. Farmers blockaded the roads around cities in Iowa and Nebraska, forcibly dumping out truckloads of produce that got close to their picket lines. They faced down police and government officials. They disrupted so many foreclosure proceedings that it "became virtually impossible," according to one observer, "to prosecute a foreclosure in counties where the Association was strong." The farmers railed against bankers and produced a manifesto that echoed one of the classic Depression themes: the common people coming together to defend themselves against a predatory world. "We pledge ourselves to protect one another in the actual possession of our necessary homes, livestock and machinery as against all claimants," it read—and by "claimants," one journalist wrote, the farmers meant "the holders of mortgages."[17]

That same journalist marveled at the farmers' old-fashioned tactics of "direct action," which he saw as a Depression-induced throwback "almost to the days of 1776." It was a comparison much in the air in those rebellious years. One Iowa picketer even justified the trashing of his fellow farmers' products as follows: "They say blockading the highway's illegal. I says, 'Seems to me there was a Tea-party in Boston that was illegal too. What about destroying property in Boston Harbor when our country was started?' "[18]

The 1932 farm strike didn't do much to raise farm prices. Instead, it was just one dreadful note in a grand chorus of hopelessness that eventually brought the various ag bills, social insurance plans, and mortgage remediation schemes of the New Deal.

Still, the plight of Iowa in the thirties is worth remembering because it provides such a stark contrast with our own, hard-bitten era. We have just come through the worst recession since the days of the Farmers' Holiday Association. And just as in the awful days of 1932, average people have risen up in outrage, fuming against the moneymen who drove the nation into the ditch and the politicians who stuck by their cronies while the rest of us lost our jobs and our savings. Thirties-style populism has made a triumphant return, claiming to juxtapose decent Americans against an uncaring, predatory world.

But should you happen to hear an homage to the spirit of the Boston Tea Party nowadays, the demands that follow will be the opposite of those of the striking farmers of 1932. What makes the rebel's blood boil today is not the plight of the debtor but the possibility that such "losers" might escape their predicament—that government might step in and do the things those Iowa farmers wanted it to do eighty years ago.

That seven lean years must follow seven fat years seems like a fair deal nowadays. What burns these modern-day populists is that anyone has the arrogance to think that human affairs might be arranged any other way; that government might allow our neighbor to evade his part of the common disaster; that some mortgage remediation scheme or farm bill might let him out of the hard-times punishment that he clearly deserves. The ones moved to protest in 2009 were all "liquidationists," as old Herbert Hoover used to call them. What they needed the world to understand was that, to quote the words I saw printed on a sign at one of the first Tea Party protests, "Your Mortgage Is Not My Problem."

CHAPTER 2

1929: The Sequel

Seventy-nine years after the Great Crash, we got our own economic calamity, a crushing bust to put the exclamation point on the end of an anemic boom. As a lesson in the built-in treachery of the system, the collapse was unexcelled in living memory. As an indictment of official America's consensus economic doctrine, it surpassed any plaint about NAFTA, any righteous editorializing about the payday loan industry, any fretting about the concentration of wealth into ever-fewer hands. If you had brought the world's teenaged anarchists together in some great international congress and asked them to design an ideal crisis, they could not have discredited market-based civilization more completely than did the crash of 2008.

Committee to Give the Huge Middle Finger

It happened, to begin with, on the watch of president George W. Bush, whose faith in the prevailing economic creed was as close to perfect as any chief executive's is likely to come. The creed itself, though, transcended the partisan divide; its merry assumptions chirped forth from the opinion pages of the *Washington Post* and the research papers of the Cato Institute. Its holy trinity of deregulation, privatization, and free trade were the accepted policy mandates of that age, and only the crustiest sort of Luddite doubted their benevolence when applied to financial services.

Over the years, visionary, tech-friendly Democrats had joined with stern, patriarchal Republicans to circumvent the country's banking rules and to mute its supervisory agencies. The winds of history were at their back, as were the gales of dollars blowing in from the private sector, and in the noblest spirit of bipartisanship they repealed what remained of the nation's basic banking laws in 1999. When market-displeasing laws remained on the books, the practice of "desupervision" ensured that they were not enforced. Enlightened governance in our advanced age meant counting on industries to comply voluntarily. Self-interest is what would make bankers play fairly and oil companies drill safely. And on these principles virtually everyone agreed.

Do you remember the smugness, reader? The sheer complacency with which the free-market catechism would be pronounced in those days? Then surely you will permit me to include the following memorable passage from a 1999 issue of *Time* magazine whose cover hailed Alan Greenspan, Robert Rubin, and Larry Summers as the "Committee to Save the World." The magazine observed, dispassionately, that "Rubin, Greenspan, and Summers have outgrown ideology." What it meant by this was that "their faith is in the markets and in their own ability to analyze them." This faith beyond ideology

> recalls nothing so much as the objectivist philosophy
> of the novelist and social critic Ayn Rand. . . . During
> long nights at Rand's apartment and through her

articles and letters, Greenspan found in objectivism a
sense that markets are an expression of the deepest
truths about human nature and that, as a result, they
will ultimately be correct.

His reverence for markets forged in the searing fire of Objectivism, Greenspan was prepared to lead his two colleagues
and the nation into a new, enlightened age. All three of them
"agree that trying to defy global market forces is in the end
futile. That imposes a limit on how much they will permit ideology to intrude on their actions."[1]

To insist that the free-market creed is beyond ideology
might sound like the baldest sort of propaganda today, but
all through the eighties, the nineties, and the zeroes our leaders whistled that happy tune, congratulating themselves for
figuring it all out. Those were the golden years of libertarianism, a time when our choice and master spirits agreed on the
uselessness of big government and took the benevolent ratio-
nality of markets for granted. And while they did so, the American financial establishment proceeded to cheat the world to
the very edge of the abyss. Indeed, what brought the nation
down were the very aspects of business practice that our
choice and master spirits admired the most—the financial
innovation and risk-taking that were routinely described in
those days as America's unique offerings to the world.

No, we didn't manufacture much anymore, but we could
sure dream up awesome ways to securitize debt and slice up
the risk in every imaginable situation. One testament to the
zesty innovativeness of markets was the industry that had
sprung up to supply credit to "subprime" borrowers, selling
off the loans thus made to the investment banking industry on
Wall Street. Then there were the geniuses at the next few steps

of the process, who bundled those subprime mortgages into bonds and those bonds into collateralized debt obligations—and then sold credit default swaps to insure against the possibility of their failure.[2]

The gospel of deregulation, meanwhile, had become such an irresistible ideological juggernaut that no amount of real-world failure could call it into question. Under the guidance of this doctrine, Federal authorities removed certain derivatives from regulatory oversight; they watered down requirements that banks balance their risk with safe assets; they exempted credit default swaps from regulation as insurance products; they dialed back the Federal Reserve's regulatory powers; they struck down a rule that required hedge-fund advisers to register with the Securities and Exchange Commission, and they pre-empted efforts by state governments to crack down on predatory lending. All these examples come from the first few chapters of a single investigative report;[3] further illustrations of the rollback of the regulatory state could be piled up by the hundreds.*

Meanwhile, anyone who knew anything about markets genuflected before the great god bonus, the pay-for-performance doctrine that was being triumphantly extended to every aspect of enterprise. Lavish incentives, the theory went, would coax superhuman labors from management and bring fantastic wealth to shareholders. In reality, as we now know, what bonuses inspired were superhuman efforts to game the system, to collect those rewards regardless of what the gaming did to stockholders, customers, or even the long-term health of the company.

---

* In fact, they *are* piled up by the hundreds in my 2008 book, *The Wrecking Crew*.

Let us recall what it all looked like at its moment of supreme triumph. In the Year of Our Market 2006, it was reported that Goldman Sachs distributed some $16.5 billion in bonuses to its employees, enriching them in a way that is probably capable of overpowering all other forms of human motivation—faith, love, duty, ethics, patriotism, the law. And in such circumstances it was understandable that the bonus would become the object of a sort of cult. The high priest of the sect—or, rather, the leader of the ravening pack—was a magazine called *Trader Monthly*, which existed not to offer economic conjecture or stock tips, but merely to drool over the bonus-driven lifestyle. "See It, Make It, Spend It" was the publication's slogan, and it stood ready to help the rising Wall Street star blow his share of the loot conspicuously, flamboyantly. Oh, there were cars: Lamborghinis, Maybachs, Ferraris, Maseratis, described in the magazine's characteristic tone of flippant indulgence. There were airplanes, reviewed and rated in a column specifically dedicated to that purpose. There were Scotches, including, in the "Bonus Guide" for 2008, a $20,000 bottle of Johnnie Walker.

One definitely did not get the sense that traders aspired to live this way because they were jolly bon vivants. Quite the opposite. At one point in its intermittent pursuit of the best possible record player, for example, *Trader Monthly* described what it claimed to be a $300,000 turntable as "a huge middle finger to everyone who enters your home."

If you didn't understand why someone would want to greet his guests in such a way, you didn't understand what made the Bush era go. But *Trader Monthly* did, and it suffused its protagonist in golden light so that all might behold his glory. A trader was not just an überconsumer but a bullying, self-maximizing, wealth-extracting he-man: a lout in full. The magazine's panting worship of the truculent personality culminated in a bizarre spectacle it arranged in November of 2007: trader boxing. Before an audience chewing steak and guzzling luxury vodka, the furious fists of junk bond specialists would connect with the jaws of private equity managers, and the world would enjoy a graphic representation of the primal drama of capitalism.

I bring up this forgotten catalog of crassness not merely because its pages are such an amusing trove of bull-market ephemera but because the attitude it celebrated was instrumental in bringing disaster down on the nation. Those turntables and cars and jets were not just evidence of wastefulness at the top; they were pretty much all that Americans got in exchange for the decades of regulatory rollback. Professionals did OK during the Bush years; hourly wage earners gradually lost ground during the boom; but traders got to shop for private jets. Economists can talk in their abstract way about incentives and self-correcting markets, but this is what the free-market faith looks like in concrete reality. These tacky souvenirs were the reason for the whole mortgage catastrophe, the rewards that caused so many to cut corners and break rules and hire lobbyists and palm it all off on the next guy downstream. Not so *you* could prosper; so *they* could.

If ever a financial order deserved a thirties-style repudiation, this one did. Its gods were false. Its taste was bad. Its heroes were oafs and brutes and thieves and bullies. And all of them failed, even on their own stunted terms: the "MBA president" and his "market-based" government; the "K Street Project" and the "superlobbyists" who epitomized it; the federal agencies that had learned to think of private industry as their "customers"; the sleepy regulators, ignoring that red telephone ringing in the next room; and our fleet of hedge-fund billionaires, chortling on their yachts, as they all steered toward the iceberg. All of it should by rights have met its end.

Crime Pays

Instead, it got a bailout. Having let the louts in the nation's financial industry do as they chose for decades, Washington suddenly swung into action when it became clear that those selfsame louts had sold one another trillions of dollars of booby-trapped investments. In March of 2008, the Federal Reserve facilitated the takeover of Bear Stearns by JP Morgan. In September, after Lehman Brothers was allowed to fail and financial markets began to panic, the Fed and the Treasury Department began bailing with both hands. They put together an emergency package for AIG, an unregulated hedge fund grafted onto an insurance company; they took over Fannie Mae and Freddie Mac, the mortgage companies; they rode to the rescue of the nation's money-market funds and organized the distress-takeover of the huge Wachovia bank. And then, having warmed themselves up with these exercises, they went to Congress and asked for that notorious intervention known as the Troubled Asset Relief Program (TARP): $700 billion as a generalized rescue fund for the nation's banks, to be administered however the former Goldman Sachs chairman, Treasury Secretary Hank Paulson, saw fit.

The larger economy spun into the worst slump since the Depression. Over the next year, millions would lose their houses, millions more would lose their jobs, and countless small businesses would be wiped out. But the banks and brokerages and jerry-rigged venture capital concerns that had propelled the tainted boom—that had done everything wrong—*these* businesses could not be permitted to fail. *They* had to be recapitalized, propped up, dusted off, and sent back out into the world to swagger and bully and fly that huge middle finger all over again.

Yes, I know: Drastic action was undoubtedly necessary.

But the financial rescue could have taken any of a dozen different forms. It could have put the "zombie banks" into receivership and commenced an orderly bankruptcy process, with no one allowed to get out of it by accounting gimmicks. It could have broken up the banking industry and brought back strict regulation, along with a policy of zero tolerance for financial entities that are "too big to fail," so that the temptation to rescue such institutions would disappear. Instead, our leaders allowed the biggest banks to get even bigger. They offered the banks an open-ended guarantee against failing without really restricting their activities—a guarantee that might well encourage them to bet on the riskiest propositions available, secure in the knowledge that the taxpayer would make good their losses.

The bailouts were one of those moments that crushes the faith of a nation. Wall Street had gambled with the world's prosperity; Wall Street had brought about a financial catastrophe; and yet Wall Street was now to get the kind of government help that you and I will never receive. When you decided, reader, to spend your life making things/designing things/writing things instead of trading risky financial instruments, perhaps you thought that you were doing something productive, something our society valued. But here now was the truth, as revealed by Hank Paulson and Co.: In the land of the red, white, and blue, only one calling mattered. To go into any line of work other than finance was to confess yourself a fool. To play by the rules was a chump's game.*

To believe in the fairness of the system was just as naive.

---

* When one trader in a 2010 account of the disaster asks another trader to identify the people buying mortgage-backed securities, he gets this answer: "Stupid Germans. They take rating agencies seriously. They believe in the rules." Michael Lewis, *The Big Short: Inside the Doomsday Machine* (New York: Norton, 2010), p. 93.

The awful but unmistakable message of the bailouts was that the lords of Wall Street owned the government. First, they rewrote the nation's banking laws in a grotesquely self-serving way. Then, once they had got themselves in trouble, they simply whistled up the resources of the public treasury: our tax money. Federal agencies, we now learned, were honeycombed with alumni and future employees of the banks; Washington's officials all bowed before Wall Street's pat economic ideology; both parties were in on it. The feeling that arose from this awful enlightenment was one of almost physical nausea. It was like finding out that the CIA had murdered President Kennedy, or that President Eisenhower really was a communist agent, like the Birchers used to say.

The Populist Moment

You can quibble with my language, but little of the foregoing is a matter of opinion or controversy. Most responsible accounts of the Crash of 2008 emphasize the role of deregulation, incentives, and the free-market faith in the building of the bubble. I repeat all these well-known tales here for this reason: according to the logic of hard times—according to logic *tout court*—the Crash of '08 should have kick-started the hard-times scenario in the same way the events of 1929–32 did.

And for a while it seemed as though matters were moving inexorably down those Depression-era tracks. The financial heroes of previous years became objects of public wrath almost immediately. We turned on the politicians who bailed out their friends. Our fury spiked every time we heard some dispatch on the bankers' still-posh lives.

In October of 2008, we learned about the lavish corporate retreats enjoyed by executives at financial firms even after they were bailed out. In November, there was a wave of anger at auto executives who flew to DC in private jets to ask for their own lifeline. In January of 2009, news broke that the CEO of Merrill Lynch had approved extravagant bonuses even as the company headed for disaster; he had also spent a cool million redecorating his office. In March, it was the turn of the CNBC business news network, as the comedian Jon Stewart reminded the world of the channel's smiling sycophancy toward CEOs and its clueless optimism regarding all things Dow.

In politics, the Crash of '08 ended the prospects of that year's Republican candidate for president, Arizona senator John McCain, who had the bad fortune to be the standard-bearer of the party that had ruled for most of the preceding seven years. With the stock market plummeting in the background, a jittery nation chose as its president the Democrat Barack Obama, a first-term Illinois senator whose chances, in the usual scheme of American political things, would have been virtually nil: not only was he a professorial, big-city northerner, but he was black.

At the time, Obama appeared to be the ideal figure for the moment. Alone among the candidates competing for the presidency in 2008, he seemed to have some grasp of what caused the financial crisis. In a famous speech in March of 2008, he had actually offered a spirited defense of the regulatory state, something few politicians of our time dare to do. As the financial crisis unfolded, comparisons of him to Franklin Roosevelt became common; a *Time* magazine cover, for example, morphed his face onto a famous photo of FDR.

With the presidency in their hands, the Democrats proceeded to take certain distinctly thirties-style actions, like implementing measures to encourage mortgage modifications and establishing a commission to investigate the financial crisis. The brand-new president persuaded Congress to approve a $787 billion stimulus package early in 2009 and to partially reregulate Wall Street. He even managed to push through a universal health-insurance bill. It looked at times as though Roosevelt really was riding again.

From grandees of the old order, meanwhile, came the same cries of recantation that one heard in 1932. The most remarkable disavowal was that of Alan Greenspan, a member of the aforementioned "Committee to Save the World." As Fed chairman, Greenspan had fought fiercely to keep derivatives markets unregulated and took a comfy snooze when called upon to supervise the nation's intoxicated mortgage lenders. But now Greenspan confessed to feeling "shocked disbelief" at all that had gone on. Testifying to a House committee in October 2008, he said, "I made a mistake in presuming that the self-interest of organizations, specifically banks and others, [was] such that they were best capable of protecting their own shareholders and their equity in the firms." "You found that your view of the world, your ideology was not right," the committee chairman coaxed him. "Precisely," answered the maestro.

There was a brief vogue for stories about troubled economists brooding in the limestone halls of the University of Chicago. Among that institution's celebrated champions of efficient market theory, the Nobel laureate Robert Lucas was reported in 2008 to be doubting his former belief in bank deregulation.[4] The Nobel laureate Gary Becker confessed in 2009, "There are a lot of things that people got wrong, and I got wrong, and Chicago got wrong."[5] But the most astonishing conversion was that of Richard Posner, another knight-errant of the Chicago school. His 2009 book, *A Failure of Capitalism*, placed the blame for the cataclysm squarely on his former comrades in the deregulation movement. The collapse "hit economic libertarians in their solar plexus," he wrote, because it had discredited their free-market philosophy so utterly, so undeniably.[6] In 2010, Posner called for the revival of thirties-era banking rules and penned the unthinkable: an homage to John Maynard Keynes, the genius of deficit spending and the bête noire of the free-market crowd.

Just as readers of the thirties snapped up books trashing the great capitalists and picking apart classical economics, so did the book-buying public of our own time seem ready to read about the folly of orthodoxy. In 2009, a *Time* magazine columnist named Justin Fox scored an unlikely hit with *The Myth of the Rational Market*, a careful takedown of academic economics. Michael Lewis, who had once laughed at those who warned of a real-estate bubble, now walked readers through the descending levels of the Wall Street ripoff in *The Big Short*. And there was a sudden mania for Great Depression comparisons: Paul Krugman reissued his 1999 work, *The Return of Depression Economics*—this time they had truly returned—and a book about the blundering central bankers of the twenties actually made the bestseller list.

Waiting for Lefty

For those on the receiving end of this rising discontent, the unfolding of the hard-times scenario seemed just as certain, as unavoidable. But the fear itself was different: What these people dreaded about hard times was not unemployment or homelessness; it was the left-wing politics that traditionally accompany such things. The Jacobin jitters gripped this group suddenly and would not let go.

One who sounded an early alarm was Charles Koch, the oil baron and influential funder of libertarian organizations; in his company's newsletter, he groaned that we were reliving the disasters of the Depression and were on the verge of making the "same mistakes" as our ancestors—by which he meant installing new regulations, public works programs, ncw government agencies. As a result, he wrote, we were "facing the greatest loss of liberty and prosperity since the 1930s."[7]

"Capitalism is under siege, its future unclear," moaned the economics columnist Robert Samuelson a short while later. On CNBC, the various personalities could be heard chatting anxiously about the uptick in "class war," by which they meant public contempt for investment bankers.[8] Those investment bankers, meanwhile, were reportedly buying ranches in western states in preparation for the economic helter-skelter.[9] *Forbes* magazine fairly trembled with ancien régime anxiety. Its May 11, 2009, edition featured a wealthy cartoon family walking through a nightmare landscape, haunted by a ghoulish Uncle Sam preparing to raise their taxes and menaced by a crowd of protesters holding a placard marked "Kill the Rich!" A teaser for the story warned that "Uncle Sam wants your money, and the crowd outside the gate wants your head."

The escalating class-war danger was taken up by *Newsweek* in a screaming cover issued in February of 2009: "We Are All Socialists Now." The nation was only three weeks into the new Obama administration, but it seemed the socialist nightmare that had haunted William Randolph Hearst in the darkest days of the New Deal had already come to pass.*

---

* In reality, the premise of *Newsweek*'s "socialism" cover story—that bailing out banks was equivalent to "nationalizing" them, like British coal mines in the forties—was little more than an insult to socialism. You might, however, call what happened "socialism for the rich," since the state had been used to rescue executives, shareholders, and counterparties of big financial institutions, at the expense of millions of citizens who enjoy no such safety net.

For what it's worth, here is what the self-identifying, big-*S* Socialist Norman Thomas had to say in 1936: "There is no Socialism at all about taking over all the banks which fell in Uncle Sam's lap, putting them on their feet again, and turning them back to the bankers to see if they can bring them once more to ruin." As quoted in the *Progressive*, February 15, 1936. (And again in the *Progressive*, April 2009, p. 39.)

We had no Socialist Party to speak of, but here was a leading journal announcing that it had happened to us just the same.

The *Newsweek* cover vindicated the scariest of hard-times fears. Over the years since its publication, I have seen it waved in the air at conservative rallies; summoned up as damning evidence in popular right-wing books; and held aloft like a trump card for the TV cameras by the Republican leader Ken Blackwell. And a few weeks into his new show on Fox News, a former radio DJ named Glenn Beck displayed the *Newsweek* cover before his own cameras as proof that "the rich are being demonized" just as they were in the thirties.

The anxieties of the business class were not without reason. Public fury was mounting steadily; it reached its peak in March of 2009, when managers of the bailed-out financial supermarket AIG handed out $165 million in bonuses to the division that invented the derivatives that brought the company down. Bonuses! The nation was already in flames over the bailouts by then, of course. But now this comatose, money-hole of a corporation—AIG was being kept alive only so its bad bets could be unwound in an orderly way—showed us that the bonus-grabbing culture of the trader would not die.

It was an inconceivable ripoff. The people who had nearly succeeded in shoving the world off a cliff were now going to walk away rich. Wall Street pay, we suddenly understood, had never been a reward for "performance" or a grateful recognition of what financial innovation did for the nation—it was strictly about what Wall Streeters could get away with. The AIG bonus scandal thus became a symbol for the larger scandal of the crisis/bailout, another one of those moments that shreds people's faith.

The public's disgust was volcanic this time; it seemed to erupt more violently with each passing day. A Bloomberg story that appeared on March 18 observed that "Americans want to see heads roll. They are calling National Public Radio to accuse AIG of 'legalized robbery without a gun.' They are telling CNN to put photographs of AIG executives on the air and 'expose them like America's Most Wanted.'"

The firestorm quickly overtook mainstream, business-friendly Democrats. Connecticut senator Chris Dodd had been a loyal friend of AIG, it was now angrily remembered. President Obama himself had received campaign contributions from the company's executives. Larry Summers, formerly of the "Committee to Save the World" and now director of the National Economic Council, thought the way to respond was to lecture Americans on the rule of law and the sanctity of contract. And with every snooty dismissal, matters only got worse.

Now *Newsweek* published a "thinking man's guide to populist rage," depicting the reaction to the AIG bonuses as a replay of the sentiments of the Depression. The wise men warned President Obama that he had to keep a lid on this populist thing; the country was being swept up in a whirl-wind of class antagonism, as in the thirties, and matters could easily get out of control.[10] Obama himself then extended the warning to Wall Street. When he met with a delegation of Wall Street bankers in April of 2009, the new president told them, "My administration is the only thing between you and the pitchforks."

The World Turned Right Side Up

Those pitchforks showed up, all right. But Wall Street had nothing to fear from them. Almost none of the elements of the hard-times scenario outlasted the early months of the slump. There was no surge in formal worker militance, although there was soon a determined effort by state governments to kill off organized labor. There was no wave of defiance by the foreclosed-upon, but instead a successful campaign to destroy ACORN, the fair-housing advocate. It would be two more years before Occupy Wall Street would materialize.

By that time, Wall Street compensation had been lifted back where it belonged. In April 2011, *New York* magazine carried on its cover a photo of a satisfied young investment banker with a wad of C-notes gripped in his taunting hand. "Wall Street Won," sneered the caption. If it had been briefly unfashionable to rub the world's face in one's plundrous glory, now the hairshirt days were over. The louts were swinging wide once again.

But the populist fury of March 2009 lived on in a thousand Tea Party gatherings in parks and convention centers all across the nation. In April, there were Tea Party events in nearly every city of any size in the land. All through that summer, protesters attended town hall meetings to make things hot for our elected representatives. In Washington that autumn, they paraded by the hundreds of thousands down the National Mall; the following spring, they filled the west lawn of the Capitol; and in August 2010, they showed up at the Lincoln Memorial to lay claim to the memory of Martin Luther King Jr.

And through it all the protesters' sense of the injuries suffered by average Americans stayed fresh; their anger at the elites did not dim. They cursed the high and the mighty using the unmistakable terms of the democratic tradition: quoting Jefferson, quoting Franklin, quoting Tom Paine. The zeal of some was so great that they waved "Don't Tread on Me" rattlesnake flags and wore powdered wigs.

Theirs was a different populism than the one we started with, however. In the early months of 2009, it was mass public outrage against bankers that threatened to pull Americans out of their chairs and into the streets. By the time a year had elapsed, however, the bonus boys' misbehavior had been pretty much forgotten. In no time at all, the public's rage had migrated from Wall Street to Washington. Before long the only populism available in the land was an uprising against government and taxes and federal directives—in other words, it was now a movement in favor of the very conditions that had allowed Wall Street to loot the world. In fact, nearly every aspect of the culture responsible for the collapse—from deregulation to Ayn Rand's novels—quickly became the subject of roaring enthusiasm. Old man Greenspan may finally have found a "flaw" in his system, but outside the hearing-room windows of the nation the people themselves were swearing that their faith would never die.

For the antigovernment Republican Party, the shift brought an amazing revival. What seemed to be a suicidal maneuver by GOP leaders turned out to be just the thing for the time and the place. In January of 2010, voters in liberal Massachusetts enthusiastically filled the Senate seat of the recently deceased Ted Kennedy with a little-known Republican named Scott Brown. In that contest, a core Democratic group—blue-collar workers—showed the most remarkable swing of all. Among this demographic, the results were so lopsided that the AFL-CIO's national political-action director called the Massachusetts election a "working class revolt."[11]

And on it rolled. A month after the Massachusetts upset, a *Washington Post* headline observed that "Appalachia Is Slipping from Grip of Democrats"; the story that followed described a down-and-out coal-mining area in western Virginia where the forgotten man's response to the slump was a headlong flight into the arms of the GOP.[12]

The general election that November was a full-blown Republican triumph. The House of Representatives saw its biggest midterm swing since 1938, with an amazing sixty-three seats changing from blue to red.* It had been only two years since the Democrats' own great victory, but now the populist fury was all on the other side.

The story was the same just about everywhere. *National Journal* went through the exit polls and discovered that blue-collar whites chose Republican congressional candidates by an amazing margin of two to one nationwide. In a demonstration of "profound resistance to Obama and his agenda," the demographic that had been moved by capitalism's last systemic crisis to hand the presidency to Franklin Roosevelt four times in a row now resurrected the politics of Herbert Hoover.[13]

It was an astonishing reversal, to be sure, but it was hardly the guileless upsurge that its fans have made it out to be. Most of the people involved were well-meaning citizens caught up in the spirit of the times. But the larger political operation in which they enlisted themselves has been like a gigantic game of three-card monte, in which the deck is shuffled and one card takes the place of another. Before our eyes, imaginary terrors have been substituted for real ones. All that remains is for the nation to pay up.

---

* In state legislatures, over 650 seats swung from the Democrats to the Republicans.

CHAPTER 3

Hold the Note and Change the Key

Maybe a more appropriate metaphor for the conservative revival is the classic switcheroo, with one fear replacing another, theoretical emergencies substituting for authentic ones, and a new villain shuffling onstage to absorb the brickbats meant for another. The conservative renaissance rewrites history according to the political demands of the moment, generates thick smokescreens of deliberate bewilderment, grabs for itself the nobility of the common toiler, and projects onto its rivals the arrogance of the aristocrat. Nor is this constant redirection of public ire a characteristic the movement developed as it went along; it was present at the creation. Indeed, redirection *was* the creation.

Drawer of Water, Hewer of Bullshit

The call that awakened the rebellion came not from some itinerant IWW organizer but from a TV "rant" delivered on February 19, 2009, by one Rick Santelli, a business reporter standing on the floor of the Chicago Board of Trade—a reporter ranting, let us be clear, not *against* the traders who surrounded him but *on their behalf*. In retrospect, there would be few better examples of the spirit of inversion that drives the conservative revival.

Rick Santelli had criticized many aspects of the bank bailouts over the preceding months, but on that day in February when he had the ear of the nation, the part of the TARP that drew his disgust was, significantly, the element designed to help homeowners modify the terms of certain underwater mortgages, making payments more affordable and thus preventing foreclosures. It was the only part of the TARP that was intended to directly benefit individual borrowers rather than institutional players, and thus it was supposed to help make the program popular. Instead, it brought down the wrath of this man Santelli, who found it inconceivable that such an initiative was even under consideration. "This is America!" he yelled, working himself into a rage.

And in Santelli's trading-floor "America," such a program was "promoting bad behavior," "subsidiz[ing] the losers' mortgages" with public money that, were it directed to society's winners, would presumably be spent on better, shinier things. Santelli's outrage at these "losers" was inexhaustible, incandescent. They "drink the water" while others "carry the water." Raising his arms and turning to his friends, the Chicago traders, he asked, "How many people want to pay for your neighbor's mortgage that has an extra bathroom and can't pay their bills?"*

---

* Let us compare Rick Santelli's fears to the reality of the Home Affordable Modification Program (HAMP) as it unfolded over the following years.

　　As it happens, the HAMP was the subject of considerable journalistic scrutiny. The ProPublica website, in particular, carefully tracked the program's record, in part by interviewing people the program was supposed to help—the ones Santelli called "the losers." What ProPublica found was that countless

Boo, went the traders: Down with neighbors! To hell with their extra bathrooms, their arrogant water-drinking, their hard luck.

The next step, should government proceed along the mortgage-modifying paths of tyranny, the reporter reported, would be communist Cuba. But before Big Brother clapped us in statist irons, he'd have to deal with Rick Santelli, friend of the trader and scourge of the thirsty. Santelli was going to defy the Obama administration with a "Chicago Tea Party," and he invited "all you capitalists."

Over the following days, the question that seemed to transfix commentators was whether or not Santelli's instantly famous tirade had been scripted or sincerely felt. But what interested me was the elephantine perversity of the moment. The country was then teetering on the edge of economic disaster; one reason it so teetered was due to the bonus-driven doings of people like the traders who cheered for Santelli. And one reason so many of us teetered along with it was that business-news outlets like CNBC had almost entirely failed to warn us about the mounting problems in investment banking and mortgage lending.

But this CNBC host and his trader friends weren't the villains; they were the guys with a grievance.

One point remained. Who were these disgruntled traders, the body politic for whom Rick Santelli was the eloquent voice? Well, he told a CNBC colleague, they were "pretty

---

people who could no longer afford their payments were unable to take advantage of the program because their lenders dragged their feet, did not cooperate, or simply denied their requests. It seems the communists in the White House had neglected to supervise the lenders or make sure they complied. (See also the *New York Times*' gloomy postmortem on the program, dated March 30, 2011.)

So good news! We're still in Rick Santelli's "America": The law was on the books, but it wasn't enforced. It was a colossal flop, with "the losers" proceeding to lose their homes, just as God and the Market intended them to.

straightforward . . . a pretty good statistical cross section of America, the silent majority."

Of all the capsized reasoning Rick Santelli used on that fateful February day, this was the most perverse. Traders may come in different shades and prefer different foods, but by definition they represent only one walk of life: they are people who buy and sell abstract commodities. They make nothing. They move nothing (except prices). They are the financial industry distilled down to its grasping essence. And if we are to judge by *Trader Monthly*, traders are a "cross section of America" only if "America" is a place where truculence and bullying are the great national virtues and financial legerdemain is considered the noblest way of earning a living.

To others, however, the equation of traders with America, with We-the-People—why, that was the wisest thing to pass Rick Santelli's lips that morning. By sheer force of assertion, Santelli erased the stigma that had marked financiers ever since the start of the downturn. Now we could see, as one Tea Party organizer wrote later, that those traders were "simply working people who wanted the freedom to continue working and to enjoy the fruits of their labor in a fair way."[1]

As for Santelli himself, his oneness with the common man had been established even before his great moment in February. According to a *Washington Post* profile of the TV personality that was published in November of 2008, Santelli "is usually perched in a lower corner of the TV screen and is filmed from above, shouting up from a trading pit at the Chicago Board of Trade. It gives his rants a classic plain-speaking-little-man-against-the-system feel."[2]

And so the inversion was complete. For the original Populists, the Chicago Board of Trade was the very pit of hell, the seat of a financial elite who impoverished workers and robbed consumers while creating nothing themselves. For the populist rebels of our own time, however, the business reporter speaking for the "working people" of the derivatives pits is, obviously, a "little man" standing up to "the system" in classic thirties fashion.

Santelli's rant caught the insurrectionary spirit of the times. Public choler at the powerful was blowing out the stops in those first few months of 2009, and the reporter's outburst was an immediate sensation, replayed millions of times by the angry YouTubing multitude. The instant comparison was to Howard Beale, the populist anchorman character in the 1976 movie *Network*, raging against the system while the cameras rolled.

That the broadcaster was, in point of fact, speaking on behalf of the system and against the claims of the average people who were its victims was a subtlety Americans found easy to overlook. It was a time of confusion, and just about wherever you looked, the frustrated expressions of the powerful were being characterized as spontaneous eruptions of the American everyman, taking matters into his own hands.

Conditions were right for grand-scale perplexity of this kind. Who really knew, for example, what caused the cascading bank failures of the financial crisis? Or what a credit-default swap was? And who could explain the process by which such an instrument had brought the mightiest economy on earth to a standstill?

Amid the tides of bewilderment, though, one piece of deviltry stood solid and unmoving, a sort of Gibraltar of populist outrage: the TARP bailout bill. Now, here was a bit of villainy people could understand. It would be costlier, Americans were told, than the entire Vietnam War, or the Louisiana Purchase, or just about anything else. And it was unmistakably bad: the bailouts were the avenues by which our government obligingly moved the financial industry's losings over to the taxpayers.

In different times, the TARP might have become the rallying point of a revitalized Left. After all, the bailouts were clearly of a piece with the misbehavior that had come before: the deregulation of the banks, the bonus culture, the wrecking of the supervisory state. Business-friendly conservatives had been behind each of these, and then business-friendly conservatives had knitted together the TARP for the same rotten reason: to give their pals the bankers whatever they wanted. Had they mobilized themselves quickly, reformers might have depicted the TARP as the final chapter in the great book of fraud, the episode in which Wall Street used the captured state to transfer its debts to the public.

But it was the Right that grabbed the opportunity to define the debate, using bailouts to shift the burden of villainy from Wall Street to government. For them, the TARP was the only part of the crisis story that mattered—not the derivatives or the deregulation—and its conservative-Republican parentage made no difference. (That congressional Democrats voted for it, on the other hand, was deeply meaningful.) *They* were the sole rightful opponents of the TARP, conservatives insisted, because they opposed federal interventions in the market, and bailouts violated strict laissez-faire orthodoxy—*their* orthodoxy. Bailouts allowed government to decide who won and lost; they replaced the forces of competition with those of administrative fiat; and they puffed up the deficit, to boot. And so the Right staked its claim, making the TARP into the liberal outrage that lifted a thousand snake flags.[3]

"Let the Failures Fail"

The first of those snake flags was hoisted at a Tea Party rally in Washington eight days after the Santelli broadcast, and it was as perfect an example as any of the Right's ability to capitalize on public confusion. That original Tea Party rally sure didn't look spontaneous or grassroots to me when I showed up. In fact, it had every appearance of being one of those staged protests that happen all the time in Washington, in which a handful of people from a pressure group pose with signs for the media. I had heard about the plans for the gathering not from some radical handbill picked up on a street corner, but in an online message from an editor at the *American Spectator*, a sturdy pillar of right-wing Washington. The rally was to be held at the park across the street from the White House, the traditional staging ground for phony right-wing protest going back (at least) to the days when Jack Abramoff ran the College Republicans.

This was no act of defiance by the little man. It was Astroturf of the most ersatz kind; plastic grass with extra vinyl content. The event was swarming with well-known conservative movement personnel. The blogger Michelle Malkin took a turn with the megaphone, as did Joe the Plumber, the itinerant proletarian, who was there to show working-class America's faith in the cynical idealism of billionaire America. Lots of people were in suits, and some were wearing name tags from the Conservative Political Action Conference, which was going on a few subway stops away.

The protesters denounced deficit spending and bailouts and the item that had triggered Santelli's explosion: the possibility that government might help people modify their mortgages. Where communities once used to rally to help out a foreclosed-upon neighbor, the prototypical populists now wanted to see that uppity neighbor get evicted from the oversized home the rascal had no business buying in the first place.

The symbols, costumes, and confusion that the nation would soon come to know so well were all pretty much present at that first gathering: the snake flags, the three-cornered hats, the Constitution worship, even the epidemic of spelling errors. And, of course, the small-minded vindictiveness that for years now has masqueraded as brave back-talk to arrogant authority. Photographing Tea Party protest signs would soon become something of a cliché, but on that first occasion, a woman proudly held up for my camera a homemade declaration of befuddled outrage that read as follows:

> Can anyone on
> Capital Hill read?
> If so read the
> Constitution
> As Americans we do not
> have the right:
> To a house
> To a car
> To an education
> Americans have a right
> to per sue happiness
> not to have it given to
> them!*

There was talk about the conflict of "freedom versus tyranny," as though the real danger Americans faced was not economic collapse but some bid to crack down on personal liberty. And there was a slogan, a cry of existential anxiety from the bitter seventies—or, rather, a confused homage to Rick Santelli—as speakers began one after another to repeat

* The "pursuit of happiness" is a phrase from the Declaration of Independence, not the Constitution.

a famous line from *Network*: "I'm as mad as hell and I'm not going to take this anymore." *

"Anymore"? Barack Obama had been in the White House for a little over a month at that point, and yet already their suffering at his hands was more than they could bear. "They're" not going to "take this"? For decades, politicians had catered to every short-fused demand that economic conservatives raised. This was a group that had been singularly well served by the political system; they had received exactly the deregulated world they now said they wanted.

But "mad as hell"? Oh, that note rang true. Even I could be roped into that sentiment. And for everyone who was livid about the financial crisis and the bailouts, those first-generation Tea Partiers had a simple proposal: "Let the Failures Fail." That was the slogan I saw on one protest sign, and I have probably heard some echo of it hundreds of times since then.†

"Let the failures fail." Here, in one sentence, was a key to the amazing success the Right would shortly enjoy. They had an answer to the bailout outrage, and it was not modulated by lawyerly subtleties or votes-taken-with-nose-held, like the House Democrats who had voted for the TARP. "Let the failures fail": it was a line that would allow the revived Right to

---

* The line has a long history on the right. Howard Jarvis made it the rallying cry of the Prop 13 tax revolt in California in the seventies; Arnold Schwarzenegger picked it up from him. Journalists have used some variation of it to summarize the appeal of Ronald Reagan, Newt Gingrich, and Fox News boss Roger Ailes. It has been processed into titles for histories of both the populist Right in the seventies and the Tea Party movement. And about a month after Santelli was widely compared to Howard Beale, Glenn Beck claimed that he, too, had been inspired by the Beale character. See the profile of the star in the *New York Times*, March 29, 2009.

† Example: Glenn Beck, about a month later, monologuing to the camera just before letting his famous TV tears roll down his cheeks. "Those who screwed up must be allowed to fail, those who broke the law must go to jail."

depict itself as an enemy of big business, rooting for the collapse of the megabanks. The Tea Partiers may have looked ridiculous in their costumes, but their central demand was anything but.

The Bad Neighbor Doctrine

Not all "failure" is the same, however. What the newest Right has in mind is something philosophical, something both personal and sweeping. It demands liquidation across the board, a sort of deserved doomsday for the borrowing-based way of life. But in the great die-off it delights in imagining, the real culprits of 2008 have a way of disappearing from view.

If we watch closely, we can see the cards being switched. Whenever our tea-partying friends warm to the subject of letting-the-failures-fail—and they do so often[4]—sooner or later they inevitably turn from the bailed-out banks to those spendthrift "neighbors" identified by Santelli, those dissolute people down the street who borrowed in order to live above their station. These are the failures who need to be made to fail. It is always personal. Here are conservative warriors Dick Armey and Matt Kibbe, in a chapter of their "Tea Party Manifesto" called "Bailout."

> Many of us knew instinctually the bailout was wrong. We understood that in order for capitalism to work we need to be able to not only keep the potential gains from the risks we take but also accept the losses that may come. With profit comes the potential of loss. *Many of us had a neighbor or heard about someone who had been living too high on the hog for too long and were wondering why we were now supposed to pay for it.*[5]

At other times, the failure they long to see is cosmic failure, a "day of reckoning," as Senator Rand Paul likes to say: failure as nature's response to the hubris of big government, failure as our richly deserved punishment for our bad values. According to the former Fox News personality Glenn Beck, failure is a way of atoning for American materialism. Failure is a morally necessary and even a healthful thing, he wrote in a 2009 bestseller, "a necessary step in achieving success—a step that safety nets and bailouts attempt to take a shortcut around." These bailouts are, in fact, an offense against nature and republican virtue itself, an extension of the same selfishness that saw consumers go into debt and "politicians and the media" assure "us that America is about having the most stuff, the nicest cars, and the biggest homes." *

So let a thousand failures fail. Let all the losers go down. Government agencies that handed out the bailouts, banks that received them, greedy neighbors that took out mortgages, and everybody in between: Let them all fall flat. Let the jobless go without unemployment benefits. Let the farmers go without subsidies. Let depositors in failed banks walk away empty-handed. Let the dollar fail, too, and let those who didn't hoard gold coins for retirement in their own private hidey-hole suffer the consequences.

For decades, goes the sweet, scolding refrain, we've been living beyond our means. We thought we could waft to riches on flowery beds of ease, but now the bill has come due. The

---

* Aside from exhortations to go shopping after 9/11, I can think of no really prominent American "politicians" who have celebrated consumption in such a crass way. In fact, the only big-league politician I know of who has come close is China's Deng Xiaoping, who said, "To get rich is glorious." The quotations are from *Glenn Beck's Common Sense: The Case Against an Out-of-Control Government, Inspired by Thomas Paine* (New York: Threshold Editions, 2009), pp. 12, 14.

country is "broke," as Glenn Beck and countless other conservatives love to remind us; we can no longer defy the "Laws of Nature."[6] The thrifty and productive can no longer support the profligate. Only those who sow get to reap. Life is harsh, and Americans need to get used to it.

A few years down the road, this dogma would lead the rejuvenated Right to attempt actually to bring failure down on the nation, via the federal debt-ceiling showdown. But in the meantime, it was an attractive moral doctrine; a sweeping condemnation of a society that has lost its way, that worships false gods, that has become besotted with affluence. But the cult of failure appealed for another, subtler reason. It allowed the resurgent Right to shuffle the bitter mood of the moment and generate an outcome that was more to its liking—to deflect public anger from the obvious targets.

To Muddle Is Divine

For this sleight-of-hand to work, conservatives had to surmount an enormous cognitive barrier. By and large, the people who designed the hated bailouts—and the banks that benefited from them—had played on the conservative team. It was no problem to cast the Democrat Barack Obama, who continued the Bush administration's bailout policy, as a freedom-crushing dictator. But what to make of the fact that the ones who hustled the nation into this state of tyrannical unfreedom were, to all appearances and just a few short years ago, free-market paladins themselves?

The reviving Right could not accept the obvious answer to this question: that free markets were never really a holy cause at all; that for bankers, politicians, and corporate managers, the call for free markets has always been a high-minded way of saying "gimme," to be replaced by more direct methods, like demanding bailouts, whenever the situation changes.*

For the conservatives of 2008 and 2009, that left only one possibility: to declare that *their* faith in the myth was true, was pure; and to cast out the previous generations of conservatives as heretics to free-market orthodoxy. They even excommunicated their old hero, George W. Bush, as a traitor to the cause of freedom. Bush helped matters along by confessing, "I've abandoned free-market principles to save the free-market system," a line that will no doubt live forever on the websites of the insurgent Right.

Bush was not the only hurdle, however. In order for the rebellion to make sense—in order for the blame to fall where it needed to fall, the entire history of the last few decades would have to be rewritten. Instead of the global turn toward the market that historians see beginning in the seventies, we were now to understand that socialism had never been vanquished at all, that nearly every so-called conservative politician in those years was actually a liberal in disguise, that no one (with the peculiar exception of Ronald Reagan) had really been faithful to the free-market dogma.[7] The era of regulatory permissiveness that allowed the financial crisis to happen had to become unmentionable, deliberately erased. It could not have happened, since conservatives knew now that progressives and crypto-socialists had controlled both parties and called the disastrous shots from the days of Woodrow Wilson to those of Hank Paulson and Ben Bernanke.

---

* 'Twas ever thus. In *Age of Greed*, the financial journalist Jeff Madrick tells the story of Citibank CEO Walter Wriston, an outspoken free-market zealot (see, for example, Wriston's book, *The Twilight of Sovereignty*) who nevertheless demanded and received government bailouts for his bank on several notable occasions. See Madrick, *Age of Greed: The Triumph of Finance and the Decline of America, 1970 to the Present* (New York: Knopf, 2011), chapter 1.

Trickiest of all was what to make of the Wall Street banks. These had once been the crown of free-market creation, happy hives buzzing with humanity's highest incarnation, the trader. The bailouts, however, made them seem like the greatest welfare queens of all time. Or could the story be different? Maybe the government's villainy was so great that it had *forced* the bailouts on the banks as a means of taking them over. Maybe the banks were actually the *victims* of the politicians' meddling, rather than the architects of it. Just as Rick Santelli's commodity traders were recast as the American everyman, so the banks became, in certain tellings, the true casualties of the crisis.

Take, for example, the famous scene from the bailout saga in which a number of bank CEOs were summoned to Washington and told by their old colleague Hank Paulson of the government's offer to recapitalize them with what one set of observers call "free money." For the libertarian activist Stephen Moore, this incident was the opposite of what it appeared to be: not an occasion for outrage at the government-assisted survival of the unfit, but for solidarity with the oppressed banker, ground under the iron heel.

> Six bank presidents were summoned by Treasury Secretary Hank Paulson to Washington, and then shuttled into a conference room and told, in effect, that they could not leave until they collectively signed a document handing over percentages of their future profits to the government. The Treasury folks insisted that this shakedown . . . was all in "the public interest."[8]

Muddlement was the mode of the moment, and the master of muddlement was the TV host Glenn Beck. One day during the AIG bonus scandal in March of 2009, for example,

Beck explained AIG's business model to his viewers as though AIG was a subprime mortgage originator, and that therefore the economy's crash "had nothing to do with the company" but instead was to be blamed on "the weasels in Washington" who, as the right-wing legend had it, had forced those unfortunate subprime lenders to issue all those lousy loans.*

The next day, the host's rage went on, but the story was slightly different. This time, Beck declared himself staggered that a "failed" company (AIG) was shelling out millions in bonuses (correct), and that its bailout had effectively sent taxpayer money to foreign banks (also correct). Sure, the bonuses were an outrage (and here the muddling begins), but the recipients were sort of entitled to them, and, besides, Democrats had approved them. In fact, Democrats were the true culprits here: They had taken campaign donations from AIG employees, he announced, and now they were following their script from "last time," which is to say, the thirties, "whipping up mob

---

* In the course of this same remarkable episode, Beck also implied that Congressman Barney Frank was responsible for the AIG bailout the year before. Beck then went into a "history of AIG," which was actually a fairly detailed attack on Fannie Mae and Freddie Mac—apparently he had confused the mortgage companies with the insurance giant. (The quotes are from Beck's TV program for March 17, 2009.)

In point of fact, the initial 2008 AIG bailout was engineered by the Federal Reserve without input from Barney Frank or any other members of Congress; Frank famously criticized the deal the day after it happened. And although nearly everything in high finance is related to everything else, Fannie and Freddie are not the same as AIG, which is an insurance company that acted like a hedge fund, investing in mortgage-related securities and issuing credit default swaps. These were the businesses that got AIG into trouble. It is true that AIG owned a subsidiary that originated subprime mortgages—all the Wall Street playaz did—but to my knowledge no one has ever thought to blame AIG's travails on that subsidiary.

Government regulations, for their part, never required anyone to make risky mortgage loans and they certainly never forced anyone to invest in securities based on risky mortgage loans. The credit-default-swaps business was almost completely unregulated.

rule" and stoking public anger against the AIG executives. They were doing nothing less than trying to "channel the outrage" and "direct it towards the faceless bonus recipients at AIG."[9]

Which was an odd thing to say because "fake populist anger," as the host described it with disgust, was Beck's very raison d'être. Channeling the outrage was what he was put on Fox News to do. In this particular case, he was using any form of reasoning he could dream up to steer the nation's outrage toward Democrats, the party of government, "the weasels in Washington."[10]

This may seem confusing to you, but to the leaders of the conservative renaissance the muddling came easy. For them, Democrats were devil figures; there was no contradiction in depicting them as both the pawns of the banks and also the persecutors of them. Democrats were so malignant they could play both roles simultaneously. That is why a characteristic text of the movement, 2010's *Red State Uprising*, seethes about the "bailouts of Obama's Wall Street friends": apparently Wall Street was bailed out because Wall Street's kept politicians give Wall Street whatever it wants. Just two pages later, however, the sinister Obama is said to use "rhetoric for job creators and Wall Street that would be better reserved for Al Qaeda"—now we are to pity the poor financiers![11]

By that fall, the muddle was canonical, the shared common sense of the millions, the stuff of TV commercials, even. Rand Paul's Senate campaign, for example, ran an advertisement called "The Machine" that shows a monstrous robotic Capitol building, reaching out with steel tentacles and "scooping up Wall Street banks [the AIG logo], businesses [the GM logo], our health care," as the narrator woefully puts it. Here AIG is the hapless *victim* of the grasping, nationalizing, socialist monster. Then, a few seconds later, the commercial accuses Paul's opponent of "raising campaign money from the very people who supported the bailouts"—including a fund-raiser "hosted by lobbyists for bailed-out AIG"—these latter words spoken with the sneer that always accompanies AIG's name. Now the company is the *villain*, buying politicians to get itself a bailout. The viewer is expected both to hate AIG and feel compassion for it in the space of thirty seconds.

Into the swirling waters of national bewilderment waded a new generation of leaders, sharp-minded individuals who saw the opportunities in all this ruination. They felt our fury, they knew where it needed to be directed, and they also seem to have had a pretty good idea of who would benefit from it all.

CHAPTER 4

Nervous System

Much of this desperate bamboozlement looks pretty transparent today. Still, the duplicity led to exactly the grassroots phenomenon that its promoters imagined. The thinking at its core was sloppy, maybe, but in its general tenor it hit precisely the right note for those anxious days. While the world was coming to pieces in the storm, the newest Right acknowledged our terror and offered a utopian ideal, a beacon of authentic Americanness that glowed like a lighthouse through the swirling muddle.

Fear Itself

The reinvigorated Right has no leader, it is often said. But it does have a favorite doomster: this man Beck, whose career at Fox News began in January of 2009 as the wave of rage was building to a crest. For three years prior to that, Beck had presided over a TV show on a CNN station, but without ever managing to achieve popular success, let alone make himself the face of an era. Now, from the stage of Fox News,

Beck would become the voice of American discontent, stoking public fury and then escorting our outrage away from any logical target and over to a quarry more to his liking.

Glenn Beck is an unlikely hero. In 2008, when I first tuned in and heard him moan about leftist conspirators, I immediately dismissed him as some programmers' bet gone wrong: How could anyone think the George W. Bush era was the time to unleash a crew-cut red hunter? Or that the age of the Internet was the moment to get behind a man whose many wrong assertions could be so easily checked?

Then there was the man's odd combination of ignorance with chalkboard-scrawling didacticism. His snarling vindictiveness, punctuated with episodes of maudlin self-pity. His boyish clothes and winsome comic voices, sprinkled with shocking expressions of pure loathing. I doubted him, but I was wrong. From the start of his Fox News program until he left the air in June of 2011, he was one of the network's biggest stars, drawing in unprecedented numbers of viewers for his 5 p.m. time slot.

During this period, Glenn Beck was the subject of cover stories in *Time* and the *New York Times Magazine*; of two biographies, one of them written by the *Washington Post* columnist Dana Milbank; and of the adulation of millions of fans, a hundred thousand of whom packed the National Mall on one occasion to watch and listen as Beck swiped the symbolism of Martin Luther King's famous 1963 March on Washington. His strange ideas spread like weeds in the fearful climate of those days. You would hear his eccentric historical interpretations repeated word for word at Tea Party rallies, and his attacks on particular individuals echoed by other institutions across the nation's right wing. He was, for those two crucial years, the man of the moment; the person whose peculiar views defined the temper of the times.

For me, the key to understanding Beck is his admiration for thirties boy genius Orson Welles; Beck's production company, Mercury Radio Arts, is actually named after Welles's Mercury Theatre group. When the latter was organized in 1937, it was hailed in the Communist *Daily Worker*, but Welles's number-one modern-day fan seems to take inspiration less from his hero's left-wing politics than from his 1938 radio drama, "War of the Worlds," which described an invasion from Mars.* The mass hysteria that Welles accidently caused back then—many listeners didn't know the radio show was a Halloween drama—seemed to be Beck's conscious objective.[1] Night after night, as the Great Recession plodded on, the announcer would send his viewers shivering from their TV sets with scary fables of onrushing doom: Constitution-tearing power-grabs, civilization-ending inflation, leftist revolutionaries in the streets. And each end-times scenario, he would swear, was really happening; the Martians were really coming; this time the end was really here—almost.

The economic collapse turned out to be the perfect environment for this peculiar act. Every afternoon at five, there Beck would be with another installment in the unfolding tale of the nation's destruction: sometimes based on fact, sometimes almost purely imaginary, but always catching the jittery mood of the moment. And the central fear in his system of dread is that the Left is on the march, as people used to say in the thirties. Not *openly* on the march, mind you. No;

---

* Welles's "War of the Worlds" looms large in Beck-land; according to Beck biographer Alexander Zaitchik, it is "a recurring motif in Beck's life and career." Beck has actually restaged the Mars-invasion broadcast on more than one occasion, and one of the photos of himself that Beck includes in his first book, *The Real America*, shows the right-wing wunderkind striking virtually the same pose as Welles in one of the famous photos taken of the latter during the original "War of the Worlds."

advances by the Left are always made *by stealth*; their marchings are largely invisible to the untrained eye. Which meant it was up to Beck to inform us that the government was crawling with secret subversives, that the president was building a private army, and that liberals were scheming to make the economy worse so that an anguished public would turn to them to fix things—the hard-times scenario as a left-wing doomsday device. In fact, one of the talker's most demented ideas—he repeated it countless times, making it something close to gospel on the newest Right—was that many of the nation's problems, from the subprime debacle to the bailouts to the health insurance crisis, were manufactured according to a leftist plan that was published in the *Nation* magazine in 1966.*

"Most people will dread economic recessions and depressions," said the TV host in March of 2010, explaining the theory that had, by then, animated his show through a year of economic disaster. "But some people don't dread them. Some people are a little more opportunistic. They view this as their big chance. A window of opportunity to seize power to fundamentally transform things.† They don't see this as, 'Oh my gosh, we're struggling,' they see this as 'Now is our time.'"

---

* This is the "Cloward-Piven Strategy," a long-ago suggestion by the sociologists Frances Fox Piven and Richard Cloward (academic experts on social movements of the thirties, incidentally) that poor people be encouraged to sign up for state welfare systems on the theory that if enough of them actually claimed the benefits to which they were legally entitled, the systems would run out of funds and stronger poverty-reducing measures would have to be put in place. The lessons Beck took from Cloward and Piven's 1966 article on the subject, however, were that leftists yearn to "collapse the system," that leftists have an occult power actually to collapse systems, and that therefore leftists can be blamed whenever any system does, in fact, go astray.

† "Window of opportunity," "seize power," and "fundamentally transform" are trademark Beck characterizations of liberal thinking.

If the hard-times scenario was unfolding, it was coming not as an inevitable public response to Wall Street chicanery, Glenn Beck seemed to believe, but because leftists had carefully arranged matters to make all this happen. First they caused the financial crisis, Beck charged, then they seized power in response to it, and now they were pressing forward with a socialist program that would only make matters worse and thus increase demand for their brand of politics.

Blaming economic downturns on liberals—meaning everyone from academic leftists to labor unions to our bleeding-heart government—is a time-honored practice on the Right. You simply match up the crash, recession, or disaster in question with some contemporaneous expression of doubt about markets by a liberal politician, or with the announcement of some plan for a tax increase or a tariff hike. They happened at the same time, you announce; therefore, one caused the other. For larger, more systemic disasters, you simply heap the blame on grander works of liberalism like the Community Reinvestment Act, Fannie Mae, or the existence of the Federal Reserve System.

But Beck took the scapegoat strategy far beyond these terrestrial conventions. Liberals hadn't merely blundered us into downturns with well-meaning regulations; they had done it deliberately, in order to put the hard-times scenario into effect. They are, in Beck's imagination, what Beck is in reality: entrepreneurs of fear.

Conspiracy theorists have always been with us. But Glenn Beck brought them into the mainstream. And so began one of the most distinctive features of the right-wing renaissance: a rhetorical rapture-race in which pundits, bloggers, and candidates for high office competed to paint the most alarming end-times picture. Suddenly everyone was talking about the Martian invasion. The nation was being destroyed from within, the Constitution subverted, Freedom itself placed in mortal danger. We were on a march to socialism, a roller coaster to socialism, a bullet train to socialism—no, wait: socialism was already here, being crammed down our throats by the well-known socialist Barack Obama.

I myself got an unforgettable taste of this doomsday mania in March 2010, standing in a Tea Party crowd on the lawn of the Capitol building, listening to angry speeches in the open air while the members of Congress droned over the Democrats' health-care bill inside. A few of the speakers addressed some contested aspect of the measure, but the crowd's favorites were the ones who saw it as a colossal battle between good and evil—like the actor Jon Voight, who told us he prayed that legislators would find "the will, the strength, the courage to turn [their] back[s] on this destruction of America."

"Destruction of America": those were the words that rang the bell, that brought down the house in this new age of panic. During the health-care debate of 2009 and 2010, when it looked like the government was going to provide universal health insurance for all citizens—another big intervention into the marketplace—end-times foreboding ran riot. "The end of America as you know it" was the modest way Glenn Beck described the health-care measure. Its object was "robbing you of your humanity," protested Rush Limbaugh; another radio talker said it was "the end of the Republic."[2]

Although Newt Gingrich's contributions to the genre were not the spiciest, they were remarkable because he had once been a man we entrusted with weighty governing responsibilities. In 2010, however, Gingrich stepped forward to tell us the Obama administration "represents as great a threat to America as Nazi Germany or the Soviet Union once did." The question before us, he continued, is "whether the United States as we know it will cease to exist."[3]

Gingrich didn't say these things off the cuff in a TV interview; he wrote them with deliberation and put the lines right smack at the beginning of his book *To Save America*. Not "To *Renew* America"—that had been Newt's title back in 1995, when he was bubbling over with big ideas about the information age. But mere "renewal" wouldn't cut it now. Things had gotten so inconceivably worse that our requirement now was existential. We needed salvation.

Newt's ridiculous proclamations should have disqualified him from the political debate; instead, they made him, briefly, a front-runner in his party's presidential primaries. To judge by the thousands and maybe millions of people who were saying similar things, warning of betrayal from on high—of a corruption so universal, of a conspiracy so immense, of a crisis so dire—was now the way to speak convincingly to the anxiety gripping the land.

Fear was all the rage. The celebrated "red state" blogger Erick Erickson (along with his coauthor, Lewis Uhler) has given an almost clinically precise description of what he and his fellow alarmists achieved.

> Many Americans who had never been politically active, never walked a precinct, never interrupted their golf games, family gatherings, or vacations to discuss politics, government, or the Constitution, were suddenly gripped with the sense that their government, nation, and way of life were being stolen from them.[4]

People all across the nation were tuned to the Mars-invasion broadcast this time, and they found the coming catastrophe satisfying, delicious, even addictive. It was the orgasmaclysm: They tingled to imagine the outrageous injustices that would be done to them by the coming "death panels." They purred to hear about the campaign of "indoctrination" that the new president had planned for their innocent kids; their pulse quickened to think of the "chains" he was preparing for their mighty wrists; and they swelled with imagined bravery to picture how they would be targeted by "the coming insurrection." Their heroes, they quivered to learn, were victims of "persecution," their nation was under "systematic assault" by its own leaders, and they who had defeated Soviet communism; they who rejoiced to see their enemies writhe in the dungeons of Guantánamo—why, now they were "Gulag Bound," as a popular website of the day moaned rapturously.[5] This time it was apocalypse that moved the needle, that swayed the undecided, that made the sale.

We the Market

And what it sold was the great god Market. If only Americans would return to the paths of mercantile righteousness, we were told, the market's invisible hand would lift the threat of "destruction" from the land. It would restore fairness to a nation laid waste by cronyism and bailouts. It would let the failures fail, while comforting the thrifty and the diligent. Under its benevolent gaze, rewards would be proportionate to effort; the lazy and the deceiving would be turned away empty-handed, and once again would justice and stability prevail.

From the day the newest Right emerged from the shell of its rattlesnake egg, apocalypse (on the one hand) and perfect capitalism (on the other) have been its two lodestars, its omega and its alpha, its fear and its hope. "What do we say to socialism?" went the rallying cry at a Los Angeles Tea Party protest in 2009, according to two pollsters who have studied the movement. "Nooooo," yelled the crowd on hand. "What do we say to free market?" "Yesssssssssss."[6]

"The most powerful, proven instrument of material and

social progress is the free market," declares the preamble of the 2009 Tea Party manifesto, the "Contract from America." Or heed the words of the publishing magnate Steve Forbes, who maintains in his 2009 book, *How Capitalism Will Save Us*, that "*markets are people voting with their money.*" And then in the very next sentence, that "in many ways, a market is an ecosystem."[7]

This gets us closer to the grand social vision of the newest Right. Markets are both natural and democratic; they are, in fact, naturally occurring democracies, places of innocence and wonder. Just as we don't want to interfere in the fragile and no doubt democratic community of the coral reef, so we must leave (say) suburban developers alone to do their equally natural thing and express the popular will.

A particularly telling expression of the free-market faith occurs in a 2009 Tea Party pamphlet called *Spread* This *Wealth*. In order to teach readers about the nature of capitalism, the author, C. Jesse Duke—like many market-minded thinkers before him—describes the doings of an imaginary primitive man who finds a stick, kills a deer, and trades things with other primitive men. Duke then makes the following pronouncement.

> *This whole process of free markets and the trading of time and energy is just the natural order of the world.* A tree exchanges oxygen for carbon dioxide. A fire exchanges heat for oxygen. Atoms exchange electrons to become other atoms. Plants collect light to make chlorophyll, which nourishes animals, which become food for other animals and man, and so on. Everything in nature is constantly exchanging. So the free exchange of time and energy between people is the God-designed, natural order. Conflicts erupt when this order is upset.[8]

Remember the larger situation in which Duke (and Forbes and the anonymous contributors to the contract) felt moved to spin these fantasies. Our economy was in ruins thanks largely to unfettered investment banks trading complex financial derivatives that not even experts could understand. Monopolies and oligopolies were everywhere. Hourly wages had been falling for decades. But according to these voices of protest, the way to make sense of it all was *by imagining a state of economic nature.* By presuming that God Himself wants government to stay out of it.

I quote Mr. Duke here not to rain down mockery on his works but because the above passage is the clearest distillation I have yet seen of the movement's deliberate naïveté concerning economics. Capitalism is a system of balance and harmony and simplicity, the latest generation of conservatives insisted, regardless of what the newspapers say about shadow banks or credit default swaps. Armed with this universal truth, the newest Right vowed to accept no compromises, like better rules for Wall Street or smarter supervision; this was to be a war over ideals, over clashing utopias, over fundamentals. Economic policy needed to be understood as a quest for authenticity. And when that was clear, you understood that what we were suffering from was a conflict between true, natural capitalism and some phony, gimcrack amalgam slapped together by politicians over decades of compromises. As Glenn Beck asked his radio audience in September 2008:

> Why did Fannie and Freddie not work? Because it is the hybrid between government and capitalism. It is taking political power and injecting money into it. That's why it didn't work. Socialism doesn't work. Marxism

doesn't work. Fascism doesn't work. Capitalism works.
Capitalism put a man on the moon.*

Capitalism was a simple thing, once you stripped away the complexities with which progressives had saddled it over the years—so simple that Beck actually painted a picture of it, titled *Capitalism*, that he offers for sale as a lithograph: a red rectangle with smokestacks attached, peacefully pooting out little dollar signs. There are no human figures complicating the picture, and no cars or power lines or anything else surrounding the object. Just a basic shape in red with its name underneath: Capitalism. In its bricklike simplicity it's a sort of counterpoint to Beck's tangled world of conspiracies and disaster schemes—his serenity space, maybe, whither he travels mentally to escape from what must be his constant anxiety. Serene, soothing capitalism.

The problem that confronts us isn't how to fine-tune the controls; it's how to get back to that tranquil place. The only system that works is the real system—the true system, the system God made.[9] With the economy in ruins, our mission was to recover that authentic state of pure capitalism, rediscovering in the process what the Founders really meant and

* In truth, however, NASA circa 1969 was far more directly run by government than were Fannie Mae and Freddie Mac circa 2007. (It was also unionized.) While there was no profitable reason to send men to the moon, there were all sorts of profit motives at work at Fannie and Freddie. In fact, economists who have studied the two mortgage companies believe their failures arose not from their government-ness but from their leaders' desire to emulate the profits and bonuses of the private sector. "Fannie and Freddie caused such horrific losses because they were private institutions run by officers who obtained a 'sure thing,'" writes Bill Black, a professor at the University of Missouri, Kansas City, in his Benzinga column for January 10, 2011—"great wealth through booking high yield in the near term without establishing meaningful loss reserves."

what the Constitution really instructed us to do. It was as simple as one of those self-help recovery books where we come face-to-face with our honest selves: we had to take our country back, purge the body politic of compromises and alien ideas.

They Are Us

It is strange for the free market's reputation to have bounced back so quickly after its devotees came close to ruining us all, but it is doubly strange when you consider the nature of free-market fandom. Aside from the occasional Steve Forbes, the conservatives who are proclaiming their market-love these days are not tycoons or economists or bankers; they are average people.

And the markets that the people love, according to the newest conservatism's way of thinking, love the people right back. According to the populism of the revitalized Right, markets are democratic systems, with consumers and investors making their desires known through the channels of supply and demand. When markets are allowed to function without interference, this form of populism holds, they are essentially elections, perfectly articulating the will of the people. That's why those who participate most intimately in the market's doings—like Rick Santelli's bond traders—wear the halo of common-man averageness (they are the "silent majority," you will recall), while those who regulate markets from the outside are invariably "elitists": autocratic eggheads thwarting the will of the people with their iron fists.

A reverse Marxism like this appeals to the country's winners for obvious reasons: it casts their success as the thundering approbation of the public, while depicting their traditional enemies—especially those parasitical government bureaucrats—as arrogant know-it-alls. That's why the idea's origins are found in the literature of wealth: management books that tell bosses they are liberating humanity when they outsource the work to China; investment guides that extol the stock-picking genius of the small-town grandma; and those grand historical tracts that retired bank presidents like to write, assuring us that free markets are fueling popular uprisings in all countries.

Many years ago, when I first started writing about market populism, it was almost exclusively a faith of the wealthy. To write about it was to write about propaganda. Average people, I thought, no more believed that the corporations of America were democracies than they believe that a Pontiac is "fuel for the soul."

But then came a near-catastrophic failure of the economic system, and market populism, the sole utopian scheme available to the disgruntled American, went from being a CEO's dream to the fighting faith of the millions. One reason for this is that utopian capitalism can look pretty good in a time of disillusionment and collapse. It is a doctrine that seems to have all the answers. We were suffering, it held, because our leaders had broken faith with American tradition, meaning the laissez-faire system that prevailed before the dawn of organized labor and the regulatory state. The system we thought of as everyday American practice—"capitalism"—was in fact an "unknown ideal" that we had never really lived up to. Our elected officials had never been pure enough; our business leaders had always sacrificed principle to grab at subsidies; government's presence had grown and grown—and now, the story went, we would have to shape up if we wanted to prosper again.

That we don't have a pure market system in America is not some unique revelation vouchsafed to the Tea Party awakening. For decades, the idea has been a staple of the Left, where the limited-capitalist model is generally understood as a good thing. The state is involved in the economy in thousands of ways, the libs say, because it has to be. A complete free market would be a disaster, something not even the business community itself wants to try. As a famous labor historian wrote in 1975, "Not a single major American industry could survive today without government."[10] The real problem, from the liberal perspective, is that government doesn't go far enough; it merely doles out public subsidies of one kind or another while shareholders of private companies walk off with the profits, in the now-familiar scenario of socialized risk and privatized gain. The bailouts are a perfect example, the liberal critic says: the system allowed investment bankers to gamble however they wanted and then took over the losses after the bankers' bets went bad.

The revitalized Right simply turned this argument upside down. Yes, government has its finger in every segment of the economy, and that's what is to blame for everything that has happened. Market forces have never been truly free, and therefore they bear none of the blame for our current predicament. And so the obvious answer arose from a thousand megaphones: Get government out of the picture completely! Smash what's left of the liberal state! Until the day free enterprise is totally unleashed, capitalism itself can be held responsible for nothing.

Glenn Beck stages an allegory of the true faith in his 2009 book, *Arguing with Idiots*, in which a Founding Father in a powdered wig argues with a Soviet soldier over issues of the day. One of them asks whether the financial crisis was brought on "by a failure of capitalism, or by an abuse of it by the government?" The answer is simple, and Beck's Founding Father character enlightens us: "Under true free-market capitalism,

the government would have no involvement in homeownership whatsoever."

> They wouldn't encourage it through artificially low
> interest rates, Fannie and Freddie, tax breaks, or a
> "Community Reinvestment Act," but they wouldn't dis-
> courage it either.* Rates would be set by market partici-
> pants, based on risk, reward, and a clear understanding
> that making bad loans would result in bankruptcy.†

Do you see how awesome that would be, reader? Without regulation, everyone would live in harmony with nature
and the intent of the Founders, and nothing like collateralized debt obligations would ever be invented. Bubbles would
never happen. Bankers would never build systems that
rewarded them for making bad loans—their rational self-
interest wouldn't let them! To get back to Beck:

> But we've done the *complete opposite* of that. The
> housing market is manipulated by the government

---

* Chapter 11 of the *Financial Crisis Inquiry Report* compares the performance of
loans guaranteed by Fannie Mae and Freddie Mac to those issued by private
lenders. It concludes that Fannie and Freddie's loans were far less risky and
resulted in far fewer delinquencies than those issued by private companies. This
was because Fannie and Freddie, for all their faults, had higher underwriting
standards than their private-sector competitors. See in particular the chart on
page 218 of the *FCIR*. On the Community Reinvestment Act, see page 106.
(Full disclosure: My wife, Wendy Edelberg, worked for the Financial Crisis
Inquiry Commission as well as for the Council of Economic Advisers, whose
former chairman I quote below.)

† "Market participants" fully understood that the risky loans they were issuing
might result in their companies' bankruptcy during the housing bubble. They
just didn't care. This was because management had set up incentive systems
encouraging the "participants" to issue the bad loans anyway. The individuals
maximized their self-interest even though their companies died.

> every step of the way. So while some may argue that we need more regulation to prevent those future "excesses," I would argue that it's the existing regulations that created those excesses in the first place. In other words, what has failed isn't the idea of free markets, it's the idea that a market *can* be free when it's run by an increasingly activist government.[11]

In order for markets to deliver us to our destiny, we had to become mindful of their freedom. And ordinary people by the millions heard the call. In October of 2010, Glenn Beck exhorted his host of alienated followers to donate money to *the U.S. Chamber of Commerce*—the biggest, baddest business lobby in all of Washington, DC—on the grounds that "they are us." Ordinarily, of course, gifts to the chamber are denominated in the hundreds of thousands and are made by enormous corporations, but such a deluge of small donations followed Beck's appeal that it crashed the chamber's servers.[12]

CHAPTER 5

Making a Business of It

A handful of Washington's leading conservative institutions had seized the opportunity of the Santelli "rant" to stage the first Tea Party protest, and other organizations immediately scrambled on board. Certain groups could legitimately claim to have been partying since the beginning, like Grover Norquist's Americans for Tax Reform and whatever establishment Newt Gingrich was heading at the time. Outfits financed by the Koch oil billions, like Americans for Prosperity and FreedomWorks, were also quick to get on the bandwagon.

Once the Tea Parties looked like they might take off, just about everyone on the Right grabbed at the opportunity. The Fox News Channel, for example, presented the emerging protest campaign as if it was the network's own reality show. People from the Cato Institute were not hard to find at Tea Party conventions, nor were the folks from the Heritage Foundation. Ed Meese, attorney general in the Reagan administration, started the Conservative Action Project, supposedly an organization in which the new Tea Party groups could come together with existing movement leaders; its "only paid staff

member," according to a *Washington Post* story in February
of 2010, was Patrick Pizzella, a former associate of Jack
Abramoff.* And today there is no more fervent Tea Partier
than Richard Viguerie, the direct-mail genius of the seventies
who remade himself with "ConservativeHQ," a website aggre-
gating news from around the right wing.

There are former Bush administration office holders, like
John O'Hara, late of the U.S. Department of Labor, who published the first book about the Tea Party movement. There are
lobbyists, like Dick Armey, formerly of the DLA Piper firm and
now the figurehead at the Koch-backed FreedomWorks pressure group. There are the free-market policy wonks, like Phil
Kerpen of the Koch-backed Americans for Prosperity grassroots group, whose policy interests tend toward arcane corporate regulatory matters—opposing "net neutrality," fighting
proposed credit-card rules and suchlike—but who also writes
essays celebrating the Tea Party's "true populism" and boasting
of the fear it brings to the hearts of "powerful elites."[1]

Pelf and Populism

As the Tea Party grew, becoming the official populist response
to the economic disaster, opportunists both political and economic saw the gathering crowds and the spreading outrage
as their very own ship, sailing benevolently into port. Indeed,

---

* The organization also gives us a glimpse of bandwagonism at its worst. A video
produced by the Conservative Action Project in February of 2011 claims that
its manifesto of the preceding year, the Mount Vernon Statement, "sparked a
national movement," apparently taking credit for the Tea Party protests that
had actually commenced an entire year prior to that. The video also includes
comically lame footage of Ed Meese and other project leaders droning out the
lifeless words of their manifesto. If you want, you can watch it on YouTube:
http://www.youtube.com/watch?v=Pl6nJna-bl8.

the categories of "politics" and "profit" became so thoroughly scrambled on the resurgent Right that by September of 2010 it was possible for Mike Pompeo, a Republican candidate for Congress in Wichita, Kansas, to describe the political movement itself as "a restoration of the great American entrepreneurial spirit."[2] There were so many entrepreneurs, and they swung into action so quickly in the wake of the protests, that you sometimes wondered if their affluence wasn't the object of the agitation all along.

The most famous example was the National Tea Party Convention, held in Nashville in February of 2010, which featured an appearance by Sarah Palin and charged attendees $549 each. What's more, the sponsoring organization turned out to be a for-profit outfit headed by a man who was reportedly trying to set up a kind of Facebook-style web empire for wingers. "What was celebrated here in Nashville," wrote the journalist Will Bunch, after cataloging the trinkets for sale there, "wasn't so much the coming out of the conservative movement as the commoditization of it."[3]

The commodification continued wherever the movement pitched its tent. There were Tea Party cigars, $125 per box, perfect for those moments when you want to relax and "contemplate what has gone wrong and how to fix our government." An outfit called 912 Citizens, Inc. offered for sale a silver coin commemorating the movement's big Washington, DC, rally of September 12, 2009; it could be yours for $59.99.*

---

* "The Tea Party has been a fantastic success across our country due to real everyday people getting involved," declared the group's website. "At 912 Citizens, Inc. we believe using that same grassroots effort to promote our commemorative coins is not only a smart move but the right move. By allowing you to take part in our new reseller program you or your organization can use the extra income as a buffer in today's economic flat line or as a fund raiser to help your organization get the word out."

The commemorative coins on sale at the September 12 rally the following year were of some baser metal, but they were painted in full color; I picked one up at the Liberty XPO held at the Shoreham Hotel in Washington for a mere sixteen dollars. At that same trade fair, I perused a collection of tiny tea bag jewelry, countless T-shirt designs, bumper stickers that deliver "stinging slogans," a self-published book offering success tips distilled from Army field manuals, and a "hand signed lithograph" of American soldiers, with a wordy homage at the bottom proclaiming the man-at-arms' superiority over various civilian occupations.

This robust synergy of politics and profit extends to the highest reaches of the right-wing revival. It is, to name but the most obvious case, the signature approach of the movement's snarling sweetheart, Sarah Palin, who gave up her elected post as governor of Alaska in order to indulge in a series of cash-in opportunities: books, speaking gigs, TV shows. Let someone else do the scut work of governing.

Then there's Glenn Beck, who went from being a TV performer able to cry on cue to a one-man brand in a few short years. For example, his nightly forecasts of onrushing doom dovetailed nicely with the paranoid marketing strategy of his gold-vending sponsor—an outfit for which he also cut commercials.* Another product of Beck's preternatural opportun-

---

* Possibly in order to generate feelings of capitalist solidarity with his audience, Beck used to make much of his role as boss of Mercury Radio Arts, his production company. See in particular *The Making of GBTV*, a promotional video from June 2011 in which various Mercury personnel speak with reverence about Beck's entrepreneurial savvy and his idiosyncratic but brilliant way of making business decisions.

Beck is also a master of the politicized brand extension. During his heyday of 2008–11, he and his staff authored no fewer than ten books and booklike objects (three nonfiction humor books, two novels, one self-help book, one original audiobook, one children's book, and two works of commentary on the

ism is the 9/12 Project, whose putative object was to promote a vague civic togetherness of the kind Americans supposedly felt on September 12, 2001, along with a passel of antigovernment sentiments that the TV host associated, inexplicably, with that occasion. The "project" did much to inspire a large rally that took place in Washington, DC, in the fall of 2009. But to me the 9/12 effort always looked like something knocked together in a hurry in order to slap a proprietary claim on the then-emerging Tea Party—to brand the larger movement as a project of the empire of Glenn.*

And from the ever-shrewd Richard Viguerie there came an expensive DVD set revealing "Fundraising Secrets for Tea Party Leaders." Not only was he charging $297 for the DVDs—hopefully yielding a profit for Viguerie's outfit—but the declared goal of the instruction was to teach you to take advantage of the right-wing ferment to raise money for your own outfit. "Not since the late 1970s has there been a more favorable climate for you to launch a conservative organization," the entrepreneur Viguerie enthused in his advertisement for the DVD set. "The fundraising winds are at your back . . . and those winds are now blowing at hurricane force!"[4] It was entrepreneurship squared, with every party to the transaction an acknowledged mercenary: Viguerie would sell you the secrets of fund-raising so you could get started as a political entrepreneur in your own right.

Federalist period), and also launched Beck University, where you could take in Beck-approved lectures such as "Presidents You Should Hate."

* The shoddiness of the whole thing was apparent from the 9/12 Project's symbol: the familiar old rattlesnake, only cut into pieces like the one in the famous 1754 cartoon by Ben Franklin. What this chopped-up snake was supposed to represent, weirdly enough, were the movement's "Nine Principles"—there were nine chunks of reptile carcass, see—and its "Twelve Values," which were clearly indicated by the twelve rattles on the viper's severed tail.

I bring all this up not because I think Tea Partiers are uniquely covetous but—the very opposite—because the marketing of discontent is so typical of the way modern right-wing movements unfold. Viguerie, for example, introduces his website with a salute to political entrepreneurship from Benjamin Franklin: "It is incredible the quantity of good that may be done in a country by a single man who will make a business of it."

"Making a business of it" is exactly right. That is the formula that gave modern conservatism so many of its most notable institutions and adventures: the direct-mail revolution of the seventies, when it first became obvious that fearmongering was a profitable enterprise; the Iran-Contra episode, with its galaxy of panic-slinging fund-raising stars; the archipelago of Washington think-tanks and pressure groups that, for a modest consideration, will supply foot soldiers for your corporation's war with unions or environmentalists or consumer advocates; the careers of Jack Abramoff, Tom DeLay, Grover Norquist, and the rest of the gang; and, of course, the entrepreneurial brilliance of the K Street Project.[5]

And why shouldn't conservatives sell their services? They are cadres for capitalism, after all. When disgruntled activists criticized the 2010 National Tea Party Convention for crass commercialism, its organizer returned fire by calling those critics "socialists."[6] While his insult missed the mark, his sense of having been unfairly criticized was accurate enough. Viewed in the context of the last forty years, there is nothing strange about those who understand conservative politics as a career opportunity. Nor is there anything contrary to conservative principle in regarding grassroots movements as ready-made roundups of suckers. On the contrary; opportunism is one of the factors that has made conservatism so fantastically successful.

Still, the appearances can be off-putting, and the resurgent Right often struggles to reconcile such naked enthusiasm for gain with its self-image as the simon-pure voice of the common people. Yes, the movement loves capitalism, but even prophets of the profit motive do not like to think of themselves as exploiters or corruptionists. Markets must triumph everywhere, they tell us, but spondulics must never mix with statesmanship. This is why a Tea Party coffee-table book that includes dozens of pictures of protest signs praising capitalism also begins with a foreword (written by the action star Chuck Norris) complaining that "the Constitution has been ousted by cash" and that "the Bill of Rights has been bartered for corporate bonuses."[7]

It is another undecidable muddle, and the movement resolves it by simply having it both ways. Take lobbying, for instance, the most basic activity of commercialized politics. Tea Partiers think of lobbying as unspeakably dirty, an industry so repugnant that it can only be understood as a branch of the liberal empire. That's why few on the right are willing to embrace Abramoff or DeLay as one of their own anymore, regardless of those men's successes as political entrepreneurs. On the other hand, lobbyists like Dick Armey, who are not stained with felony convictions, are welcome in the movement's leadership. And no stigma attaches to the Tea Party Express, supposedly a mobilizer of the millions that was actually set up as a fund-raising operation by a well-known California political consultancy.[8]

Mass Individualism

The opportunism I am describing extends all the way to the newest Right's lowliest precincts. The movement's trademark expression may be the rally in the town square, but Tea

Partiers are not mass men. Attend such a rally, and you will notice that just about everyone seems to be angling for a moment in the spotlight, with shocking homemade placards or outrageous costumes. At a 2010 rally in Denver, a guy who stood a few feet away from me blew an old army bugle every time he heard from the podium a sentiment of which he approved. At the 2010 Virginia Tea Party Convention, I watched a man amble through the lecture sessions with a snake flag actually draped over his shoulders. Other men thought it was appropriate to show up wearing pistols strapped to their belts, even though the event was held in the safe, civilized, and almost antiseptic premises of the Richmond Convention Center. And, of course, people dressed in colonial garb—sometimes Revolutionary War reenactors or professional impersonators of Founding Fathers—are a well-known attraction at Tea Party events.

It can be a little embarrassing to watch the newest Right's rank and file arguing over who was the very first Tea Partier, exhorting their comrades to adopt some flag that they have designed, trying to impress one another with patriotic arcana like the *forgotten fourth verse* of the "Star Spangled Banner," or strategizing to parlay a single moment of YouTube notoriety into a lifelong career. But these stabs at personal branding, these efforts people make to transform themselves into walking advertisements—they are all of a piece, I believe, with the conservative establishment's efforts to capitalize on the grassroots awakening. Both are specimens of a kind of entrepreneurial self-assertion that distinguishes the American Right.

That's why the movement's gatherings are filled with freelance James Madisons, each one working on some patented political contraption out in the garage. Go to enough rallies, and you will learn about a group called GOOOH, which developed a plan to "evict the 435 career politicians in the U.S. House of Representatives and replace them with everyday Americans just like you." You will meet the folks from iCaucus, who promise to apply a metaphorical "Big Stick" to members of Congress in retaliation for the bank bailouts. You will discover "the answer we've all been waiting for has arrived" in the form of another group's "Redeclaration of Independence," which all are exhorted to sign.[9] Someone else has launched a movement called We Read the Constitution, which aims to have people all over America hold parties where they will declaim that document aloud. It may sound boring, but in truth it's a "profoundly moving exercise," so sign up.*

And everyone is a philosopher. This is a movement of manifestoes, blogs, and small-press books in which thousands of self-taught Montesquieus spin theories of government villainy they dreamed up using only the information provided by the Bible, the Constitution, and *The Glenn Beck Program*. Read through these brave declarations of political faith, however, and what astonishes is not their idiosyncrasy but their sameness. Using the same ingenious reasoning, each self-published *philosophe* comes to the same conclusions: The divinity of markets. The elitism of the liberals. And the extreme danger hanging over the head of the Republic.

Going Viral

All of these themes came together over the course of a story that began at a public meeting in a depressed part of Washington State in August of 2009. This was "Town Hall Summer,"

---

* After Tea Partiers helped redeem the House of Representatives in the sweeping election of 2010, the first act of the new body was—of course!—to read the Constitution aloud, with each member of Congress being assigned a different passage.

when protesters took their complaints from the streets and into the traditional Q-and-A sessions held by their elected representatives. It followed the same trajectory from contrived to genuine as did the Tea Party movement itself. At first, memos appeared from leadership groups instructing conservatives how to make themselves heard at town hall gatherings or even how to disrupt same.[10] Then, after a few town hall meetings were duly disrupted in spectacular fashion—with the disruptions captured for eternity on handheld video cameras—the fad caught on. The chance to inflict spectacular humiliation on some politician before the eyes of the nation was apparently the opportunity for which thousands had been waiting.

At the town hall meeting that concerns us here, the subject was the Democrats' various health-care proposals; the politician on stage was Brian Baird, a bland, affable Democratic congressman in khaki pants and a light-colored shirt; the local unemployment rate was well above 10 percent; and all across the country, public meetings of this kind were giving way to explosions of rage. Representative Baird had made the mistake of labeling such protests "brownshirt tactics," thus painting a big bull's-eye on himself.

Thanks to those ubiquitous video cameras, the man who would emerge from the meeting with the spotlight fixed on his burly frame was David W. Hedrick, a management consultant and former marine. At some point in the Baird gathering, participants had talked over a federal proposal to encourage the teaching of parenting skills, and now, as the cameras hummed, this man Hedrick stepped up to the microphone on the floor of the auditorium to tangle with Representative Baird. "I heard you say tonight about educating our children, indoctrinating our children, whatever you want to call it," Hedrick began, after introducing himself. On the soon-to-be-famous videotape, the congressman can be heard mumbling a reply, but before he finishes Hedrick erupts: "*Stay away from my kids!*"

The audience explodes with approval at the unprovoked assault. But the man on the floor is just beginning; thirty seconds later he is imparting "a little history lesson" to the hapless Dem: "The Nazis were the National *Socialist* Party. They were leftist." These Nazis, according to Hedrick and countless leaders of the revived Right who have seen fit to educate the nation on the subject of World War II, seized the very industries that the Democrats were now also ominously accused of coveting: banks, automakers, health care. Therefore, if liberals such as Nancy Pelosi wanted to search the country for people wearing swastikas, the angry man on the floor insisted, in a voice growing husky with righteousness, "maybe the first place she should look is the sleeve of her own arm."

The audience was on its feet now, shouting; a standing O for a guy who thinks we fought World War II to free mankind from universal health care. Or, more likely, because it's always fun to see a politician get a good verbal thrashing, regardless of the delusions involved. Hedrick, for his part, was not quite done yet; there was one more insult yet to come. He had earlier mentioned the oath to "support and defend" the Constitution that soldiers and public servants take—a matter of grave significance where Tea Partiers gather—and now he flung it in the Democrat's face. "As a marine," Hedrick insisted, "I've kept my oath. Do you ever intend to keep yours?" As the congressman mumbled again, the former marine turned his back and marched to the rear, as if from an overwhelming disgust.

The video of the confrontation "went viral," as the expression had it. Its image of a passionate everyman speaking up (literally, upward) at uncaring power was an awesome, inspiring sight, a populist moment of the most moving sort— that is, if you put aside the asinine things Hedrick actually said. In the days that followed, the clip appeared on countless conservative websites. It was played endlessly on Fox News. Someone set it to music. The former marine himself appeared on Sean Hannity's TV program several days after the show-down, informing the host that the Democratic administration's policies were the same "almost line for line" as those of the Nazis.

The world briefly seemed to be at the former marine's feet, thanks to YouTube, the revitalized Right, and an understanding of German history that bordered on complete fantasy. Hedrick was the political star of the moment, the Santelli of the summer. But the summer did not last.

Shortly after his appearance on Hannity's show, David Hedrick showed up at another town hall meeting for Congressman Baird, clearly trying to duplicate his original stunt. This time things didn't go as well. Hedrick burned up his allotted time pouting about all the abuse he had received since his last go-round on the public stage and then made the rookie mistake of asking Baird to read from the Constitution; the long, boring disquisition that followed took the wind out of the proceedings.

Still, as we media-age citizens know, it's hard to return to anonymity after a moment of stardom. Hedrick decided to run for Baird's seat in Congress; of the several Republicans vying for the post, the former marine distinguished himself by the extremist purity of his stance. It won him an intense grassroots following, Hedrick claimed.[11]

Even though he was now a congressional candidate, articles about Hedrick still usually began by noting his long-ago moment of YouTube glory, and in July of 2010 he showed up at a public budget hearing, clearly aiming to rekindle the populist magic, this time by throwing accusations at Washington governor Christine Gregoire while the cameras rolled. She ignored him. In August he lost the Republican primary to a state legislator.

Still, Hedrick could not seem to let go. Toward the end of the year he made one more attempt to capitalize on his fame: a Tea Party book for kids—the very kids that he was remembered for having warned that congressman to stay away from. As far as I can tell, the only notices the book drew were written in the key of *can-you-believe-this-shit*. But let us give Hedrick his due. He produced here one of the movement's most memorable documents: blunt, forthright, compact, insulting—and, most typically, written at an elementary-school level.*

The book was, of course, a Christmas story—which is to say, a contribution to the vast literature of complaint about how Christmas has been debased and uprooted from its rightful origins. *The Liberal Claus*, Hedrick called it, and it was a simple fable for the Tea Party era. It seems that evil liberal elves had stolen an election and installed a usurper on Santa's throne: the "Liberal Claus," a.k.a. Barack Obama. This impostor Claus ("'Are you even from the North Pole?' an elf questioned") buys off the children of David Hedrick's town, Camas, Washington, with free candy. He flouts the

---

* Perhaps because it understands politics to be such simple stuff, the conservative resurgence often chooses to express itself via children's lit. Glenn Beck's 2009 book, *Arguing with Idiots*, for example, includes a page of verse called "My Papa is a Capitalist"; it instructs kids about the power of incentives. In 2010, the Tea Party Patriots issued a coloring book that was supposed to carry the message of the Tea Party to the fat-crayon set, and the political entrepreneur behind the online "Patriot's Club," a kind of politicized Boy Scouts, offers "Patriots Qualification Cards" to kids who can declaim the Pledge of Allegiance, sing "My Country Tis of Thee," and learn sundry "survival skills." Sign up at http://www.fortpatriot.com/patriotsclub/.

"Christmastution," claiming that "very smart" people can find authorization for his misdeeds in that document even though ordinary people can't. He even requires Santa's elves to join unions, using as his enforcer an elf who uses German words and wears "jackboots," a clever nod, apparently, to Hitler's alliance with organized labor, something I had never heard of before but which I guess history-minded Tea Partiers know all about.

Spoiler alert: the kids of Camas, Washington, get their hands on a snake flag and rise up against the pretender Claus. Critical verdict: the metaphors are tortured, the prose is lousy, the caricatures are heavy-handed, and in a sort of demented homage to *Where's Waldo?* the illustrations include images of a Stalin elf, a Castro elf, and a Hugo Chávez elf, all of them lending a hand to their liberal North Pole pals. Of course, Hedrick and his singular accomplishment had to be mentioned in the story, too: at the bottom of a page of the *Christmas Times*, the reader can see the following headline: "Camas man's rant goes viral," over a caricature of Hedrick himself.

David Hedrick was not elected to Congress, but his story tells us something valuable nevertheless. The relentless grabbing of opportunities, the blending of politics with profit, the ceaseless striving to build a career on a single moment of media glory—these are the elements from which the conservative resurgence has grown. In this particular episode, the entrepreneur failed. But thanks to the many others in which entrepreneurs succeeded, the resurgent Right was able to conquer Congress and put its crippling agenda into effect.

CHAPTER 6

A Mask for Privilege

Another revealing artifact: an enormous flag, waved by a man at the Code Red rally on the west lawn of the Capitol in March of 2010. This remarkable banner featured the stripes of the traditional Old Glory but replaced the stars with the Tea Party movement's coiled-rattlesnake emblem, over the words "GET BACK!" The red and white stripes, meanwhile, were filled with carefully lettered political demands, eighteen of them in all, plus the name of the website where you could buy a flag just like it for forty dollars, plus shipping. Talk about political entrepreneurship: here was a flag with a built-in advertisement.

When I was young, I used to wonder what the elements of the American flag were supposed to represent; this particular ensign seemed to have been designed as an answer to that question, with each stripe carefully labeled so no misinterpretation was possible. It was difficult to read while flapping in the March breeze, of course, but now, after having visited the flagmaker's website, I can tell you that, among other things, the stripes call upon our elected officials to: "Balance the Budget," "Protect Free Markets," "Respect Property Rights," and to make "No Regulation Without Representation," which sounds a lot like a call to let corporations vote.

I didn't buy a "Get Back" flag. Instead, I picked up a book of political theory, *Spread This Wealth (And Pass This Ammunition)*, in which the flag designer, the aforementioned C. Jesse Duke, can be found declaring that America was "settled, built, and defended by ordinary people, just like me—laborers, lumberjacks, farmers, soldiers, share-croppers, and others who make their living by the sweat of their brow." These are also, I guess, the people who want government to keep its hands off "free markets" and to stop its infernal regulating— laborers and sharecroppers, acting through their intermediary, the Tea Party movement. "I take pride in the fact," Duke continues, "that I'm one of them and not an intellectual."[1]

But C. Jesse Duke isn't exactly "one of them." The About the Author page in his book describes him not as a lumberjack or a sharecropper but as "a self-employed small business owner for thirty-eight years." And with that mix-up about social class, I submit, we encounter the movement's most essential bit of muddling.

Duke's idea of society's structure is actually something you come across all the time in the rhetoric of the resurgent Right: America is made up of two classes, roughly speaking, "ordinary people" and "intellectuals." According to this way of thinking, as we see again and again, either you're a productive citizen, or you're some kind of snob, a university professor or an EPA bureaucrat. Compared to the vivid line separating intellectuals and productive members of society, all other distinctions fade to nothingness. Between small-business owners and sharecroppers, for example, there is no difference at all, just as other Tea Party authors saw no real difference between Rick Santelli's bond traders and "working people."*

Erasing class distinctions in this self-serving way is one of the conservative revival's great recurring techniques. There is no better instance of this erasure than the enormous rally held in West Virginia on Labor Day 2009 for the express purpose of announcing the solidarity between coal miners and the coal mine operators who employ them. The get-together featured the protest favorites Sean Hannity and Ted Nugent and was presided over by Don Blankenship, the CEO of Massey Energy, a pollution-spewing, strikebreaking mogul of the old school.[2] Dressed in American flag clothing and boasting that the gathering had cost him "a million dollars or so," Blankenship took the stage and declared that he was there to "defend American labor because no one else will." Specifically, the CEO was standing tall against "our government leaders," who are, with their safety and environmental meddling, "American workers' worst nightmare."

Eight months after that rally, twenty-nine workers in Massey's Upper Big Branch mine were dead from a huge underground explosion that almost certainly would have been minimized if Massey had followed standard safety and ventilation practices—or if U.S. mine inspectors had backed up their many citations of the operation with proper enforcement.[3]

Now, when we find a mine *operator* claiming that his own struggles against regulation are actually the struggles of mine *workers*—workers who are then killed because mine regulations are not properly observed by said operator—we have

---

* "Capitalism is NOT the problem; Ivy League politicians ARE" is one of the ready-made protest slogans that blogger Bruce Bexley suggests in *The Tea Party Movement: Why It Started, What It's About, and How You Can Get Involved* (NP: Seattle, 2009), one of the first bound works to appear on the subject. The quote can be found on p. 53.

stumbled upon a nearly perfect example of what the sociologists call "complete horseshit." The man's ideas about class are so contrary to reality, so absurdly false, that they serve to bring into sharp focus precisely the difference they are meant to conceal.

By the end of 2011, Americans would have a name for Blankenship's class—the one percent—as well as for the 99 percent of the population on whose behalf he claimed to speak. But for the conservatives who had by then taken control of Congress, class is never about income or wealth; it's about learning. Intellectuals are the villains at the top of the great pyramid, just as they were during the years of the culture wars. To be sure, the reasons we are supposed to hate intellectuals have changed slightly this time around. Back in the Bush years, the crime of the intellectuals was always supposed to be their contempt for the values of the red-state heartland—their disrespect for the sanctity of the fetus as well as the fine points of NASCAR. In the present situation, though, the intellectuals' sin is different: they doubt the hand of the almighty Market.

The common people, by contrast, supposedly understand their place in the Market's order, whether they trade bonds or dig ditches. Indeed, these humble souls are indistinguishable from the Market Itself since It is an expression of their wants and aspirations. And the embodiment of this populist spirit of humility before the Market is the small-business person. Unlike the bureaucrat or the college professor—or that unholy cross of the two, President Obama—the small-business person is a purely Market-made creature, an individual who gets by on his initiative alone, an entrepreneur who works hard, who reaps what he sows, who receives no assistance from government, who even accepts failure uncomplainingly if that's the way the Market wants it.

Dictatorship of the Entrepreneur

We know, anecdotally at least, that the people who show up for Tea Party rallies tend to describe themselves as victims of the recession. But this is not to say that Tea Party protesters have been pauperized by the downturn or even that they are unemployed, in the manner of 1932's Bonus Army, although individuals here and there certainly are. In fact, Tea Partiers tend to be better off than the public generally; read their accounts of hard-times suffering closely, and you will often find that the form it takes is a downturn in their business.

This is no poor people's movement. Just look around you at a Tea Party event: the protesters' clothes look new; their hair was recently barbered; and male protesters sometimes wear neckties even when not in Washington, DC. One man I met at a rally in Denver showed up in an ascot. Nor are they a desperate mob. The favored rhetorical style of the movement is vituperation with overtones of righteous bloodthirst, but when addressing one another the protesters tend to be polite—at least, in my experience.* They say "excuse me" as they make their way through the crowd, and according to right-wing legend they always put their litter in the trash can when they leave.

Management-speak saturates the movement. Tea Partiers sometimes write about "core competence" when they mean *protesting*, "political entrepreneurs" when they mean *leaders*,

* There are also a few famous examples of uncivil behavior, like the time in March 2010 when a protester allegedly spit on Representative Emanuel Cleaver and threw a racial epithet at Representative John Lewis. And the e-mails I received from Glenn Beck's fans after I became one of the anchorman's targets were far more vicious than ordinary letters to the editor. On the other hand, such bullying bravado was nowhere in evidence when a Tea Party rally that I attended in Denver drew a heckler with a bullhorn. On that occasion, the conservatives did nothing but wave their signs and call on the police to intervene.

and "early adopters" when they mean *rank and file*.[4] One of the movement's favorite texts is a work of management theory. There even used to be a Tea Party website that kept a list of favorite CEOs.[5]

The entrepreneurial personality is never absent where tea-sippers gather. Don Crist, author of the booklet *What Can I Do?: After the TEA Party*, describes himself as a "small business consultant," while Stephen D. Hanson, author of *Transcending Time with Thomas Jefferson*, is "a small business owner and mortgage loan executive." Senator Jim DeMint of South Carolina, the Tea Party kingmaker, tells fans that his prepolitical career as a "small business owner" is where he learned his signature antigovernment politics.[6] And Republican presidential candidate Herman Cain earned his own conservative spurs back in the nineties when he denounced Bill Clinton's health-care proposal on behalf of the nation's small businesses; today he presents himself as a man in touch with "the real folk."[7]

Glenn Beck also glories to remind the world of his small-town, small-business roots, and throughout the fall of 2009, the TV host could be found protecting the pale flame of small-business populism as it flickered unsteadily in the socialistic winds blowing from Washington, DC. He interviewed panels of small-business owners, talked up the number of jobs small-business owners create, and saluted their generalized, all-American greatness: "They represent the spirit of America," he said on one particularly maudlin occasion, "what used to be the American Dream."[8]

The new crop of conservatives elected to Congress in the 2010 landslide often talk as though protecting small business was the special cause for which they had been called forth from behind the plow. Mark Kirk, now a U.S. senator for Illinois, proposed a "Small Business Bill of Rights" during the 2010 campaign season,* while the campaign website of Congressman Francisco Canseco of Texas included this astounding call for the dictatorship of the entrepreneur: "We must put the reigns [*sic*] of our economy back into the hands of American small business owners."⁹ Empty rhetoric, to be sure, but consider the implications had Canseco meant this sincerely: given that small business surrendered the economy's reins to finance and large-scale manufacturing in the period after the Civil War, he would essentially be demanding the reversal of nearly a century and a half of modernity.

A survey by the *New York Times* found that small-business owners made up nearly 40 percent of the Republicans swept into the House of Representatives in 2010—a dramatic increase from small business's representation in previous years.¹⁰ If we count the GOP freshmen who were endorsed by the National Federation of Independent Business (NFIB, the main small-business trade association), our census of small business allies comes to 74 percent of the new Republicans in Congress.† Soon after arriving in Washington, a bunch of these

---

* Item number one of Kirk's rights was, oddly, to "Protect secret ballots in union elections." Now, protecting workplace democracy seems like a strange concern for small businesses, which traditionally are sworn enemies of labor unions. Then you remember that the "card check" bill, a high-profile Democratic proposal which would have allowed workers to replace ballots with signed cards, would have made it much easier for workers to unionize. Therefore, it had to be opposed by any rhetorical means necessary. And so, in the funhouse mirror of contemporary conservatism, the greatest foes of workplace democracy became its biggest champions.

† Representatives of the NFIB were much in evidence during the 2010 crusade. At a Tea Party gathering in Wisconsin, for example, a local NFIB officer assured the disgruntled that the federation stood shoulder to shoulder with them in the fight against "un-American socialistic behavior." "NFIB believes exactly what you do," he told the throng: "We need to stop big government." Fortunately for the world, his speech has been preserved on YouTube: http://www.youtube.com /watch?v=jA5ftE4B0lQ.

entrepreneurial legislators got together in what they called the "Congressional Job Creators Caucus," open only to small-business types. And when they held the economy hostage during the 2011 debt-ceiling debate, they did so because they knew government had to operate like a small business.[11]

Wait, go back: *the Job Creators Caucus?* Let me admit here that, for all my skepticism, I was a little startled by the epic fraudulence of that phrase, the fake sense of accomplishment that it must require to call yourself a "job creator" while excluding almost all of your colleagues from the designation. Nearly everyone in Congress believes they're helping to create jobs, whether they're voting for the giant stimulus package of 2009, writing up a tax loophole for a campaign contributor, or earmarking a "bridge to nowhere"—heck, even supporters of the Obama administration's hated cap-and-trade proposal believe it will create jobs.

Ah, but according to the purified market populism of the conservative renaissance, those other members of Congress are simply mistaken. Forget the WPA and the millions of people it put to work during the Depression: Government simply cannot create jobs; it's impossible by definition. The only entity endowed with this power is business, and the smaller that business is, the more potent its job-generating magic. Thus one of the great catchphrases of the period: "Government doesn't create jobs; you do," as Republican freshman Nan Hayworth of New York put it in a speech to business leaders in her district.

One reason the Right fastened on the "job creator" line so avidly is because it allowed them to flip the script of the hard-times scenario. In years past, high unemployment had led almost automatically to liberal victories, since liberals were historically the most willing to take action on behalf of the jobless. But now we knew that the only possible way to help the unemployed was to help entrepreneurs. When people were out of work, the important thing was not stimulus packages or public works or social insurance: it was giving small-biz trade associations every last little item on their legislative wish list. The nation's job creators had to know they were loved. Their confidence had to be carefully built up; their biases had to be catered to; their every caprice had to be enshrined in state policy.

Unfortunately, no one seemed to know for sure the exact quantity of jobs these job creators actually created. In 2009, President Obama credited small business with 70 percent of the new jobs in the economy, but conservatives sneered at such a feeble number. Ninety-seven percent of new jobs was the figure Glenn Beck gave during an interview with the president of the American Small Business League in March of 2009; by October of that year, his views had moderated slightly, and small business was said to be creating only 80 percent of the new jobs in America.[12]

The reason no one can give a definite answer is that small-business job creation is a myth. It has been thoroughly debunked by journalists and academics over the years; it only got its start thanks to a statistical illusion created during the eighties, when big businesses were beginning to outsource everything they could to small, no-benefits firms in order to suppress labor costs.[13]

But against the amplified righteousness of the conservative revival, such facts had as much chance of being heard as does a kitten's gentle purring while a freight train roars by ten feet away. The country was in a deep recession; unemployment was high; the job creators must be empowered to do their thing.

So it was that David Rivera, a GOP freshman from Florida, was able to declare on his campaign website that "the biggest problem our economy is facing"—the biggest problem, mind you, even after the near collapse of the nation's financial structure—"is that business owners, especially small business owners are nervous, and reluctant to start hiring again."[14] And since small-business owners were such world-champion job creators, their nervousness was a matter of grave public concern. If we wanted to help the unemployed, we had to soothe small business's jitters. We had to assuage their fears. We had to grant their wishes.

Let's Drink to the Salt of the Earth

Small business is traditionally cloaked in a haze of populist heroism. Like family farmers before them, entrepreneurs are thought to be sacred: they are individualism in the flesh, the plucky strivers who have always made the American economy go. If you put aside details like the benefits that mom-and-pop stores generally don't provide their workers, small business can sometimes seem like the last redoubt of Jefferson's independent yeomanry.

In a 1983 speech commemorating Small Business Week, for example, Ronald Reagan started off by saying, "Every week should be Small Business Week, because America is small business."* It just got sappier from there: "entrepreneurs are forgotten heroes"; they're "the faithfuls who support our churches, schools, and communities, the brave people everywhere who produce our goods, feed a hungry world, and keep

---

* Democrats are no different. Although Barack Obama is often understood as the satanic antithesis of entrepreneurship, his own 2010 statement on Small Business Week declared small businesses to be "the engine of our prosperity and a proud reflection of our character. A healthy small business sector will give us vibrant communities, cutting edge technology, and an American economy that can compete and win in the 21st century." Read more at http://www.whitehouse.gov/sites/default/files/2010smallbusiness_web.pdf.

our homes and families warm while they invest in the future to build a better America."[15] Oh, they're the salt of the earth. The roots of the grass, the dreamers of the dream, the vox of the populi, the common man in all his upstanding righteousness.

And everyone wants a piece of that righteousness. Liberals, for example, like to salute small business because that way they can seem to be "pro-business" without openly endorsing Walmart or Exxon or JPMorgan.[16] Perhaps also, deep in their subconscious, lingers a tribal memory of the days when small businessmen were members of the progressive coalition, soldiers in William Jennings Bryan's crusade against monopoly, and reliable supporters of reform because reformers used to make a point of enforcing the nation's antitrust laws.

Not only has the conservative revival harvested the righteousness of the brave little entrepreneur; it has adopted the small-business mind-set. With this understood, several of the peculiar ideas of the newest Right immediately make sense. Its insistence that an alliance of big government, big business, and big labor have come together under the banner of "socialism" and closed off true competition in America, for example, might have been drawn from some pamphlet circulated by a small-business trade association generations ago.[17] The movement's undimming rage against organized labor, otherwise so pointless in the largely union-free twenty-first century, is one of the fixed obsessions of the small-business mind. And the notion that "real" capitalism can and should be quickly restored has been the entrepreneur's panacea pretty much ever since small business surrendered pride of place to large-scale industry in the mid-nineteenth century.

Similarly, the movement's reverence for an imaginary past, for "taking our country back," is merely a displaced longing for the distant days when small-business people were men of preeminence in their community. The conservative revival's single-minded focus on bailouts stems from small business's historic hostility toward monster banks, now reincarnated as "too big to fail" institutions and locked in an unholy union with monster government.* ("Congress spent billions of dollars in stimulus money to bail out big banks and financial institutions," declared Congressman-to-be Pat Meehan of Pennsylvania in 2010. "But your average small business owner simply has not seen the benefits.") Even the Tea Party's famous agnosticism on social issues reflects small-business priorities. While almost all entrepreneurs tend to be conservatives on matters economic, according to the NFIB, many of them take a liberal stance on social issues like school prayer.[18]

But it is the movement's obsessive fear of "burdensome regulation" that really marks it as a product of the small-business mind.

For decades, middle-class Americans loved telling one another scary stories about Invasive Regulators. The tales always unfolded in the same way: A small businessman was doing something eminently reasonable, minding his own beeswax, when—out of nowhere—he was hit with some outrageous EPA fine or tripped up by some hypertechnical OSHA demand. Obvious realities would be disregarded in the bureaucrat's zeal for rule-following; time would be wasted; business

---

* Although I have never seen it mentioned in any reporting on the Tea Party, small-business people have special reason to be aggrieved in the particular economic situation of the last few years. As a class, entrepreneurs tend to borrow against their houses far more than other social groups; this is how they finance their businesses. When real-estate prices collapsed, many of them found themselves underwater and closed off from an important avenue of credit. This has undoubtedly made the spectacle of the Wall Street bailouts that much more galling. See Mark Schweitzer and Scott Shane, "The Effect of Falling Home Prices on Small Business Borrowing," a commentary dated December 20, 2010, and posted on the website of the Federal Reserve Bank of Cleveland: http://www.clevelandfed .org/research/commentary/2010/2010-18.cfm.

would not get done. *It was as though our government wished to punish productive effort!*

Stories of Invasive Regulators were a constant feature of the comfortable midwestern milieu into which I was born. Ronald Reagan tossed them off all the time on his way to the White House. The plot of *Ghostbusters* (1984) turned on just such a small-business set piece. And the Republican Revolution of 1994 was largely driven by small-business anecdotes like these—that is, if the account of that revolution written by the then president of the U.S. Chamber of Commerce is to be credited.[19]

But it's no longer so much fun to swap stories about the ignorant overreaching of the Consumer Product Safety Commission, a favorite target of the storytellers of old. That particular agency was lobotomized so effectively by the George W. Bush administration it couldn't spot the lead paint on imported Chinese toys. Toothless regulatory agencies are what allowed the rampant safety violations at both the ill-fated Deepwater Horizon oil rig and the ill-fated West Virginia coal mine mentioned earlier. And the idea of a bank regulator getting up in an entrepreneur's grill is the real joke nowadays. Bank regulators! They're the ones who did so much to protect the big banks from nosy state-level officials who actually wanted to stop fraudulent mortgage lending.

One reason the bogeyman of the Invasive Regulator can still mobilize the troops, I think, is that small businesses actually experience the regulatory presence, such as it is, far more acutely than do their big-business colleagues. When we talk about the age of deregulation or the era of "neoliberalism," we are referring to the gradual rollback of certain banking rules, the rise of a certain school of economic thought, and the privatizing of certain government functions. These are important developments in the grand, historical sense, but to a struggling small-business owner they might seem completely irrelevant. It's hard to convince a man sweating over a fifty-page income-tax return that the state has gone away or that markets are now in charge.

And after 2008 there were some good reasons to believe—to fear—that the regulatory state was back, most obviously the universal health-care law signed by President Obama in 2010. Not only did Obamacare contain a—yes—burden-some provision that would have required businesses to issue 1099 forms for nearly every expenditure they made (it was promptly repealed in early 2011), but it required businesses with fifty or more employees to provide health insurance for workers, possibly stripping away one of the greatest com-petitive advantages that such firms possess.*

If "capitalism" is the system in which you eke out a living installing plumbing or selling farm equipment, it is under-standable that you feel that government interferes enough in capitalism already. If "capitalism" is the system in which no-doc loans are handed out indiscriminately in order for the management of some mortgage firm to hit some bonus tar-get, then packaged up and sold off to some hedge fund so that *its* management can hit another bonus target, well, we are talking about something entirely different. The journalist Matt Taibbi got this aspect of the right-wing renaissance exactly right when he recounted, in a 2010 interview, how

> most of the Tea Party people I talk to—a lot of them are
> small business owners. They have hardware stores or

---

* Another famous example of clumsy regulatory overreach was the Consumer Product Safety Improvement Act of 2008, which was designed to get lead toys out of the market, but which was so poorly written that it seemed to threaten the existence of thrift stores.

restaurants, and they see regulation as an ADA inspector or a health inspector coming to bother them and ring them up with little fines here and there. That's their experience with government regulation. And so when they think about JP Morgan Chase and Goldman Sachs and regulating those banks, to them it's the same thing. They have no idea that regulation for these big companies is really a law enforcement problem, that it's not this little niggling health inspector type of business.[20]

The distinction between these two kinds of capitalist practice is not something the renewed Right has much interest in clarifying. Rather than acknowledging the outlandish practices that actually went on in the mortgage industry, to name the most important chapter of recent business history, conservatives push the blame back where many business owners suspect the blame belongs: the deadbeats who took out all those mortgages in the first place.

And also back to the usual, all-purpose culprit: government. If you ask a random sample of Americans what caused the financial crisis, you will almost inevitably hear that it happened because government forced banks to hand out risky loans to poor people. Sometimes the story is embellished with lurid details like an imaginary lawsuit with which Bill Clinton supposedly threatened bankers if they didn't hand over money to his minority constituents. But always it comes back to the familiar villain: Big government, using the 1977 Community Reinvestment Act (CRA) to force the poor bankers to do something they wouldn't otherwise have done.

It is true that this myth gets the beloved Market off the hook for our economic disaster, but in terms of what actually happened, the myth is completely wrong. Banks handed out subprime loans because it was profitable to do so, not because a thirty-year-old law suddenly kicked in and forced their hands. In fact, the CRA was basically not enforced, and everyone in banking knew it. Furthermore, the CRA did not apply to the fly-by-night mortgage originators or shadow banks who were the actual prime movers in the disaster, and the traditional banks that were subject to it were not required to hand out risky or fraudulent loans. On the contrary: The Financial Crisis Inquiry Commission studied mortgages written under CRA commitments and discovered that such loans were generally prime loans which have performed well over the intervening years.[21]

Once again, however, when facts get in the way of idealistic preconceptions, preconceptions win. The only way lending standards get weakened, in many businesspeople's experience, is when federal agencies get involved. And where they've seen such weakening most prominently—or believe they've seen it, as certain historians of small business attest[22]—is with minority-owned enterprises, which are sometimes granted set-aside government contracts. It's simple enough to imagine that the pattern extended to mortgages as well; that the feds forced banks to hand out special loans to minority borrowers; and thus to conclude that the entire financial crisis was a consequence of government interference in what ought to be—used to be!—private affairs.

And the bailouts! To your average entrepreneur, it was an unmitigated insult to watch the big banks get an injection of capital from the Fed and the Treasury on terms that no local business ever receives. For some, the bitterness still lingered nearly three years later. When it was revealed in August 2011 that the bailouts had been far larger than originally reported, conservative leader Richard Viguerie took the occasion to look back in anger. Recalling the optimistic statements issued by Morgan Stanley at around the time the firm was borrowing almost a hundred billion dollars from the Fed, Viguerie wrote, "Try that line with your bank examiner and securities regulators if you are a local banker." Describing the deal's outrageously favorable terms, he steamed, "Try getting that deal if you are a small manufacturer anywhere in America."[23]

For Viguerie and for thousands of others, the bailouts confirmed one of the baseline convictions of the small-business mind: that big business is in league with big government. The idea is powerful because it is essentially true; it has been around for a long time; in fact, in 1962 the political scientist John Bunzel unearthed an expression of this bitter sentiment that, though written in the mid-fifties by an officer of a small-business trade association, might have been published on a Tea Party blog last week. Big business, the accusation went,

> goes along with big labor, with big government, with fascist [!] and corporative tendencies in the government—with NRA first and then with OPA and OPM and WPB industry committees—anything for harmony and convenience and *job safety for management*, regardless of what happens either to the country or to the other fellow.[24]

It is because of fixed images like these that the bailouts triggered such an immediate reaction on the Right: it was the entrepreneur's nightmare fear coming true in broad daylight.

The age of the giant corporation is here to stay of course, and as long as it is, big government must be on hand to curb its abuses. When the system is corrupted, as it clearly was in the case of the bailouts—and the subprime lending spree, and the West Virginia mine disaster, and the BP oil spill—the obvious answer is to clean up government so it can perform its police function properly.

But that's not how the revivified Right understands things. Instead, they blast the entire structure of the modern economy as "crony capitalism" or "socialism" and find, conveniently, that we can only cure its ills by doing away with the big-government side of the equation—with the regulating and taxing and pension-giving side.

And thus are our choices spread before us. On the one hand, the small-business utopia; on the other, "socialism." One system is "capitalism," the "American Way of Life"; it is in harmony with the rhythms of nature itself; but the other is something alien, something impure, something dishonest.[25]

Taking this tack allowed the renaissance Right to do a very remarkable thing: to pretend to be an enemy of big business. Not because market actors misbehave, of course, but because big business is not really a market actor in the pure sense. There is some truth to the accusation, naturally, since megacorporations do indeed lobby for subsidies, and bailouts, and government contracts, and even sometimes for regulation, which in a few well-known cases has been designed to protect existing players from new competition.

But the real reason for the claim was obvious: to capture the populist sentiment of the moment. The convoluted argument that the struggle for a purified free-market system was a revolt against big money as well as big government probably convinced very few. But its rhetorical thrust was powerful. It gave us, for example, the amazing 2009 essay in *Forbes* magazine penned by soon-to-be-famous Congressman Paul Ryan titled "Down with Big Business." The giant corporation, Ryan wrote, could not be counted upon to defend capitalism in its hour of need: "It's up to the American people—innovators and entrepreneurs, small business owners . . . to take a stand."[26]

Ryan's essay was just the beginning. Anticorporate statements are so common among conservatives today that sometimes the contorted reasoning undergirding them is completely omitted. It is simply taken for granted that opponents of corporate power belong on the far Right. Recall, in this connection, the evocative TV commercials aired in 2012 by the SuperPAC backing Newt Gingrich's presidential campaign that assailed the former venture capitalist Mitt Romney for his role in various corporate takeovers. Or the ferocious expression of anticorporate sentiment made by a DC political consultant who was working for the Tea Party. In a 2010 article in *Playboy*, this worthy described the targeted mail he was planning to send that fall, which would steer clear of the culture wars and zero in on public anger at the bailouts:

> Designing a thank-you note from an imaginary Wall Street executive to working-class taxpayers is so much more rewarding than most other messaging campaigns. With new variable-print technology, the postcard can be personalized and won't look as though it was printed overnight at Kinko's.

> *Dear [insert name],*
> *I received my Troubled Asset Relief Program check from you and other taxpayers and wanted to personally thank you for your money. I will now be able to keep the third car and vacation home by [insert name of nearby vacation area].*[27]

False Flag

It's exciting to imagine a vigilant small-business everyman disciplining the giant corporation for its deviations from free-market orthodoxy, but that's almost completely the reverse of what's actually happening. The famous hedge fund manager Cliff Asness didn't buy "Down with Big Business" author Paul Ryan $700 worth of wine at dinner one night in the summer of 2011 in order to placate a dangerous enemy and quell the possibility that an angry crowd of Wisconsin roofing contractors might soon come marching down Wall Street. He almost certainly did it because he approves of what Ryan and his fellow Republicans are doing in Congress. Small business is the face of the Right today because its pugnacious, anti-big-business message catches the bitter national mood; what the Right actually does is deliver the same favors to the same people as always.

Which is to say that behind the mask stands the hated megacorporation itself, making all its usual demands for lower taxes, sedated regulators, and free-trade deals with countries where labor unions are unknown. It is a familiar phenomenon. In a famous 1951 study, the sociologist C. Wright Mills observed that the "fetish of the American entrepreneur" did not arise from small business's actual economic accomplishments, but rather from "the usefulness of its image to the political interests of larger business." Small business served big business, he observed, as a "front," as a "concealing façade," as a "shield," as "shock troops in the battle against labor unions and government controls." The entrepreneur

> has become the man through whom the ideology of utopian capitalism is still attractively presented to many of our contemporaries. Over the last hundred years, the United States has been transformed from a nation of small capitalists into a nation of hired employees; but the ideology suitable for the nation of small capitalists persists, as if that small-propertied world were still a going concern. It has become the

grab-bag of defenders and apologists, and so little is it challenged that in the minds of many it seems the very latest model of reality.[28]

Here in the twenty-first century, we don't have to do a lot of sociological research to figure out that small business often acts as the populist front for the country's most powerful actors; we need only turn on our TV and watch the muddlement fly. The inheritance tax must go, we are told, not because it discomfits the rich but because it threatens family farmers. The Bush tax cuts must stay because small businesses will go under without them. Banking deregulation was done to help out small-town main streets. NAFTA was sold as a boon for entrepreneurial start-ups.[29] Every now and then, someone will even come out and insist that there is no daylight between the interests of Wall Street and those of Main Street.[30]

Let us take this moment to recall the loyalties of the remarkable Texas senator Phil Gramm, who delivered so many favors to the financial industry in the course of his career, like the repeal of the nation's Depression-era bank laws and the passage of the Commodity Futures Modernization Act, which made possible the energy-derivative trading business of Enron. Remember, though: Gramm did it all for the little guy. He fought to overturn those 1933 banking laws not to clear the way for lucrative and disastrous corporate mergers, but just to "make things simpler for anyone who has a checking account, car insurance or a share of stock."[31] Gramm even came up with his own salt-of-the-earth stock character to champion: one Dickey Flatt, a small businessman whose tax burden had to be weighed against the cost of any federal program before it could win the senator's assent.

Some on the revivified Right find it so easy to substitute small-business folklore for the complexities of the actual economy that it has apparently become a mental habit, a way of blocking out the unpleasant world we live in. Consider the example of Representative Nan Hayworth, whom we have already met flattering a group of small-business types for heroically creating jobs. In August 2011, Hayworth faced a group of constituents concerned about the opposite problem—the rampant offshoring of jobs by Verizon, one of the biggest companies in America. When those constituents asked Hayworth what she would do to solve the problem, the congresswoman launched instead into an elementary-school lecture on how small businesses operate—how people work hard, how they add value, and so on. "And that's the way opportunity grows," she summed up. This pleasant fable had nothing to do with the matter at hand, as Hayworth's annoyed audience pointed out. For Hayworth, however, the political implication of her lesson was undoubtedly obvious: government must let the little guy do his thing—meaning entrepreneurs in their garages and global telecom conglomerates alike.[32]

Nowhere is this kind of posturing more transparent than in the Tea Party movement, which understands itself as an expression of "the great American entrepreneurial spirit," to use Representative Pompeo's words again, but whose actual function has been to ensure that an economic collapse brought on by Wall Street does not result in any unpleasant consequences for Wall Street. Pompeo himself might serve as Exhibit A in this regard. During his run for Congress, he made much of his small-business experience and the number of jobs he had thereby created, as the expression goes. Upon closer inspection, however, Mike Pompeo's organization seems like an extension of Wichita-based Koch Industries, the enormous oil-and-gas concern whose owners, as we have had occasion to note before, are generous funders of Tea Party institutions. Pompeo's small business had been supported in its 1990s infancy by Koch venture capital; Pompeo's bid for Congress in 2010 was underwritten by Koch employees; Pompeo spoke at Tea Party rallies organized by the Koch-funded Americans for Prosperity; Pompeo's chief of staff, once he was ensconced in Washington, turned out to have come from Koch, too. Even the issues on which Pompeo focused his efforts were also, according to the *Washington Post*, signature Koch concerns: zapping EPA regulations and defunding an online database where people can look up product recalls.[33]

But what the sociologist Mills called "the ideology of utopian capitalism" blurs all this. The Tea Partiers aren't the pawns of big business; because they believe in markets, they're the sworn enemies of big business. Got that? And the way they're going to take their revenge on the crony-capitalist behemoth is by attacking government.

Recall, again, Paul Ryan's famous *Forbes* essay, "Down with Big Business." In it this conservative's conservative painted a noxious picture of "crony capitalism," telling us how lobbyists for the biggest firms cut deals with government and secured favors like the hated TARP, which Ryan called "an ad hoc, opaque slush fund for large institutions that are able to influence the Treasury Department's investment decisions behind-the-scenes." Which was accurate enough. What surprises is the direction Ryan's animus takes us from this starting point: the problem, in his telling, was not lousy decisions by government; it was that government made any decisions at all. Thus his bizarre prescription for the situation: the way to bring big business "down" is to get government out of the game altogether. The problem with big business is big government.[34]

The bald hypocrisy of this stuff should be obvious to anyone with an Internet connection. Once the GOP had reconquered the House of Representatives with talk like this, Paul Ryan became the instant crush of big-business donors, raking in massive sums from the banking industry (among others) within weeks of taking his place in the new majority.[35] Money knew all along that his threat to bring it "down" was just another way of saying "I love you."

Paul Ryan wasn't alone in trying to capitalize on the populist sentiment sweeping the land. One of the usual DC conservative outfits launched a website called "Big Business Watch"; the group's director—another former colleague of Jack Abramoff's, as it happens—insisted that "the tea party movement is as distrustful of big business as it is of politicians." The only "big business" the group really cared to "watch," however, was General Electric, which it accused in classic populist terms of being "an opportunistic parasite feeding on the expansion of government." The company's sin wasn't offshoring or anything like that; it was that GE wasn't capitalist enough: it subsisted on government contracts; it stood to profit from new, "green" energy rules; and most important of all, one suspects, it owned the liberal cable news channel MSNBC.[36]

The muddle kept right on puddling. In 2010 there was even a proposal afoot for a "National Day of Strike" in which Tea Partiers were to take to the streets and confront big business—in order to stop it from backing liberal measures in Congress! On the surface, this too sounded like a full-blown uprising against capitalism. "Congress is controlled by powerful business interests," one gung-ho strike supporter wrote. "Congress won't listen to us, so it's time to by-pass them and go above their heads on the totem pole of power." A strike, the theory went, would force big business to restrain its lobbyists and stop the flow of "bribe money" to Washington; only then would liberalism finally cease. The plan, in other words, was to stage the biggest industrial showdown of all time on the basis of a colossal mix-up: the idea that big business was bankrolling liberalism; that liberalism existed because of corporate bribes; and that only through a general strike against corporate America could capitalism be saved. Over the last few years we have watched any number of lousy schemes win out, but here, for once, was an idea so breathtakingly bad that not even the Tea Party could make it work. Cars built with their wheels on the roof have trouble moving, and the great proletarian walkout on behalf of markets never came to pass.[37]

CHAPTER 7

Mimesis

Mimicry is a familiar phenomenon in the animal kingdom, where moths have developed spots on their wings that look like the eyes of an owl, inoffensive bugs fly about in black and yellow stripes, and harmless snakes have learned, over the millennia, to frighten predators by shaking their tails in the dead leaves. They are mimic rattlesnakes, not the real deal. Don't be afraid. Go ahead and tread on them.

And in human affairs we have a conservative movement that has learned, over the decades, to mimic many of the characteristics of its enemies. The crushing experience of the thirties taught conservative leaders that it wasn't a good idea to speak in the accent of aristocratic disdain, blasting the poor for not knowing their place. During times of economic collapse, no one loves a defender of orthodoxy or a self-appointed spokesman for society's rightful rulers.

And so, over the years, the movement came to affect a revolutionary posture toward the state that it might have borrowed from Karl Marx or Jean-Paul Sartre. It imitated the protest culture of the sixties, right down to a feigned reverence for anticommunist guerrilla fighters who were its version of Ho and Che. Conservative leaders studied the tactics of communists, applying them to their own struggles. And the movement learned to understand itself not as a defender of "the status quo," in the famous formulation of the conservative organizer Paul Weyrich, but as a group of "radicals, working to overturn the present power structure of the country."[1]

When the economic collapse of 2008 and 2009 came along, conservatism immediately positioned itself as a protest movement for hard times. Aspects of the conservative tradition that were haughty or aristocratic were attributed to liberals. Symbols that seemed noble or democratic or populist, even if they were the traditional property of the other side, were snapped up and claimed by the Right for itself.

Bounces Off Me . . .

There was, to begin with, a useful confusion in the early days of the economic debacle: was the Tea Party a phenomenon of the Left or of the Right? Its participants certainly didn't accept the GOP label, which was still radioactive in 2009, thanks to the doings of George W. Bush and Tom DeLay. Maybe, certain commentators thought, this novel form of protest represented something altogether new.

Glenn Beck, the emblematic figure in this mix-up, ritually claims to be a man beyond partisanship. He has deliberately imitated Martin Luther King Jr.'s 1963 march on Washington, and at one point in 2009 he suggested that he might have voted for Hillary Clinton had she won the Democratic nomination for the presidency. In order to round out his right-wing conspiracy theories, Beck constantly pilfers left-wing imagery and arguments: his critique of the public relations industry, for example, seems to come straight from the pages of Noam Chomsky,[2] while his famous charge of racism against President Obama was a clumsy attempt to use a weapon that conservatives feel is usually directed against themselves.* The host has also hinted at the reason for his constant swiping from liberaldom. "America needs revolutionaries," he says he once told Newt Gingrich. "Because what you are fighting are revolutionaries."[3]

The burning need to mimic the Left is also the theme of the *National Review Online* contributor Michael Walsh, who came up with a novel way to persuade conservatives to adopt the strategy. Walsh dreamed up a pseudonym, "David Kahane," supposedly a rich, arrogant Hollywood radical, and proceeded to confess to his right-wing readers that liberalism was, in fact, an orchestrated, demonic assault on the responsible and productive, with every federal regulation and insulting TV show and crazy lawsuit part of liberalism's grand plan for disaster. Rightists, "Kahane" insisted in his 2010 book, *Rules for Radical Conservatives*, were "in the fight of your life, up against an implacable foe that has loathed you and sought your destruction not for years or even centuries, but for millennia," and they needed to understand how to fight back. The prescription for activist conservatives was obvious: Do exactly as those nefarious, successful liberals

---

* A more tragic example was furnished by Internet personality Andrew Breitbart, who made a career out of mimicking what he believed to be the "smashmouth" tactics of the all-powerful Left and who deeply resented the false accusations of racism that are routinely hurled at conservatives. And so he became a false accuser himself, posting on one of his websites a video excerpt from an address to the NAACP by Shirley Sherrod, a Department of Agriculture official in Georgia. The speech, as it was edited, seemed to show Sherrod making a startling admission of racism toward a white farmer who came to her for help, while in the unedited version, Sherrod went on to tell how she overcame her prejudices and saved the white man's farm.

(are imagined to) do. "Pretend to be like us, so do what we do: lie. Adopt all of our manners and mores, right down to our mannerisms."[4]

Wingers needed to mimic the libs and "give no quarter." They needed to act like ancient Visigoths turned loose on "the effete Romans." Above all, they needed to reverse the age-old perceptions of which party represented the establishment and which the insurgent public. "We're the Man now—fat, sassy, and socialist," "Kahane" confessed on behalf of his fellow libs. "Which means we're also ripe for a takedown."[5]

This is a pretty fair description of how the Right played things as conservatism signed up the nation's unfortunates in what appeared to be a classic hard-times social uprising. On the surface, this uprising seemed to have all the necessary indicators: people with placards, people protesting banks and big corporations, people yelling through bullhorns, people organizing boycotts. There were marches on Washington and big talk about strikes.

What's more, it was cast as a people's movement with no leaders. A movement that was so profoundly democratic, so virtuously rank-and-file, so punk rock, that it was actively *against* leaders. A movement that was downright obsessed with being "sold out" by traditional politicians, with betrayal, with guarding its independence and its precious authenticity.[6]

At its most primitive, the crypto-leftism of the conservative revival took the form of simple duplication, in which the signature images and catchphrases of liberals during the Bush years were swiped and echoed simply because it is perfectly legal to do so. Thus Michelle Malkin appears to have titled her 2009 Obama book *Culture of Corruption* for no other reason than that "culture of corruption" was a famous phrase

applied to Republican officeholders in 2005 by Nancy Pelosi.*
In 2010 Ben Quayle, son of Dan, announced his candidacy
for Congress with TV commercials proclaiming, "Barack
Obama is the worst president in history"—a description of
George W. Bush that libs had been repeating constantly a
short while before. (Quayle won, of course.) Conservative
pundits learned to frighten their flock by describing Democratic plans to grab a permanent lock on the electoral system,
a repurposed liberal fear from 2004 and 2005.[7] Tea Partiers
favored a variation on another famous Bush-era put-down—
"Somewhere in Kenya a Village Is Missing Its Idiot"—while
others on the Right sold clocks that would count down the
days until Obama left office, just as their counterparts had
done in the Bush years. Images of Constitutions being sucked
into paper shredders, a popular motif during the early days
of the Patriot Act, were picked up by an entirely new demographic. Meanwhile, opponents of the administration's health-
care reform also imagined—and boasted, with stickers and
T-shirts—that they were on "Obama's Enemy List," thus shifting one of Richard Nixon's most famous sins onto the shoulders of a man who was twelve when the enemies list was
made public.

Of course, all of this is much like writing a book called
Michael Moore Is a Big Fat Stupid White Man as a response
to a book called *Rush Limbaugh Is a Big Fat Idiot*—the
I'm-rubber-you're-glue school of disputation. It serves no
purpose greater than sowing confusion.

The mimicry becomes more interesting when it is taken

* The book has little to do with actual Obama administration corruption, as it was
published only a few months after Obama took office. Instead it details the shady
histories of the administration's appointees, highlighting the many lobbyists who
were nominated and the many "czars" the administration hired, and suggesting
that Michelle Obama's father may once have held a patronage job in Chicago.

to the next level, where an ideologue projects the sins of his own movement onto his adversary. Take, for example, that phrase of Barack Obama's—that he would "fundamentally transform" America, a throwaway line Obama used a handful of times on the campaign trail but which was quickly magnified into a favorite Tea Party nightmare, sending a thousand would-be Paul Reveres through every cyber-age village and town. On the basis of one ten-second video clip, the new Minutemen have determined that tyranny is on the way, courtesy of a would-be king who thinks he's so smart that he can dispense with the work of God, the Founders, and all the accretions of the centuries.

Admittedly, the fear is a catchy one: beware the politician who thinks he knows all the answers and holds in his hands the true design for human civilization. But the only first-world politician who ever deliberately tried to "transform" a society in this way in my lifetime was Margaret Thatcher, and the abstract blueprint around which she aimed to remake Britain was . . . the Right's beloved free market. Her own words on the matter are far more frightening than any progressive bromide uttered by Barack Obama: "Economics are the method; the object is to change the soul." (Incidentally, encouraging homeownership was a large part of her intended transformation.)

Those fantastic ambitions were widely exported. Over the last four decades, Thatcher's ideological comrades brought their free-market plans to countries all around the globe, remaking the souls of Chileans, Argentines, Poles, and Iraqis as the opportunities presented. Societies were "transformed," all right: dynamited, bulldozed, privatized, swept away. And in the classic 2007 account of this particular chapter in civilization's development, the journalist Naomi Klein explains that it often happened in the aftermath of crises: hurricanes, military coups, civil wars. An entire program of market-based reforms would be installed all of a sudden as a sort of "shock therapy" when traditional social systems had been knocked off balance.[8]

Let me repeat, before we proceed, that what I am describing were the acts of conservatives: professional economists using crisis to impose what they knew to be the correct social model—the market model—on nations that were not really interested in it. Also: that this really happened, that the economists talked about it openly.

To hear the resurgent Right tell it, however, the only place where you'll find such ruinous strategies in discussion are in the war rooms of the sneaky Left, as they plot to destroy the free market itself. In a curious inversion of Naomi Klein's argument, the rejuvenated Right fastened on a single flippant 2008 remark from then-incoming White House chief of staff Rahm Emanuel—"You never want a serious crisis to go to waste"—and convinced itself on the basis of this one clue that a cadre of left-wingers were planning all manner of offenses against democracy including, in some tellings, the overthrow of capitalism itself, with the financial crisis as a pretext.

The Spider, the Starfish, and the Bull Snake

Actually, "pretext" is too small a word for the vast array of liberal shams, fakes, tricks, and black ops that haunt the imagination of the revitalized Right. The liberal stratagems they see around them are the stuff of Cold War duplicity—only with the roles reversed: it's the liberals who are forever peddling crisis, not the people who used to insist that we were about to lose to the Soviets because we weren't spending enough on the military. The best expression of this fear of trumped-up crisis comes in the 2010 "thriller" by Glenn

Beck, *The Overton Window*. At one point in the novel, the son of an evil progressive PR genius is explaining his dad's methods to his rebel-conservative girlfriend. "We never let a good crisis go to waste," he says, echoing Emanuel, "and if no crisis exists, it's easy enough to make one."

> Saddam's on the verge of getting nuclear weapons, so we have to invade before he wipes out Cleveland. If we don't hand AIG a seventy-billion-dollar bailout there'll be a depression and martial law by Monday. If we don't all get vaccinated one hundred thousand people will die in a super swine-flu pandemic. . . . Now they're telling us that if we don't pass this worldwide carbon tax right now the world will soon be underwater.[9]

As Beck's plot unfolds, the reader learns of the most diabolical fake crisis of them all: a "false-flag domestic attack" in which these nefarious libs set off an atomic bomb near Las Vegas, blame the deed on Tea Party types, and then, in the ensuing hysteria, put over their grand plan for remaking the country according to their enlightened theories.

But wait: go back a step. Of the several fake crises Beck's PR boy mentions to his girlfriend, three are standard-issue right-wing talking points. But one of them is not: the 2003 wave of fear that Saddam Hussein had weapons of mass destruction and that the Iraq war was therefore justified. As it happens, one of the most enthusiastic peddlers of this particular line was none other than the network that made Glenn Beck famous, Fox News. Beck himself, back in those days, was leading "Rallies for America" across the country, patriotic demonstrations that often featured a video message from President Bush. Liberals, you will recall, were the wimps on the other side of the issue—the ones like Barack

Obama, who called the impending invasion "a dumb war." To read *The Overton Window* eight years later, however, the whole episode was just another malevolent deed of the big-government conspiracy, to which only right-wing rebels are wise.

Conservative populists, meanwhile, are imagined by the novelist Beck to be victims of everything big brother can throw at them. They are jailed on the flimsiest of charges. They endure savage beatings by police. The book's hero is even waterboarded after he signs up with the Tea Party resistance. Their patriotic meetings are infiltrated by police spies and broken up by mysterious *agents provocateurs*—the descendants, I suppose, of the Red Squads that real-life city governments actually fielded in order to suppress left-wing radicals in the old days.

Similar fears come up all the time in the larger conservative movement culture. In 2009, for example, the populist right was swept by panic that the new Democratic administration was preparing internment camps for conservatives. On TV, Glenn Beck managed to feed this peculiar fear even as he debunked it, and in *The Overton Window* he plays it the same way: the existence of the camps is first suggested by an unreliable person, yet the main character seems to end up in just such a facility after his waterboarding. Fortunately, Beck has attached a nonfictional "Afterword" to the end of the novel to sort things out, and here he reminds the reader that a former director of the Federal Emergency Management Agency once proposed rounding up undesirables during a national emergency.[10]

This historical factoid is a favorite of conspiracy theorists and *X-Files* fans, but it is generally discussed absent an important detail: the FEMA boss who suggested those infamous plans was brought to Washington by Ronald Reagan; he was a close friend of the Reagan adviser and Tea Party sympathizer Ed Meese, and the object of his emergency scheme was to prevent a recurrence of the antiwar agitation of the sixties.[11] The McCarran Act of 1950 also authorized a big roundup of left-wing radicals should a "national emergency" arise.[12] And exactly such a roundup actually occurred in 1919, during the first red scare, when radicals and labor organizers were arrested and, in many cases, deported.

The truth is that neither federal nor state governments have ever mounted a campaign to intern the free-market faithful or blacklist the hardworking proletarians in the Chicago futures pits. However, they have used force over the years to break up strikes, imprison labor organizers, keep minorities from voting, round up people of Japanese descent, and disrupt antiwar movements. Today, though, it suits the resurgent Right to imagine itself as the real victim of state persecution, which no doubt enhances its aura as a dissident movement taking on a merciless establishment.

To see the sort of passions that drove America's actual history of politicized prosecution, conservatives need only consult the *Official Tea Party Handbook*, a 2009 booklet authored by an Arizona activist named Charly Gullett. "Socialism is treason," Mr. Gullett proclaims.

> It is criminally motivated political terrorism. Both terrorism and treason are anathema to Liberty and those who advocate it are political criminals. This is not complicated. Clear-thinking Americans must begin to view Socialism as a prosecutable crime and recognize those who conspire to advance it are in fact criminals to be adjudicated in courts of Federal law. We must embrace

the notion our Founding Fathers defined high crimes because they are real, they are being perpetrated against America and they need to be prosecuted.[13]

The Political Economy of Self-Pity

Reminding our conservative friends of their mile-wide law-and-order streak seems a little unfair. Their movement has got such a beautiful heroic-outlaw thing going that it seems almost a deliberate buzzkill to point out their slips into Grand Inquisitor mode, hunting down the heretics. So let us stay on the well-marked trail, descending now from the misty heights of conspiracy theory and approaching the river of tears the new conservatives cry for their own sufferings, bawling that they, not liberal darlings like minorities or the poor, are society's true victims.

As we approach this raging torrent, however, let us remember that it was not always such a swiftly flowing stream. The first Tea Party rally I attended was largely devoid of self-pity; it was a straightforward political *j'accuse*. The protesters were there because they disliked the TARP and the stimulus package; as far as I recall, none of them took it to the second remove by moaning about being persecuted because they were protesting. True, at a CPAC speech I went to a little later on the same day as the protest, I heard Mitt Romney say that he needed to get through his prepared script "before federal officials come here to arrest me for practicing capitalism." But the prosperous crowd in attendance there got the joke: arrested for practicing capitalism—*that's a hot one!*

A year later, though, and that second-remove grievance had far overshadowed the original cause. Now people protested not only to advertise their views on a given issue but *out of resentment at the insults heaped upon protesters*. The collecting and categorizing of these insults had by then become such an absorbing pursuit among Tea Partiers that it made up a good part of one of the earliest Tea Party books to appear, the radio talker Michael Graham's 2010 effort, *That's No Angry Mob, That's My Mom*. In his book's first chapter ("My Mother, the Terrorist"), Graham proposes a theory of political motivation that begins and ends with liberal insults heaped on "normal" Americans, veering off into actual issues only incidentally.

> Stupid, backward, bigoted, racist. You've probably been called all this and more. . . . Then one day, you had enough. You got tired of the attacks on private enterprise. [!] . . . Then you went to a tea party, and that's when you really crossed the line. Every morning the newspaper calls you a dangerous, hate-filled kook. Every night, the TV news declares you an ignorant, potentially violent redneck. And in between, political pundits and even politicians denounce you with juvenile insults like "teabagger."[14]

These details may amuse, but it is the paradox of the phenomenon that I wish to emphasize, the unconflicted way in which these proud voices of the strong—these hymners of Darwinian struggle, of the freedom to fail, of competition to the death—advance their war on the world by means of tearful weepy-woo.

Self-pity has become central in the consciousness of the resurgent Right. Depicting themselves as victimized in any and every situation is not merely a fun game of upside down; it is essential to their self-understanding. They are the ones to whom things are done. This is the reason they have taken as their banner a flag that reads, "Don't Tread on Me." The slogan is a concise expression of the grand distortion that undergirds everything I have been describing: the belief that we are living in an age of rampant leftism; that decades of unrelieved progressivism are what brought the nation to its awful straits; that markets were born free but are everywhere in chains.

Consider the amazing rise of Tea Party darling Sarah Palin, a former governor of Alaska and a one-time Republican vice presidential candidate. Even those who followed her career don't really know where Palin stood on many issues. We know only that she was constantly being maligned, that whenever we turned on the TV and saw her fair face beaming, we were about to hear that some liberal someone had slurred this noble lady yet again. Indeed, if political figures stand for ideas, victimization was what Sarah Palin was all about. It was her brand, her myth. But to become such a symbol, Palin had to do the opposite of most public figures: where others learn to take hostility in stride, she and her fans developed the thinnest of skins. They found offense in the most harmless commentator remarks and diabolical calculation in the inflections of the anchorman's voice. They took insults out of context to make them seem even more insulting. They paid close attention to voices that are ordinarily ignored, relishing every blogger's sneer, every celebrity's slight, every crazy Internet rumor.

One of the adoring biographies of the former would-be veep was called *The Persecution of Sarah Palin*; it is a catalog of just about every nasty thing anyone has ever said about the woman. Its author, Matthew Continetti, actually seems to specialize in such profiles in victimhood: He has also written a cover story for the *Weekly Standard* about the persecution of the Koch brothers, two of the nation's richest men and most influential political donors, but who, it is Continetti's solemn duty to report, receive mean e-mails every day. They are in fact "the latest victims of the left's lean, mean cyber-vilification machine."[15] Pity these billionaires, reader.

And we have the latest bestseller by David Limbaugh, a book that understands both the health-care debate and the financial crisis largely in terms of the slurs that Democrats have cast upon the insurance and banking industries. These dirty things-that-were-said are "Crimes Against the Private Sector," which are in turn a form of *Crimes Against Liberty* (the title of Limbaugh's book), and the author lists them in the detailed manner of a man in whom indignation throbs righteously: There was "slander"; there was "vilifying"; there was "derogatory and bellicose language." There were "malicious claims" made against doctors and harsh words "castigating Wall Street bankers"; there is a president who "delights in bashing American businesspeople"; and there is Tim Geithner's "Chicago-style machismo"*: "'As the [financial reform] bill moves to the floor,'" quoth that brute, "'we will fight any attempt to weaken it.'"[16] Tremble before the iron Treasurer, reader, as he muscles a bill through Congress! And weep for the Nation as the insolent words of the liberals fasten fast the chainy chains of Servitude around the neck of Liberty!

If this is the first time you've encountered the Right's victimhood rap, you might feel that it's just a mild irritant, an unconvincing act meant to becloud the Democrats' traditional appeal to society's actual outsiders. But this is only part of the story. Understanding themselves as the true victims is, in fact, essential to the conservative revival. There are few political or cultural situations in which they don't instinctively reach for the mantle of the wronged, holler about bias, or protest about how unfairly they've been treated. It goes on even in the most improbable precincts. Army generals

---

* Geithner is a New Yorker. He is not particularly macho. He was also a Republican for much of his adult life, which would exclude him by definition from the machine politics of Chicago.

must be consoled. Job creators must be honored by those they employ. Billionaires must know we love them. And former majority leaders of the House of Representatives need your sympathy.

I refer, of course, to Dick Armey, who, along with his coauthor, Matt Kibbe, chooses to enliven the pages of his "Tea Party Manifesto," *Give Us Liberty*, with a chapter that catalogs every insult directed against him and the Tea Party movement over the last three years. Oh, reader, they called what Armey's group did "Astroturfing," he remembers. They objected when people organized by his group disrupted town hall meetings; they called him names; they said his movement was racist; they made fun of his hat.

But before you weep for poor ragged Dick, recall that Armey was a congressional bigwig who eventually cashed in his legislative chips for a lobbying job at the enormous international law firm DLA Piper (which also employs former Democratic Senate majority leader Tom Daschle). When not himself one of the most powerful men on the planet, Armey has been an adviser to the most powerful men. From his 2003 book of market-worshipping aphorisms to his labors on behalf of the Marianas Islands sweatshops, he has consistently sided with the moneyed and against the weak. But now, with tearful self-regard, he asks us to consider all the slights and insults he has endured in the course of his long career.

Why must the world be persuaded to think of Dick Armey as a victim? For the same reason that Glenn Beck channels Martin Luther King Jr., that Paul Ryan shouts, "Down with big business," and that conservatives generally have learned to apply the term "fascist" to their foes: because, consciously or not, all of them are following a political strategy that works in hard times.

At Armey's FreedomWorks pressure group, for example,

there is reportedly a deliberate effort to look and sound like a left-wing organization. The idea, according to Armey, was "not just to learn from their opponents on the left but to beat them at their own game." The outfit's leaders write that after the Tea Party conquers the GOP and Congress, it "will take America back from The Man," explaining helpfully to readers that this is "the term the New Left used to refer to the political establishment." Activists that the group trains are asked to learn the leadership secrets of the Communist Party* and to read a book by the famous neighborhood organizer Saul Alinsky; their idea for a big march on Washington came to them from another favorite text: a famous history of nonviolent protest. To fill the streets with demonstrators rallying for free markets—why, according to Armey and Kibbe, "in Washington, D.C., this is known as radical. Even dangerous." It is so radical, so dangerous, that "the establishment doesn't like it one bit."[17]

"Hard work beats Daddy's money," the revolutionaries of FreedomWorks like to say, since they are such jolly, wisecracking opponents of privilege.[18] And I suppose the slogan is true enough, if by "beats" you mean "protects" or "increases" or "compounds" Daddy's money. So off they go, studying communist tactics and doing everything in their power to make market utopianism sound like legitimate democratic protest—and behold: Daddy's money multiplies and reproduces and turns cartwheels of joy; Daddy's money comes zooming into Dulles airport in its private jet, wreathed in smiles, to help elect you to a long career in the DC wrecking crew.

---

* The book they read is Douglas Hyde's *Dedication and Leadership: Learning from the Communists*, a 1966 work by a former officer of the Communist Party of Great Britain.

CHAPTER 8

Say, Don't You Remember

"Brother, Can You Spare a Dime?" was the so-called anthem of the Depression, a transcendent expression—if such a thing is possible—of the hopeless disillusionment of 1932. It derides patriotism, the American dream, and even the promise of the future, mocking them all in the voice of a working-class every-man.

> They used to tell me I was building a dream,
>   and so I followed the mob.
> When there was earth to plough or guns to bear,
>   I was always there, right on the job.
> They used to tell me I was building a dream,
>   with peace and glory ahead.
> Why should I be standing in line,
>   just waiting for bread?
>
> Once I built a railroad, made it run,
>   made it race against time.
> Once I built a railroad; now it's done.
>   Brother, can you spare a dime?

Once I built a tower to the sun, brick, and rivet,
and lime;
Once I built a tower, now it's done.
Brother, can you spare a dime?

Once in khaki suits, gee, we looked swell,
Full of that Yankee Doodle-de-dum,
Half a million boots went sloggin' through hell,
And I was the kid with the drum.

Its obvious incitement of unrest got the song banned by certain radio stations. In the grand history of cynicism, the only other hit record I know of that comes close to it is the Sex Pistols' "God Save the Queen," or maybe the Vietnam-era song "Fortunate Son."

In 2009, someone posted Rudy Vallee's recording of "Brother" on YouTube; immediately people began to share their reactions to that wrenching bit of Depressiana. Here are a few entries that caught my eye.

> This song speaks to the failures of Keynesian Economics. Public spending on infrastructure to stimulate the slowing econonmy—it has never worked, and never will. It turns recessions into depressions like it did in the 30's, and like it is doing now.

> Kinda sounds like today, with the bailouts and stimulus packages. The whole, government making it worse thing.

> This song is terrific!!! The theme applys again to us in 2009 like it did in 1929. Please "world leaders" give us "Hope for a brighter Future" not this thing called "Change" spoken by every two-bit politician since Hitler.

Brother, can you spare a trillion dollars?
America is staring this in the face again, watch
closely what's happening. April/May . . . will be the
"dropping off the cliff" reality.
Call your reps and tell them NO to the proposed
"stimulus." It's not going to help Americans when it's
spreading pork around for all the special interests
groups and delayed for years. Not gonna work.
Stock up on supplies that are necessities, and hold
on. We're in for a spin.

The song's famous lyrics were written by Yip Harburg,
a socialist who was later blacklisted during the McCarthy
period. But in our own enlightened age, it is evidently possible to listen to "Brother, Can You Spare a Dime?" and hear it
as a call for a purified form of free-market economics, as a
warning against public works projects, maybe as an endorse-
ment of the Hoover administration, even.

I do not bring all this up in order to score easy points at
the expense of confused YouTubers. I mean merely to high-
light what the posters themselves assume: That conservatives
are the rightful heirs to Depression culture. That the songs
and books and movies of the thirties abound with lessons on
the wisdom of markets and the folly of government; that the
Red Decade is in fact some kind of spiritual homeland for
the free-market sensibility.

It is an understandable mistake. The thirties, as we know
them in the Internet age, are very different from the thirties
we know from the canonical literature of the time or the
standard histories of the period. To Google nearly any aspect
of the first two Roosevelt administrations is to encounter
almost immediately the obsessive loathing for the New Deal
felt by conservative entertainers and libertarian economists.
You can find the works of scholars like Arthur Schlesinger or

Irving Bernstein or Michael Denning or Robert McElvaine down at the library if you wish, but if you begin your research on the Internet, the experts you will encounter first are likely to be Amity Shlaes, the author who has tried to recapture FDR's expression "the forgotten man" for conservatism;* or the bitter libertarian economists of the Ludwig von Mises Institute, proving to one another over and over again that the New Deal was not necessary, did not help, and very probably made the Depression worse. *Of course* Yip Harburg was bemoaning government meddling when he wrote "Brother, Can You Spare a Dime?" What else was there to bemoan?

If the strategy of the contemporary Right is, roughly speaking, to mimic successful leftist movements, it is only natural

---

* Before Roosevelt, according to Shlaes, "the forgotten man" referred to the average taxpayer, who was forcibly enlisted in whatever altruistic project government was undertaking. She extends the phrase to encompass such pitiable billionaires as Andrew Mellon and Samuel Insull, the *real* victims of the thirties.

The larger object of Shlaes's 2007 book, *The Forgotten Man*, is to document the conservative article of faith that Roosevelt's New Deal did not help the nation recover from the Depression. The author uses two measurements of the national economy to accomplish this goal: the Dow Jones Industrial Average and unemployment numbers. The first metric had little to do with the economy as average people experienced it; the second metric is actually rigged against Roosevelt—Shlaes counts people who held temporary government jobs as having been unemployed. The author thereby makes a mystery of the enthusiasm for FDR felt by the millions of people who were saved by jobs with the WPA. As for the standard yardstick of economic well-being—GDP growth—Shlaes does not mention it at all.

On the chance that anyone gives a damn about what actually happened in the thirties, here are the numbers. GDP shrank dramatically from 1929 to 1933, then abruptly reversed course in the year after Roosevelt took office. "Real GDP increased 11% in 1934, 9% in 1935, and 13% in 1936," writes the economist Christina Romer—and those percentages, incidentally, dwarf the growth levels of the eighties, nineties, and zeroes. In fact, Romer continues, "the growth between 1933 and 1937 was the highest we have ever experienced outside of wartime." (Romer, "Lessons from the Great Depression for Economic Recovery in 2009," a paper given at the Brookings Institution on March 9, 2009. Romer was then the chair of Obama's Council of Economic Advisers.) See also the critique of the book by historian Eric Rauchway in *Slate*, July 5, 2007.

that they have sought to swipe the memory of liberalism's defining era—the Depression, the period that our own times so closely resemble. For anyone wishing to present themselves as a friend of the common man, standing up to society's masters, it is to the cultural patterns of the thirties that they must ultimately turn. And so the revitalized Right has set out to commit the consummate act of cultural theft.

Full of That Yankee Doodle-De-Dum

Again Glenn Beck, during his moment as conservatism's face, supplies the extreme case. He is a man of distinct Depression sensibilities, routinely paying homage to the cultural forms of the Red Decade. His constant worry about the coming of fascism, for example, was a characteristic fear of that period. So it is with his hate for Woodrow Wilson, an opinion that can seem bizarre today but that was common enough during the pacifist years after World War I. And in classic thirties style, he warns the honest people of America against a vigorous and resourceful Left that is swarming with radicals and communists.

Much has been made of Beck's rhetorical similarity to the notorious "radio priest," Father Charles Coughlin, but Beck's populist habits actually seem to be drawn from a whole range of Depression-era figures. His trick of concealing his intelligence behind a facade of boyishness and buffoonery might be borrowed from the Louisiana "Kingfish," Huey Long: garish suits in Long's case, clashing patterns in Beck's, plus those unlaced sneakers and those untucked shirts. Beck's one-man red scare, in which he hounds professors, foundation figures, and intellectuals on flimsy charges of secret radicalism could have been lifted from the career of the newspaper titan

William Randolph Hearst. From the 1939 movie *The Wizard of Oz* comes Beck's favorite metaphor for the deceivers who rule us: "the man behind the curtain," pulling the levers and pretending to be all-powerful.[1] From Franklin Delano Roosevelt himself comes such rhetoric as the following, which Beck uttered in a special TV program in March of 2009:

> What happened to the country that loved the underdog and stood up for the little guy? What happened to the voice of the forgotten man? The forgotten man is you.[2]

Back in 2003, when the conservative entertainer was touring the country celebrating what he called "the real America," Beck made a point of locating heartland authenticity not merely in the red states but also in the past, in the ways of the "Depression people" who were his grandparents.[3] On one emotional occasion in 2009, he told his TV audience that the answers to present-day economic distress lay in remembering the lessons of the Depression—by which he meant being thrifty and neighborly, not signing up for a labor union or voting for a New Deal—and the following year, a collection of documentary Depression photos produced from him an outpouring of workerist sentimentality that was almost Soviet in its proletarian bathos.[4] Gazing upon a photograph of a farmer and his wife, Beck burbled,

> Look at how proud she is. Look at the confidence. Look at the way she is standing. Look at her face. She's proud. She's strong.

Depression people were both the fount of American authenticity and the source of our material well-being. "These are the people that built America into what it is," he declared. "We have been feasting off of their labors for seventy years! They built it, and we're just using it all up!"*

Beck's most telling homage to the Depression sensibility was the 9/12 Project, which aimed to rekindle hard-times neighborliness. He announced it with great fanfare on his TV show one night in March of 2009, after a dizzy prologue listing all the scary problems Americans were then facing. Beck became so overwhelmed by the nobility of what he was doing that he actually began to cry as he spoke these words: "I toldja—for weeks—you're not alone!"

And so Beck launched the 9/12 Project with the above-cited tribute to the "forgotten man" and an invitation to meet people from "all across the country," that is, "regular people like you."[5] The movement was to be a thing of local chapters, mass rallies, mosaics made up of thousands of snapshots, and saccharine talk about how capitalist salvation lay somehow in the collective—that when angry citizens got together to revel in their Americanness they would no longer "feel powerless." As it always does with Beck, the proposal immediately went from all-American solidarity to a dark vision of the insiders who are manipulating us.

> Once you pull the curtain away you realize that there are only a few people pressing the buttons, and their voices are weak. The truth is that they don't surround us at all.
>   We surround them.[6]

---

* Many if not most of the monumental things that were "built" in that period were constructed with the help of government public works programs. In fact, the very pictures over which Beck enthused so emotionally were taken by photographers employed by the Farm Security Administration. The Depression generation achieved all of this by the use of Beck's bête noire: massive deficit spending.

It was a powerful invocation of the archetypal thirties image: the masses; the righteous millions; the people, yes.

After writing the above paragraphs describing the 9/12 Project, I realized that I was basically describing the plot of one of the most famous films of the Depression era: Frank Capra's *Meet John Doe* (1941). It is the story of a mass movement in which ordinary people get together in a spirit of vague civic togetherness under the leadership of a popular radio frontman who often talks about suicide, as Beck does. The politics of the John Doe Movement are never made clear in the movie, but both the movement and its putative leader are definitely controlled by a wealthy media mogul, like Beck's then-boss, Rupert Murdoch, who plans to use them for his own quasi-fascist purposes. As the movie's plot unfolds, it seems as though everyone is a sucker except the evil wealthy guy, who is certain to get what he wants.*

The movie, which was a commentary on the manipulation of political clubs during the Depression, tells us all we need to know about Beck's modern-day galaxy of political clubs. The 9/12 Project doesn't so much mimic thirties populism as it mimics *fake* thirties populism. It is a replica of a replica in which bogus populism shores up ironclad elitism and where bogus enlightenment serves the most grotesque form of dupery. Bogusness squared; that is the story of Glenn Beck.

---

* Second bizarre coincidence: Two years before Beck launched the 9/12 Project, the right-wing blogger Michelle Malkin announced her own "John Doe Movement." The idea was for ordinary citizens to report suspicious characters they thought might be terrorists; such alert citizens were, Malkin wrote, "9/12 people." Talk of a John Doe Movement disappeared soon afterward, but while it lasted the idea was apparently to bring together average Americans from all walks of life in a common purpose and, like Beck's 9/12 Project, it featured a mosaic made of dozens of snapshots. See Malkin's 2007 essay, "John Doe in Post-9/11 America," and her "John Doe Manifesto."

Waiting for Righty

From President Roosevelt on down, Depression-era Americans reviled the upper class that had steered them into disaster, and as Americans of the twenty-first century took their own turn on the toboggan ride to economic calamity, they once again began to grumble about what they called the "ruling class." But this time around it wasn't leftists who introduced the phrase, and it wasn't organized workers who dreamed of shutting the oligarchy down; it was the revitalized Right.

The existence of a "ruling class" dawned on the conservative revival very suddenly in the summer of 2010, the way a vogue for Marxism overtook American literati in the early thirties. For example, Beck's *Overton Window* warned readers of "the inevitable rise of tyranny from the greed and gluttony of a ruling class," while a Tea Party leader in Saint Louis could be found crowing that "the Tea Party scares the hell out of the ruling class" and speculating that the coming elections would mark nothing less than "the beginning of the end of elitism in America."[7]

Richard Viguerie's daily e-mail newsletter increasingly made "ruling class" its pet expression. The "ruling class" was sneering at Sarah Palin, it told readers; the "ruling class" was trying to silence a controversial radio commentator; the "ruling class" was made up of sore losers, and so on. Viguerie eventually became so attached to the phrase that his 2010 election-night watch party actually bore the Jacobin name "Out with the Ruling Class"; the roster of "special guests" included such lifelong foes of aristocratic privilege as Grover Norquist, the Lenin of the tax cut, and Tim Phillips, the leader of a grassroots group whose insurgencies are made possible by the Moscow gold of the oil billionaires Koch and Koch.[8]

The unlikely Engels of this strange class war was a retired professor of international relations named Angelo Codevilla; his manifesto, "America's Ruling Class," was published in the summer of 2010 by the *American Spectator* and was issued a short while later in a longer version by that magazine's book-publishing arm.

There are but two social groupings that matter in America, the retired professor maintained, a "ruling class" that legitimizes itself as the nation's intellectual superiors but that is actually defined by its control of the machinery of government, and a "country class" made up of nearly everyone else. The core of the idea was not new, but the bailouts and economic disasters of our own times allowed Codevilla to apply it in a new and uncompromising way. His indictment of the "ruling class" fell on anyone connected with government, Republicans as well as Democrats, both of whom were said to hand out economic favors to the connected. Big business was implicated too, insofar as it was in cahoots with big government; in fact, "the upper tiers of the U.S. economy are now nothing but networks of special deals with one part of government or another," Codevilla wrote. And from the remorseless workings of this system there was no reprieve and virtually no chance for reform. Only "revolution" of some vague but noninvasive kind would do. "There is no escape from the conflict between the classes."[9]

It was a strangely bolshie line for a conservative hero, weirdly akin to Marx's dictum that "the history of all hitherto existing society is the history of class struggles." But Codevilla's thesis was an immediate sensation nevertheless, with Rush Limbaugh devoting a large part of his radio program to it when it first appeared. For the newest Right, all this hard-boiled prole-talk was invigorating stuff. Now it was conservatism's turn to gasp at the horrors our society had blithely tolerated all these years. The affluence of the "ruling class," Codevilla taught, was almost entirely ill-gotten, the result of government meddling with nature—which is to say, with the free market. Using regulation, bailouts, and taxes, government rigs the game this way and that, and regardless of whether the people doing the rigging are Republicans or Democrats, the beneficiaries are always the same: what Codevilla calls the "Ins." The well-educated snobs. The conspirators. The ruling class.

> The regulators and the regulated become indistinguishable, and they prosper together because they have the power to restrict the public's choices in ways that channel money to themselves and their political supporters. Most of the world is too well acquainted with this way of economic life. Americans are just starting to find out.[10]

For Angelo Codevilla, there was nothing redeeming about these people or the system that has sluiced life's rewards in their direction. A real meritocracy, he allowed, might have its virtues, but that's not what we have in America. We are taught to bow before scientific expertise, but when viewed in the harsh light of class analysis, we can see that the expertise itself is rotten: expensive American colleges simply hand out As to everyone, while professional associations prevent the public from influencing or investigating academic work. Their expertise, their social concern—it is, all of it, merely a mask for arbitrary power.

Just as in the thirties, ordinary people are now said to be wise to the game. They are aware, Codevilla writes, "that government is not the friend of the friendless. The Country Class knows that the government is there to serve the strong: the

Ruling Class' members and supporters." They owe the established order no deference or respect; they have seen through its deceptions, swept aside its gauzy myths, shed its bunk forever. They know that the "tyranny" so many have been fretting about is in fact here. We are in its cruel grip already.[11]

Once She Built a Railroad

The ultimate act of thirties usurpation is Ayn Rand's thousand-page 1957 novel, *Atlas Shrugged*. To its present-day fans, it is a work of amazing prescience, the story of the overregulating, liberty-smothering Obama administration told more than fifty years before it actually happened. For me, it is the political flimflam of our times wrapped up in one big package: the manifesto of the traders and deregulators who caused the economic disaster, embraced without a glimmer of awareness by the protest movement that the disaster stirred up.

The story of a group of business leaders fighting big-government oppression, *Atlas Shrugged* has been popular since it was first published, especially among the sort of self-pitying mogul types who see themselves in the book's tycoon heroes. For free-market true believers, the tome is their very own *Uncle Tom's Cabin*, or, more accurately, their *Caesar's Column*.

With Barack Obama's inauguration in January of 2009, sales of *Atlas Shrugged* registered a remarkable uptick. Everyone could see that it was the novel for the era. The opinion page of the *Wall Street Journal* hailed it as the tale of our times foretold. The influential blogger Michelle Malkin urged readers to emulate the book's entrepreneurial heroes. Officers of the Ayn Rand legacy organizations began appearing at Tea Party rallies, stoking the fires of discontent; protest signs started quoting famous lines from the novel; someone issued silver coins emblazoned with the name of the book's main character; and a movie based on the book was released to the great anticipation of the resurgent Right. (It flopped.)

Rand fans heard the call to the colors. Among our characters, Rick Santelli, Mike Pompeo, and Paul Ryan are all disciples; Ryan suggested in 2009 that "we are right now living in an Ayn Rand novel, metaphorically speaking." Among the freshman class in Congress, the fandom burns particularly brightly. Senator Ron Johnson of Wisconsin refers to *Atlas Shrugged* as his "foundational book."[12] Representative David Schweikert of Arizona cites *Atlas Shrugged* as his favorite book, Representative Rick Crawford of Arkansas quotes Rand on his Twitter feed, and Senator Rand Paul describes *Atlas Shrugged* as a "must-read classic in the cause of liberty."[13]

The novelist's biographer Jennifer Burns expressed puzzlement at the book's post-crash popularity. When the economic collapse disgraced certain Ayn Rand acolytes, she told *Politico* in 2009, "I thought, 'Wow. Ayn Rand. Dead and buried forever.' But she's come roaring right back."[14]

Actually, Rand's revival makes perfect sense in our upside-down age. *Atlas Shrugged* is the story of an alternative Great Depression in which everything happens the way market-minded conservatives would have had it happen: meddling government is the obvious culprit of the economic slowdown; business types are both heroes and victims; and the gigantic strike that is the book's central thread is led not by some labor type but by genius entrepreneurs who are sick of being told what to do by politicians.

Atlas Shrugged was published in 1957 and is set in the indefinite future, but to judge by its account of American life it is actually a commentary on events of several decades previous.

It chronicles an era when steel and railroads, the two industries described most prominently in the novel, were at the vanguard of American enterprise. That era is most definitely not the fifties, when railroads were in catastrophic decline, but it could well be the thirties, when streamlined trains and massive steel mills were the symbols of American economic might. And although the book was published well into the television age, the various speeches in which the characters mouth Rand's market-friendly Nietzscheanism are all radio broadcasts, the great medium of the thirties. TV is mentioned only in passing.

The novel seems in many of its details to be an artifact of the Depression. Its first page describes an exchange between one of the main characters and a "bum" who has "asked for a dime." Its main story line—capitalists go on strike and shut the nation down—echoes a well-known liberal talking point from 1937, when the economy slid into recession and certain senior Roosevelt advisers attributed the downturn to politically motivated sabotage by the wealthy, a so-called capital strike. And illustrating the great literary fear of 1932—the sense that society itself was disintegrating—is one of Rand's few points of aesthetic strength. *Atlas Shrugged* gives us scene after scene of rural poverty, of listless people who don't know what to do with themselves, of houses and towns overgrown with weeds, of desperate humans carting their belongings down the road, of children turned into roving animals; each might have appeared in some collection of essays surveying the ruins of the nation in the days of Herbert Hoover.

The same is true of Rand's cast of capitalist hero-victims. One of them was reportedly inspired by the financier Ivar Kreuger, a villain of the Depression years.[15] The travails of another of her main characters, a steel manufacturer, appear to have been borrowed wholesale from a 1935 episode in the comic strip *Little Orphan Annie*.* And of course there's a righteous gangster we are supposed to admire in the manner of Woody Guthrie's 1939 song "Pretty Boy Floyd," only with the poles reversed: he robs the government to fill the bank accounts of the deserving rich.

The book's Depression flavor goes beyond its setting and characters; it is also a thirties novel thematically and philosophically. *Atlas Shrugged* may be the favorite novel of the millionaire class, but it is also the most commercially successful exemplar of that short-lived literary vogue of the thirties, proletarian fiction. If that literary school is remembered at all anymore, it is for its stereotyped businessmen-parasites, its hackneyed plots in which a worker-hero attains class consciousness, and the climactic strikes toward which its plots seem always to steer. The genre was a species of propaganda that shunned wit and seemed to privilege leaden

---

* The steel man is Hank Rearden, who invents a superstrong, superlight metal. *Atlas Shrugged* is, in large part, the story of Rearden's travails at the hands of the government, which first tries to buy his patent, then takes his patent away and permits others to manufacture his metal. Despite being beloved by his workers, Rearden suffers a climactic mob attack on his factory.

The 1935 *Little Orphan Annie* episode features the chemist Eli Eon, inventor of an indestructible substance, Eonite, which he begins to produce with the assistance of the business genius Daddy Warbucks, who is also beloved by his workers. Eon and Warbucks turn down offers to buy their patent, and then are set upon by a gang of business rivals, labor leaders, and a Huey Long–style demagogue who want a piece of the Eonite action.

When Warbucks is urged to fight back with propaganda of his own, he gives this succinct Randian reply: "I'm a worker—a producer—a business man—I'm not a cheap politician—what did any politician ever produce?" Eventually, Warbucks's enemies incite a mob which destroys the Eonite factory and kills Eli Eon. Warbucks had aimed to bring "prosperity and happiness" to the world with Eonite; the fake altruism of the leftists destroyed that dream.

It is almost precisely the lesson taught by *Atlas Shrugged*. And yes, it appeared in the funny pages first. See Harold Gray, *Arf! The Life and Hard Times of Little Orphan Annie, 1935–1945* (New Rochelle, NY: Arlington House, 1970). The quotes from Warbucks are found in the strip for August 8, 1935.

writing; it was only slightly more sophisticated than a comic book. It was also the paradigmatic hard-times literary style.

Atlas Shrugged deserves to be considered part of the genre.* It retains the wit-free writing and the heavy-handed propaganda, with conversations between characters frequently devolving into multipage philosophical monologues. (How any real human could stand to listen to these tedious stem-winders is one of the points of disbelief that this Rand reader found it most difficult to suspend.) As far as its characters are concerned, appearances are almost always reliable indicators of essence: bad guys are usually 100 percent bad, as the reader knows from their first step upon the stage, while good guys are uniformly awesome, endowed with the same good taste, the same weird syntax, the same mechanical

---

* "*Atlas Shrugged* was a throwback to Socialist realism," writes the Rand biographer Jennifer Burns, "with its cardboard characters in the service of an overarching ideology." (Burns, *Goddess of the Market* [New York: Oxford University Press, 2009], p. 179.)

The novel's similarity to the proletarian style is no accident. As a student in the Soviet Union, Rand absorbed a politicized communist pedagogy, and once she had escaped to America and embarked on a life of fighting communism, it was as though she resolved to do it by mimicking what the hated Reds said and did. "I loathe your ideals," says the Rand alter-ego character to a Soviet commissar in her 1936 novel, *We the Living*. "I admire your methods." (See Burns, *Goddess of the Market*, p. 16, and Anne Heller, *Ayn Rand and the World She Made* [New York: Anchor, 2010], p. 87.)

In later years Rand wrote a "Manifesto of Individualism" that was supposed to be the answer to *The Communist Manifesto* and expressed her longing to write novels that functioned as propaganda. Her goal, according to biographer Burns, was to "become the right-wing equivalent of John Steinbeck," author of the 1939 migrant-labor classic *The Grapes of Wrath*. In a letter to a friend in the forties, Rand wrote, "It's time we realize—as the Reds do—that spreading our ideas in the form of fiction is a great weapon." In her later days, presiding over a cult of followers, Rand went on to enforce a line of political and aesthetic orthodoxy as rigid as anything to come out of the CPUSA in its heyday, with "show trials" for people suspected of doctrinal schism and excommunication for those who showed insufficient contrition. (Burns, *Goddess of the Market*, pp. 61, 95, 92, 182.)

aptitude, the same marksmanship, even names with the same crackling consonant clusters.* For some reason, they almost all seem to know how to fly airplanes.

It is, of course, a novel about a strike, a standard plot device of the Popular Front era. As per the genre's requirements, its protagonists are noble producers who are unfairly oppressed. But in this iteration of the proletarian novel, the self-interested businessman is the hero instead of the villain. The parasites are the rest of us, the rabble and the intellectuals who use government to mooch and freeload on the labors of the virtuous capitalist.

In Rand's dystopic America, government meddling of the New Deal variety has been allowed to run wild. Washington interferes constantly in the affairs of private businesses, from big decisions to small ones, and then interferes more when the first interference doesn't achieve the desired result. The government forces inventors to surrender their inventions, rich men to turn over their income, producers of raw materials to divert supplies from their rightful clients to more politically favored ones. The business class resents the threats and the meddling, and, as in standard Marxist agitprop, slowly becomes aware of their exalted nature and their victimization at the hands of politicians and intellectuals. Class consciousness!

Billionaire solidarity having been achieved, the great tycoons disappear one after another into a mountain hideout pioneered for them by the genius inventor John Galt. This

---

* The names of the book's heroes fall into three general groups.

1. The Dens and the Dans: Hank Rearden, Ragnar Danneskjöld, Ken Danagger, Quentin Daniels, Francisco d'Anconia.
2. The Aggs, Oggs, and Acks: Dagny Taggart, Judge Narragansett, Owen Kellogg, Hugh Akston.
3. The Hard Aitches: Richard Halley, Lawrence Hammond, Dr. Hendricks.

strategic withdrawal of entrepreneurship—the strike—is so crushing that civilization itself begins to unravel. It's war between the "subhuman creatures" of the world and "their betters," as one heroic capitalist describes the two sides. But the subhumans, meaning the general public, won't give in or learn their lesson. And so Galt, the leader of the walk-out, delivers an ultimatum over the radio. "If you desire ever again to live in an industrial society," he tells the "moral cannibals" of the human race, "it will be on *our* moral terms."[16]

One of the objectives of the capitalists' strike in *Atlas Shrugged* seems to be to invert, one by one, each of the labor movement's notions about the nobility of the toiler. The cherished idea that workers can run the economy by themselves—and that capitalists are therefore unnecessary and even parasitical—is bluntly lampooned: workers in Rand's world have no idea what to do with themselves when capital withdraws. And the familiar, sentimental claim that workers built America is savagely rebuked. Indeed, at times in the novel, the very purpose of the strike seems to be to get even with organized labor for its uppity rhetoric. "We've heard so much about strikes," Galt lectures his industrialist friends, "and about the dependence of the uncommon man upon the common."

> "We've heard it shouted that the industrialist is a para-site, that his workers support him, create his wealth, make his luxury possible—and what would happen to him if they walked out? Very well. I propose to show to the world who depends on whom, who supports whom, who is the source of wealth, who makes whose livelihood possible and what happens to whom when who walks out."[17]

Maybe you had trouble following that passage, with all its interweaving "whos" and "whoms," but the general sentiment is simple enough. Successful businesspeople, which is to say, society's victims, are going to rise up and show the world who's boss. You are to acknowledge their suffering and their power at the same time. As the novel ends, they are preparing to resume their rightful position over the nation.

In pushing this absurd social theory, the novelist is most emphatic. Captains of industry are "the great victims," as one character puts it, "who have contributed the most and suffered the worst injustice in return." And as the long, long novel plods slowly on, Rand doubles down on the idea, having John Galt declare himself to be "the defender of the oppressed, the disinherited, the exploited—and when *I* use those words, they have, for once, a literal meaning."[18]

The libertarian economist Ludwig von Mises loved *Atlas Shrugged*, nailing the book's antipopulist message in a single perceptive sentence. "You have the courage to tell the masses what no politician told them," he wrote in a fan letter to Rand: "you are inferior and all the improvements in your conditions which you simply take for granted you owe to the efforts of men who are better than you."[19]

It is hardly a democratic formula. Indeed, democracy is part of the problem for Rand, since it puts "ward heelers" in legal authority over captains of industry. And so *Atlas Shrugged* pushes this political dilemma to its logical conclusion, with the politicians making crushing demands and the business elite rising up against them. It's a sort of Marxism for the master class, a hard-times story in which business is a force of pure light*

---

* At one point in the novel, Rand has John Galt, the leader of the strike, assert that capitalists "have never been on strike in human history." But as the economist Thorstein Veblen pointed out in 1921, sabotage and malingering are in fact pre-

and the "looters" in the government are responsible for every last little disaster.

Why *Atlas Shrugged* appeals to successful businesspeople is no mystery. But how does a book that tells the rest of the world *you are inferior* become the manifesto of a populist revival?

The usual explanation for the newfound popularity of *Atlas Shrugged*, as we noted, is its supposed prescience: it seems to predict the emergency bank-rescue measures of 2008 and 2009, plus the cruel hounding of business leaders by federal officials that supposedly followed. There have even been efforts to take matters to the next level. During the AIG bonus debacle, a Wall Street type published a peevish resignation announcement as an op-ed in the *New York Times*; he was walking out, he wrote, because he was sick of being "unfairly persecuted by elected officials." And in September 2011, House Speaker John Boehner announced that the economy wasn't improving because "job creators in America, basically, are on strike." We needed to "liberate" these powerful ones from taxes and an insane, meddling government—or else. If talent isn't treated the way talent wants to be treated, it will walk. Just try running your economy *then*.

But *Atlas Shrugged* also resonates on a much grander scale than this. It has all the answers—and I do mean "all"—for a

---

cisely how capitalism works in most industries. Were manufacturing plants simply to run all the time at full blast, for example, prices could not be maintained at profitable levels; overproduction would soon put the manufacturer in question out of business. "So it appears," Veblen wrote, "that the continued prosperity of the country from day to day hangs on a 'conscientious withdrawal of efficiency' [the IWW's definition of a strike] by the business men who control the country's industrial output." The business class is *always* on strike to some degree; for them to operate in any other way would be to court their own ruination. (Rand: *Atlas Shrugged* [1996 Signet edition], p. 677. Veblen: *The Engineers and the Price System*, reprinted in *The Portable Veblen* [New York: Viking, 1948], p. 436.)

world facing Great Depression II. The institutions of government have grown corrupt and misguided, Rand tells us; they have become instruments not for protecting us but for robbing us. When the economy falls into catastrophic collapse, she insists, it is always because government has interfered in its destructive and self-serving way. And salvation can only come after the producer class has been liberated from the state.

For its readers, *Atlas Shrugged* acts as a sort of exposé, pulling back the curtain to reveal the powers that manipulate our world. Angelo Codevilla's Country Class is figuring out the essential perfidy of the "ruling class," and this great novel of the age of Obama is there to assist them in the project of unmasking. The resurgent Right regards it as a powerful cry for justice.

But what starts out as a cry for justice quickly becomes a sort of bonus track from that event where the coal-mine CEO claimed to speak for the working people of West Virginia. Rand fandom is the equivalent of those working people rushing the stage to acclaim that CEO's wisdom, cheering hip-hip-hooray for that government-damning tycoon.

And so average Americans declare that they are joining the great strike of the producer class, shouting to the world that they have had it, that henceforth they will shut down their restaurants, fill no more cavities, paint no more houses. They link arms in solidarity with John Galt and announce from their websites that they, too, hereby declare war on the government for all the ways it has stifled their ambitions, pocketed the fruits of their hard work, and coddled the lazy. They are "going Galt," they proclaim.

We have seen a proud, strong country fall to her knees. Her people have become slovenly, inept and irresponsible. We do not see any morality in working hard for the benefit of those who choose not to. We do not see any moral value in contributing to a society that seeks to rule, rather than govern and steal from the Producers to give to them who are Looters and Moochers. We herby [*sic*] withdraw our Producing abilities, from a society that is unworthy of such contributions.

You, who would damn us, for a pursuit of success, for aspiring to our greatest human potential; yet who depend on our contributions to a society which you leach [*sic*] from.

Have you missed it?

Atlas WILL Shrug!![20]

That 99 percent of us will not, in fact, prosper in some every-man-for-himself Rand-land is a fine point that pretty much drops from view among the resurgent Right. They do not really comprehend that the only winners from a campaign to hack government down, deregulate everything, abolish taxes, and restore the gold standard would be people like that coal-mine CEO—or that the fate of most of us would be closer to that of the country's miners, toiling in a dangerous place for lousy wages and powerless to do anything about it.

Those who think they have something to look forward to in the libertarian future would do well to reread the famous scene in *Atlas Shrugged* where the author illustrates the breakdown of society with a colossal train accident. Rand arranges this disaster in such a way that the crash is attributable not to some act of negligence by the railroad but to the arrogance of one of the train's passengers, a powerful politician who forces the train's crew to proceed into a dangerous tunnel.* And then, in a notorious passage, the narrator goes through all the other passenger cars on the train and tells us why each casualty-to-be deserves the fate that is coming to him or her. One of them, she points out, received government loans; another doesn't like businessmen; a third is married to a federal regulator; a fourth foolishly thinks she has a right to ride on a train even when she doesn't personally own the train in question. For each one of these subhumans, the sentence is death.

For a reader like me, Ayn Rand's almost total contempt for humanity is her most repugnant point. For the master spirits of our contemporary Right, though, I sometimes suspect that's the stuff that sends the thrill up their spine: straightforward sympathy for the billionaire plus tangled rationalizations for the death or humiliation of everyone else. The game is finally up for the whiners of the world, they exult. The first shall be first. Root, hog, or die.

---

* Rand's train wreck is her great metaphor for the failure of socialism. It is another inversion of classic liberal concerns as train accidents were, in the nineteenth century, the source of countless lawsuits, regulations, investigations, and anti-business rhetoric.

The train wreck that is the central event in *Atlas Shrugged* seems to have been based very loosely on an actual disaster that took place in 1910 on the Great Northern Railway near the Cascade Tunnel in Washington State; Rand adapts the story in such a way that the responsibility for the accident is shunted from the railroad to one of the victims himself. For more on this story, please see note 21, page 212.

CHAPTER 9

He Whom a Dream Hath Possessed Knoweth No More of Doubting

One sunny morning in August of 2010, I drove up to the old Carnegie Library in Port Townsend, Washington, to work on the project that eventually became this book. Out in the rest of the country, according to a much-publicized poll, a majority of Americans believed the word "socialist" described President Obama well. Conservative entertainers were in full-throated denunciation of the collectivists running America into the ground, and a wave of revulsion against overreaching government was fixing to deliver a huge Republican victory that fall.

And yet none of the fears propelling the country to the right were even close to being realized. Lying on one of those big, old-fashioned tables as I walked into the library was the new edition of the *Guardian Weekly*, the British newspaper; its headline proclaimed, "Capitalism Is Still the Only Game in Town." By then it had been three years since the first shocks hit international credit markets, and yet politically nothing had changed. The free-market ideology was still in the saddle, the paper reported; the creed of

Davos still ruled the world; the near collapse of the financial system had barely caused it to break its stride. A high official from the Bank of England told the paper that "there have been far fewer repercussions than there were after the 1930s."

> "Then there was a real contest in the world about what was the right model for a modern society, and the crash convinced many people that capitalism and free markets were not the right way forward, but there has been no echo of that this time.
>
> "Maybe India and China have slowed down on deregulating their financial industries, but broadly speaking, the direction the world had been moving in is continuing. It reflects an end of ideology. Capitalism is still the only game in town."[1]

I thought about the hardworking Americans who were, at that moment, dutifully responding to the Tea Party's clanging emergency call. Here they were, raging against the socialist takeover, swearing to resist the leftist usurpers in Washington, and there in the paper a central banker was explaining that none of it had happened. From the *Newsweek* "socialism" cover to last week's bestseller about liberal tyranny, it had all been a false alarm.

Nothing had changed. We weren't going to be rounded up for the Gulag. Capitalism wasn't going to be abolished. The financial crisis hadn't put radicals in charge of America after all. Essence was in such violent disagreement with appearance that the force of it seemed likely to snap one's neck.

This is the enigma we turn to now: the resurgent Right's epistemology; its way of perceiving the world around it—or, more accurately, its way of not perceiving; its ability to keep the fear of a Martian invasion stoked for years despite the Martians' stubborn refusal to appear.

What kind of misapprehension permits the newest Right to brush off truths that everyone else can see so plainly? What backfiring form of cognition convinces them that critics of bailouts were in fact responsible for those bailouts? That deregulation is not the problem but the solution? That Ayn Rand is the hero rather than the villain of the present disaster? What allows this tremendous divergence between fact and appearance?

An End of Ideology?

To understand, we might want to take into consideration other examples of conservatism's dalliance with error. We might cast our eyes back over the long, embarrassing story of the evolution debate or the global warming controversy. We might recall the Bush administration's various campaigns against government scientists and those who doubted the official rationale for the Iraq war. We might examine the GOP's tenacious adherence to the "supply side" theory of budget-balancing despite that theory's persistent failure to work.

We might decide to put a spotlight on the outright falsehoods that the conservative movement lists among its articles of faith: Its idea that the Franklin Roosevelt administration either caused or worsened the Great Depression. That progressives have been in control of the nation ever since the days of Woodrow Wilson. That George W. Bush was just pretending to be a conservative. That bond traders are ordinary workers. That government bears the entire responsibility for the mortgage meltdown and its every little ramification. (And I have not bothered with the strange ideas that some on the newest Right hold about Barack Obama's true birth-place, or his secret army, or who wrote his first book.)

There is no level of scrutiny permissive enough to let these absurdities get by. After reviewing such a list, a certain variety of liberal likes to apply the word "liar" to the leaders of the Right. But that's not the whole story. Yes, there have been attempts to deceive in some quarters, and even deliberate misrepresentation of the facts from time to time. But more disturbingly, there is a certain remoteness from reality, a kind of politicized groupthink that seems to get worse each year as the Right withdraws ever farther into a world of its own.

That Americans are increasingly separated from social reality is not some secret that I alone have deciphered; it is the logical result of decades of increasingly specialized market segmentation. It goes back at least to the days of sociological worries about the "mass society" and the things that TV was doing to our perceptions. Ironically, one of the most memo-rable expressions of this fear comes in the Tea Party's favorite movie, *Network*, where the Howard Beale character—the one Rick Santelli and Glenn Beck were so widely compared to—rails on about TV's fraudulence and the gullibility of his audience: "We deal in illusions, man. None of it is true. But you people sit there day after day. . . . We're all you know."

These days Americans are ever more busily "self-segregating" into enclaves filled with people who think and vote just as they do—little Galt's Gulches scattered all across the fifty states. The Internet, of course, has provided a gigantic playground for self-segregation—that's the reason it exists; those who don't follow the rule are "trolls." There are separate sites for conservative social networking and conservative dating. Like-minded blog-gers often link only to one another—it is considered a political sin to reference the other side[2]—so that their readers' minds won't be contaminated by exposure to contrary views.

Conservatives inhabit a "very separate world," declared the Democratic pollster Stanley Greenberg in 2009; a place of intense group identity where Fox News is the medium of record and the president is believed to follow a "secret agenda" that is invisible to the rest of the nation. This culture of closure also gives us the phrase "Don't Believe the Liberal Media"— the slogan of the Media Research Center, an important player in winger Washington. When you consider that, by the standards of the MRC, virtually *all* traditional media is liberal media, you begin to understand that the Center is calling for a deliberate cognitive withdrawal from the shared world.

Although recent developments in mass communication have contributed to the malady I am describing, it is also true that times of economic catastrophe induce people to wall themselves off with airtight philosophical structures. When the credibility of tradition is shredded, it should not surprise us to see people retreat into pure utopianism, to cling to the *ought-to-be* when the *actually-is* really sucks. Despite the smug banker quoted in the *Guardian Weekly* story, ideology hasn't ended in the Great Recession; ideology has triumphed.

Intransigent Idealism

"I don't read books," a Tea Party activist once told the historian Jill Lepore. "I read blogs."[3]

The line struck a chord with me. It brought to mind a book that I had been reading of late, *Part of Our Time*, Murray Kempton's classic study of "the committed and the dedicated" during the thirties—Communists and fellow travelers, mainly—whose mind-set seemed identical to the one I saw among the blog-reading rebels of the contemporary Right.[4]

Kempton brought the matter into sharpest focus in a biographical sketch of one J. B. Matthews, a thirties radical who turned red hunter in the fifties, performing both roles with the same evangelical zeal, the same intolerance for ambiguity, the same "singular quality always to know in a flash without ever having learned."[5]

"Matthews saw what he wished to see, and he had no need of books for knowledge," Kempton writes. Matthews was one of many who made pilgrimages to the USSR in those days, and Kempton tells us that on one of his visits a colleague was brought face-to-face with the spectacular catastrophe taking place in the Ukraine: the man-made famine of 1932. Here is how Matthews dealt with this embarrassing situation: he "insisted that there was no such thing, and anyway, look at India. He knew how to protect himself against shocks of recognition."[6]

As did many of his comrades. So many, in fact, that the persistent blindness of the Americans who visited the Soviet Union in the Depression would eventually become one of the great set pieces of thirties historiography. Lefty after lefty made the trek, and even the keenest critics among them managed to overlook what was actually happening to the Soviet people. Reviewing the blithe reports of these clueless tourists many years later, the novelist Harvey Swados marveled at how "the will to believe often triumphed over the evidence of the senses."[7]

What made this possible, Swados continued, was that the thirties were a time of "intransigent idealism." No reports from the outside world could budge the certainty of the believers (until the 1939 Nazi-Soviet Pact, that is). Malcolm Cowley, a star literary critic of the era, put it slightly differently: it was an "age of faith." With social traditions shattered, people thought they had to sign up for one side or another in a coming showdown of ideological systems. It was, they thought, "either light or darkness, but nothing between."[8]

And so a generation of thinkers put themselves under the discipline of a clique of political con men. They convinced themselves that the laws of history were symmetrical, mathematical, predictable, and fully at the command of some distant Soviet generalissimo. They "set out to be redeemers," mourned Murray Kempton, and they wound up as "policemen." They excommunicated one another from their tiny Marxist conclaves over completely theoretical bits of trivia, they fully expected the world to someday come marching their way, and they deliberately taught themselves to produce awful, cartoonish art.[9]

It was not really a malady limited to the ideological Left. There was a corporate version as well: the doctrine of positive thinking, and it was just as vehemently idealistic and as closed to the evidence of the senses as was the communist "will to believe." The "age of faith" was in effect whether one was writing proletarian fiction or making the sale by adopting a positive mental attitude: both endeavors involved controlling one's mind in order to filter transmissions between oneself and the outside world.

In his towering 1937 bestseller, *Think and Grow Rich*, Napoleon Hill urged a kind of self-hypnosis on readers: they were to deliberately plunge themselves into a "faith" in their own success, visualizing money, imagining their future prosperity—and one day success, money, prosperity would actually materialize. Wishing would make it so. In *his* towering 1936 bestseller, *How to Win Friends and Influence People*, Dale Carnegie urged readers to adopt a system of feigned regard for others, a sort of propaganda of the smile. The catch was that the regard had to be genuinely felt, and therefore had to be deliberately cultivated: another act of faith.

The Consolation of Dogmatism

Intransigent idealism like this has continued to thrive in the dark corners of American life, and during our own experience with economic decline it has flourished as never before. No, there has been no Marxist revival, but in their mania for Ayn Rand, the disgruntled ones have chosen the next best thing. Inflexible dogmatism is, after sociopathic shrillness and speeding locomotives, one of the great selling points of *Atlas Shrugged*; the absolute, airtight correctness of Rand's views on all things is always played fortissimo in the novel, always spoken with maximum emphasis. And Rand's followers have traditionally brought the dogmatism to life. Among the Rand cult, "'objective reality' was what Rand said it was," remembers the libertarian writer Jerome Tuccille.

> "Morality" was conformity to the ethic of Ayn Rand.
>
> "Rationality" was synonymous with the thinking of Ayn Rand.
>
> To be in disagreement with the ideas of Ayn Rand was to be, by definition, irrational and immoral. There was no allowable deviation under the tenets of [her philosophy] Objectivism—which . . . quickly became a kind of New Marxism of the Right.[10]

When they weren't banishing one another from the inner circle of the Rand cult, the novelist and her followers were determining, by dint of pure deductive reasoning, that cigarette smoking was life-affirming. Or that monopolies could not exist absent federal regulation. Rand warred on environmentalists, whom she had rationally determined to be enemies of progress; and against American Indians, whose expropriation was deserved because their culture transgressed her philosophical system in some way.

Another place where thinking of this sort crops up constantly is in professional economics; indeed, the housing bubble itself could probably not have happened without the resolute determination of economists to blot out reality in favor of comforting myths of a superefficient market, an all-seeing financial deity that would surely defuse any dangerous situation.

The list of heavy economic thinkers who denied that there was a bubble in the real-estate market, for example, is long and shiny with glittering names, every prestigious one of them convinced that prices were being driven upward by fundamentals, as theory says such prices almost always are.[11] More disastrous by far, though, was the economists' push to roll back regulations against fraud in financial markets, on the smug belief that financiers were so keenly rational and so zealous to protect shareholder value that they simply would not allow fraud to happen. That fraud, in fact, happened in all sorts of catastrophic ways and at many different levels made no difference; theory canceled it all out.[12]

Abstract reasoning like this is not solely the province of advanced thinkers; another place where you find it is, of course, the Glenn Beck empire. Parsing a recent performance by his former fave British rock band Muse on his radio show in February 2011, the host declared that he had changed his mind about the group, that for all their rebel lyrics they didn't get what the conservative revival was about after all. Why didn't they get it? Because they were Europeans. And Europeans, as everyone knew,

> have had very few glimpses of real freedom. Even when England won the Second World War, they didn't

> go into freedom. That's where the *Road to Serfdom*
> came from. Because Winston Churchill and many oth-
> ers all said, wait, what are you doing? We're going the
> wrong direction. And it didn't go to freedom, it went
> to the Road to Serfdom.

Beck is correct that *The Road to Serfdom*, the famous
1944 book by the Austrian economist Friedrich Hayek, was
written as a critique of British politics, a warning that Labour
Party socialism might lead eventually to totalitarianism. The
book's weakest point, as critics have observed over the years, is
that Hayek's main prediction never came true. Although Britain did go enthusiastically socialist after the war, it never
abridged its traditional freedoms of speech, assembly, the press,
and so on. The country even reversed itself in the seventies and
swung energetically back in the direction of the market.

But here is Glenn Beck, deleting all that because a favorite work of political conjecture published in 1944 predicted
something else. Markets have to be free, or else other freedoms will disappear, Hayek had reasoned. Extending this
logic was simple: markets weren't free after the war; therefore freedom must have vanished from the scepter'd isle—
and from Europe generally, leaving the whole continent sadly
ignorant of "real freedom."

I quote the blundering Mr. Beck this one last time because
his casual bit of historical cleansing reminded me of those thirties leftists on their trips to Russia. They saw freedom in the
Soviet Union because they wanted to; Beck sees unfreedom in
England because that's what he believes ought to be there.
That old "will to believe" still blithely overrules the "evidence
of the senses."

We notice this intransigent idealism everywhere on the
resurgent Right once we start looking for it. Consider Texas

governor Rick Perry, briefly a front-runner for the GOP presidential nomination, whose hard-times manifesto *Fed Up!* speaks for an American people who are "over-taxed and over-regulated." The Great Recession furnishes Perry with an opportunity to contemplate previous episodes of hard times, and what he finds, when he contemplates, is that our understanding of the past needs revising. The conventional lesson of the thirties—that government can extricate us from our economic problems—is, according to the governor, a "fraud"; a "myth." It did not take a lot of study or reading to convince Perry of this daring thesis, however: He figured out that the New Deal was a failure, he writes, "in the 1980s after watching President Ronald Reagan institute market reforms to truly get us out of an economic mess. . . ." Having experienced this epiphany, this sudden certainty that "market reforms" are the only real solution to hard times, scholar Perry also developed a gift for seeing patterns in history of such subtlety that they have escaped the scrutiny of the reality-based world. He knows, for example, that the Great Depression did not end "until World War II, when FDR was finally persuaded to unleash private enterprise"—a reference, I guess, to the wartime regime of rationing, price controls, and War Production bureaucracies.

Senator Jim DeMint, another southern Republican, comes to similarly wrong conclusions by a similar process of deliberation. In the course of his 2009 bestseller, *Saving Freedom: We Can Stop America's Slide into Socialism*, the senator tells us that the nations of western Europe capitulated to "the siren song of socialism" after World War II and soon thereafter "declined into economic stagnation."[13] Like Rick Perry's claim about World War II, this happens to be incorrect, and in a really monumental way. As a brief check with the annals of reality reminds us, it was during those very postwar years that

France, Italy, Belgium, and Sweden—all of them called out by DeMint for choosing socialism after the war—embarked on their greatest boom periods in modern times. But according to Senator DeMint's theoretical guidelines, this is impossible: socialism *always* brings stagnation, and therefore socialism *brought* stagnation.

Throughout his bestselling book, in fact, the senator seems to advance on his quarry not by proofs and demonstrations in the conventional sense, but by a process of abstract moral reckoning. In an important passage describing the 2008 presidential debates, DeMint criticizes the then senator Barack Obama for referring to "markets running wild after deregulation." DeMint does not counter this statement by demonstrating that markets did *not* run wild after deregulation; he simply points out that the future president made these arguments and is therefore a man of "socialist principles."[14] DeMint's object here is not to refute; it is to unmask, to close down an unacceptable mental operation. There is only one way that believers in freedom can interpret the meltdown of 2008, and they must stick to it whether it fits the facts or not.

A taste for moral reckoning might also explain Senator DeMint's fondness for fairy tales. He introduces one chapter with a meditation on the Three Little Pigs and another with some thoughts on the story of the Gingerbread Man. We have noticed this infantilizing tendency elsewhere in the resurgent Right, and here, as well as in those other instances, its implication is obvious: that political economy can be understood as the battle of good and evil. Government is the wicked witch, while the market is the fairy godmother, magical bringer of freedom and prosperity.

What's going on here is not merely a withdrawal into simplicity. If simplicity is what you're looking for, the answers are almost too easy these days: Our leaders have been chasing the free-market dream for thirty-some years now, and for every step closer they've brought us, the more inequality has grown, the more financial bubbles have blossomed and burst, the more political corruption has metastasized, the harsher the business cycle has become. One caused the other; that's the "simple" answer.*

But the latest Right doesn't so much simplify reality as idealize it. They're in a place where beliefs don't really have consequences, where premises are not to be checked, only repeated in a louder voice. It is as though the frightening news of recent years has driven them into a defensiveness so extreme that they feel they must either deify the system that failed or lose it altogether.

In Pursuit of True Capitalism

Writing in 1936, the culture critic Gilbert Seldes marveled at the "morbid passion for absolutes" which then gripped the minds of his countrymen. Purists of all political stripes were in voice in those days, and none of them found the deeds of Franklin Roosevelt to their liking. To "the radical critic," the New Deal obviously didn't go far enough; it left the capitalist system intact. To "the reactionary," the New Deal reforms were objectionable for the opposite reason: they meant "the capitalist system has been destroyed."[15]

It is this latter complaint that concerns us today, and

---

* A good example of the reduction to simplicity—and a good demonstration of how simplicity can help us understand—can be found in Charles Ferguson's 2010 documentary about the financial crisis, *Inside Job*, where the narrator intones, "After the Great Depression, the United States had forty years of economic growth without a single financial crisis. The financial industry was tightly regulated." Regulation ended; crisis ensued.

Seldes provided a helpful gloss on its long history. People had moaned as far back as the 1840s that allowing labor unions to exist would destroy capitalism, the author recalled, and sure enough, the form of capitalism they had in those days died, to be replaced by "capitalism modified by the right of collective bargaining." The end-time fears returned, according to Seldes, when the federal government threatened to begin regulating railroads in the 1880s, and again the end of the world came to pass. Capitalism died, to be replaced this time by "capitalism modified by collective bargaining and Federal regulation."[16] Life went on.

Today, as in Gilbert Seldes's time, the fear that true capitalism is about to perish is with us again. Now, as then, only absolutes seem to matter. The panicked ones ignore the American genius for pragmatism and the long, complicated history of political compromise that actually built our economic system. Instead they yearn for some class-war Armageddon, some wretched rapture in which losers forever lose and the honorable are finally freed from any obligation to the inferior.

That there is no such thing as pure capitalism is a subtlety that eludes them. What they pine for is a system that can never exist, that has never existed, and that will never exist. And with every inch they bring us toward that ugly utopia, our society's deterioration accelerates. But still they keep on, blinking out the facts of the past as well as the disasters their bad medicine is sure to bring. Nothing matters but the dream, and in its pursuit they will risk our prosperity, our health, and yes, even our honor.

CHAPTER 10

The Silence of the Technocrats

Well, reader, we've had a lot of fun poking holes in the things conservatives say, haven't we? They blow off the facts when they feel like it; they swipe symbols from the other side; they illustrate arguments on economics with fairy tales. The reasoning you used to hear on the Glenn Beck show seems like something from a brainwashing session at Lubyanka prison. It is preposterous. It is contemptible.

But you know what it's better than?

It's better than nothing.

Let us recall, one more time, the original cataclysms whose memories today poison our every political moment: the financial crisis and the bailouts.

Remember, the culprits of those cataclysms—the ones who wrecked the economy—were not punished for what they did; they were rewarded. By this I don't mean they got away with a slap on the wrist; I mean they were laden down with billions and our blessings. Today they are rich in a way that you and I will never be able to comprehend. All of which happened courtesy of our government, the officials of which have conducted themselves ever since as though nothing really untoward happened at all. The bailout money will be recouped, they tell us. The experts understand these things.

You could not have contrived a scenario better calculated to destroy public faith in American institutions. What is the point of hard work, of scrapping for a few dollars more at some lousy hourly wage, when dishonest financial legerdemain is so profitable? Why play by the rules when they obviously don't apply to everyone? When louts and bullies and corruptionists take home society's greatest rewards?

The bailouts combined with the recession created a perfect situation for populism in the Jacksonian tradition, for old-fashioned calamity howlers, for Jeremiahs raging against the corrupt and the powerful.

This was the task of the moment, and one political faction, as we have seen, took to it immediately and with relish. They tossed inconvenient leaders overboard. They declared war on the ruling class. They assembled with megaphones in the park and gave voice to the people's outrage.

But the other faction—the actual political descendants of Jackson and Bryan and Roosevelt—took years to rise to the occasion. They didn't seem to understand that circumstances called for a profound change. They couldn't embrace the requirements of the moment even though they were the ones pledged to the traditional hard-times measures (regulation, reform, social insurance) and even though responding to hard times was once their party's very raison d'être.

Flowchart

They were offered the chance, of course. In 2008 Barack Obama seemed to be a figure of destiny like Roosevelt himself. He took the oath of office under similarly disastrous circumstances and was for a while buoyed up by exactly the sort of popular adulation that followed FDR.

Seven months later, it was clear that Obama had lost the populist momentum. It was frustrating when he turned over economic policy to Larry Summers and Tim Geithner, two well-known friends of Wall Street, and it was maddening when he insisted on following the bailout course of the Bush administration, even after the AIG debacle. But the moment I truly understood that the Dems had blown it came during the debate over health-care reform.

In years past, universal health care had been a cause that allowed liberals to connect to their working-class base regardless of everything else they did wrong. And since entrusting our health care to the private sector had allowed both unconscionable profits for the insurers and lousy service for sick people, the debate has traditionally taken a populist tone. The push for national health insurance was a fight, as President Harry Truman had put it, of the "everyday man" against "special privilege," meaning mainly the doctors' professional association, the AMA, with its predictable cries of "socialized medicine."

President Obama's strategy in 2009 was the reverse of Truman's. He would get the traditional opponents of health-care reform on board—the AMA, Big Pharma, insurance lobbyists—and do the deal as an act of cold consensus. All the experts would be heeded. All the corporate and professional "stakeholders" would be taken care of. No one would need to get their suit ruffled.

Then came the confrontations of "Town Hall Summer," when Democratic legislators talking up health-care reform faced hometown crowds of extraordinary hostility—average people yelling from the floor at the emissaries of the "grand bargain." It is true that the town hall meetings were deliberately packed by people who aimed to disrupt, but the populist spectacle they engineered was no less powerful for its agitprop origins. The Democrats appeared to be shaking hands with the Interests, while the ones screaming about "socialism" and theft through taxation this time around were Harry Truman's "everyday men."

Particularly memorable was one town hall meeting in Bremerton, Washington, when a Tea Partier named Keli Carender held up a twenty-dollar bill and challenged her Democratic congressman to come and snatch it out of her hand as "a down payment" on the health-care plan, which was surely going to soak taxpayers. (As with many of the town hall confrontations, it was not clear which plan Carender objected to.) And then she just stood there, staring at the congressman with those wild eyes, her arm in the air, immortalized in newspaper photographs like some kind of libertarian Norma Rae.

Another vivid episode was a town hall meeting I listened to on the radio in which an audience of angry Marylanders took turns abusing their U.S. senator. He had prepared a talk describing the minute details of the various health-care proposals then under consideration, but the audience didn't seem to care about that. They wanted to talk about big, philosophical things: freedom, tyranny, the Constitution, and the general incompetence of government.

If you don't remember the particulars of that summer, you might assume that the Democrats waded into the fight, the way Harry Truman used to do. You might think they relished the chance to talk about big, philosophical things, that they took the opportunity to tell how the existing system pocketed your twenty bucks, how government agencies had failed because they were designed to fail, or how social insurance strengthened freedom rather than violated it.

But that's not what happened at all. In most of the town hall meetings I reviewed, the Democrat on the hot seat seemed incapable of really engaging in a dispute about free-dom and the nature of government, or even of challenging the market orthodoxy that issued, in gathering after gather-ing, from the mouths of protesters around the nation.

It was as though the old-school liberal catechism had become forbidden language, placed on some index of pro-hibited thoughts. Instead, most of the Democrats I listened to brought the conversation relentlessly back to the baffling details of the various health-care proposals.

This failure led, in turn, to a second disaster. In full retreat before the right-wing onslaught, the Democrats threw them-selves into the arms of their corporate allies. They jettisoned the simpler, more popular, but more government-centric idea under consideration and settled on the "individual mandate," which required that everyone in the land sign up with a private insurance company. This solution would be more intrusive than the other one, more complicated, more regulatory. But since it would not create a social insurance program, it was also more "centrist." Naturally, it delighted the private insur-ance companies.

That's how a populist outburst from the Right caused the inarticulate Democrats to abandon the most populist ele-ments of their own plan and choose instead what we might call the elitist option, a crony-capitalist solution in which pub-lic choices would be diminished but corporate profits guaran-teed. What had been for decades a campaign to bring security to the average citizen thus became little more than an inside deal between members of the "ruling class," as the resurgent Right would soon be calling it.

The preoccupation with technical detail that I noticed during the health-care debate wasn't merely the failing of the unfortunate members of Congress who put on those town hall gatherings; it was the failing of the entire Democratic

Party. From its silver-tongued leader on down, Democrats simply could not tell us why our system had run aground and why we had a stake in doing things differently. They could not summon an ideology of their own.

This ideological void was apparent even when the Obama administration was moved to consider the greatest liberal triumphs of the past. Take Christina Romer's 2009 speech, "Lessons from the Great Depression," a typical administration document that I have cited several times in these pages. In it Romer, who then chaired the Council of Economic Advisers, rummaged through the thirties seeking guidance for present-day officials, but whether she was talking about monetary expansion or the need for stimulus, each of her suggestions was presented simply as a policy choice, as a thing that intelligent people would naturally decide to do in order to solve a given problem. That monetary expansion and stimulus programs were possible in the thirties only because of an ideological change in the way average Americans thought about government and the economy went unmentioned; we were supposed to know which road to choose from our study of the academic literature. Expertise would guide us. The ideology, presumably, would take care of itself.[1]

This was always how it went. Democratic leaders tried to assuage public anger over the bailouts while barely mentioning Wall Street's power over Washington—that subject they left to the resurgent Right. They gave us a stimulus package, but not a robust defense of deficit spending. They beefed up certain regulatory agencies, but they didn't dare tell the world how money had managed to wreck those agencies in the first place. And when a clearly unsafe BP oil well poured millions of gallons of poison into the Gulf of Mexico, President Obama told a reporter that before he could figure out "whose ass to kick" he had to convene a panel of experts.[2]

It is easy to understand how Democrats evolved into this tongue-tied, expert-worshipping species. Their traditional Democratic solutions may well have solved our problems, as Christina Romer maintained, but the ideology behind those solutions—as well as the solutions themselves, in many cases—are totally unacceptable to the people who increasingly fund Democratic campaigns. Instead, the Democrats tried to have it both ways: to deliver the occasional liberal measure here and there while studiously avoiding traditional liberal rhetoric. President Obama tries to stay on the good side of companies like Goldman Sachs and BP even as he desperately drives his hook-and-ladder around a world they have set on fire.

The nation, meanwhile, was begging for a round of national soul-searching. It wanted to know: How did the Crash of 2008 happen? How did government miss the warning signs? What are our responsibilities to our neighbors in hard times? Shouldn't we be worried about the national debt? In response, Democrats offered technical explanations. They simply could not talk about the disasters in a way that was resonant or compelling. Only the idealists of the Right did that. What the Democrats held out to an outraged nation was a fastidiously detailed flowchart for how things might be reorganized.

Good Bailouts and Bad

The bailouts, the stimulus, the health-care debate: with each of these issues, the path of expertise led the Obama administration toward compromise with the power of wealth. And by the thinking of Washington, that is entirely as it should have been. That is how you get things done.

But in every case, the administration compromised with the wrong party. Consider the Wall Street bailouts, the draft of political poison which Obama sipped even before his presidency began and from which he has never really recovered. Although it was not widely acknowledged at the time, bailouts on the scale of 2008 had happened before, and they had been politically deadly before as well. But there had also been bailouts that succeeded, bailouts that were even popular.

The difference, in a phrase, is Wall Street. What makes bailouts toxic is cronyism, the coming together of government and private wealth, the spectacle of Washington doing special favors for its pals in the investment banks. What makes bailouts healthful and popular is government acting as an alternative to Wall Street; government helping others recover from Wall Street's mismanagement of the economy.

It is a lesson that goes back to the earliest bailouts of them all, the ones orchestrated by the Reconstruction Finance Corporation (RFC) under Presidents Hoover and Roosevelt. Under Herbert Hoover, the bailout agency's doings were enormously unpopular, thanks to episodes that should sound very familiar to us today. In 1932, the RFC went to the rescue of railroads that were essentially fronts for Wall Street interests. (Like AIG!) Then it poured money into a big Chicago bank run by the man who had been not only the RFC's chairman a few weeks before, but also Calvin Coolidge's vice president. (Cronyism!) And it did these things while denying funds to cities that had run out of money to pay schoolteachers. (Where's my bailout?)[3]

Did Franklin Roosevelt simply accept those bailouts in the finest spirit of bipartisanship? As part of a "grand bargain"? In the serene knowledge that there were no "red states" and no "blue states" but only the United States? Of course not. He was fiercely critical of them. Although it was almost never mentioned in pundit discourse during the crucial weeks of 2008, those awful bailouts were one of the targets of Roosevelt's famous "forgotten man" speech of 1932, in which he charged that "the infantry of our economic army" had been overlooked while Hoover dispensed billions to the "big banks, the railroads, and the corporations of the nation."[4]

Did FDR's criticism of the bailouts mean there would be no more of them? Not exactly. As president, Roosevelt actually expanded the RFC and changed its direction. The man he installed as its chairman, a Texas banker named Jesse Jones, was no Tim Geithner. He was, instead, a classic populist type who regarded high finance with extreme suspicion. Jones spread the wealth around rather than dole it out to Wall Street. His RFC bailed out small-town banks, sank millions into agriculture, public works, education, insurance, and every imaginable type of small-scale financial enterprise.[5] And his RFC was far tougher on bailout recipients than we were this time around. It fired top management at bailed-out banks when Jones disapproved of them. It helped organize new banks when Jones thought they were necessary. It put compensation caps on bailed-out CEOs that were far stricter than anything contemplated by Team Obama. It took far-reaching steps to ensure that the railroads it rescued didn't turn the bailout money over to Wall Street banks. Jones even once told railroad executives that they had no business living in New York City.

The most critical thing was this: Under Jesse Jones's direction, the RFC was very clearly not an instrument of Wall Street. Instead, it was a sort of competitor, helping to organize the business structure of the nation independently of Wall Street's dictation.[6] While Jones's RFC did these things, the Democrats of the day regulated investment banking with the Securities and Exchange Commission, broke up the big banks with the Glass-Steagall Act, and reorganized the Federal Reserve in a way that diminished the power of the New York banks. And they repeatedly told the nation why they were doing these things.

Maybe the Roosevelt/Jesse Jones approach wouldn't have helped this time around. After all, the rebel conservatives of the last few years object when a helping hand is extended to the little guy just as much as they do when it's Wall Street that's soaking up the tax dollars. But at least such a technique would have made it impossible for the resurgent Right to present themselves as the only principled opponents of Wall Street or as the only ones who are wise to the banks' corrupt grip on Washington.

We'll never know. Obama chose the path of Herbert Hoover instead. Yes, the TARP aided regional banks here and there, but its obvious, overriding purpose was to get Wall Street off the hook for its disastrous mistakes, to stand the banks back up and get those bonuses flowing as in the old days.

Upon taking office, Obama did not break with Hank Paulson's campaign to restore Wall Street's preeminence or lay plans to reduce investment banking's power over American life. Instead, he took pains to let the world know that he embraced the Paulson strategy, appointing Paulson's ally Geithner to be his treasury secretary, retaining bailout mastermind Ben Bernanke at the Federal Reserve, and choosing as his chief White House economist Larry Summers—the man who had been treasury secretary when traditional banking rules were triumphantly overturned during the Clinton years. To this day, and despite the cries of "socialism" that dog them, Obama's crew has almost never voted the shares in the banks that the nation owns and has never replaced the management at a single one of those bungling institutions.*

---

* It *did* replace the management at General Motors, however, and it put a venture capitalist in charge of its auto bailouts, giving some idea of where manufacturing stands in relation to high finance in the modern-day Democrats' worldview.

And from cramdown to the so-called JOBS Act, the story is the same: each time political adversity has come, the Obama team has compromised in the direction of Wall Street, as though that was who needed to be mollified.

By Washington standards, the Obama administration played it exactly right. Voting for the TARP and then continuing the bailout policies of the Bush administration were acts of political maturity, showing the world that the Democrats could be trusted to rise above partisanship, to make the hard decisions, to swallow the bitter pills, to do what responsible adults knew they had to do, and so on down the list of Power Town clichés. In any case, the thinking goes, all political battles are battles over the "center." Since the Democrats are a party of the "left," their critics can only be placated by moves to the "right." That's why, in order to appease those who fear Obama's radicalism, the president had to make concessions to business (meaning Wall Street) and bring in nonthreatening personalities to develop his economic program.

The economic folly of this strategy should be plain by now. That it might also lead to electoral disaster probably never even occurred to the president's hard-nosed political advisers. After all, catering to Wall Street had brought only victories to Bill Clinton. Coming around to the way of the market had been regarded as high-minded stuff in the nineties, a statesmanlike acknowledgment of the obvious validity of conservative economic ideas. And Democrats in Washington look to the Clinton years as a kind of golden age.

But the advent of hard times made all that reasoning as obsolete as the floppy disk. Although Democrats apparently didn't know it, the Great Recession had repolarized the compass points. Nothing worked the way it used to in the nineties. It was no longer about "left" versus "right"; it was about special interests versus common interests. This was the time for a second FDR, not Clinton II.

The Right understood this instantly, as its many movements and ideas and manifestoes attested. The country demanded philosophical guidance, and the Right provided it. Conservatives claimed to speak for a recession-battered people, and as I have endeavored to show, they adopted the tones and markings of traditional hard-times insurgencies. Indeed, by April of 2011 it was possible for *National Review* to depict the author of "Down with Big Business," Representative Paul Ryan, as FDR, using the same image that *Time* used for Obama in 2008.

But it took the Washington Democrats years to grasp that things had changed. After the "shellacking" of 2010, for example, President Obama's response was to replace the former investment banker and Clinton retread Rahm Emanuel with . . . Bill Daley, another Clinton retread and former investment banker. Whom did the president think he was accommodating when he made this move? Your guess is as good as mine.

The low point came during the debt-ceiling debate in the summer of 2011, when the brand-new Republican House of Representatives, lost in a hallucination of populist righteousness, threatened to force a default on the national debt by the U.S. government unless it received what it wanted. The Republicans followed their playbook—moving ever farther to the right, creating the catastrophe they had pretended to foresee in the preceding years—and Obama followed his. Having nobly divested himself of bargaining chips some months before, Obama now declared that he would answer Republican demands by seeking some high-minded "grand bargain." He allowed that cuts to Social Security and Medicare, two of the proudest achievements of the Democratic Party, might well be necessary, and gave his assent as Republicans steered the economic policy of a stricken nation toward austerity.

Sometimes when I watch the Washington Democrats in action, my mind goes back to the tragically incompetent British general staff of World War I, ordering assault after gigantic assault, only to see their armies annihilated one after another. But still they kept at it, ordering up another round of the exact same thing, playing by the gentlemanly rules of combat, never doing anything remotely clever, and always completely surprised when the other side introduced them to twentieth-century warfare in some brutal new way.

It is that same blindness, that same fixed thinking, that we see in the strategizing of the Washington Democrats. No one among them seems to have wondered if bailouts might be done in a different way, or foreseen that Republicans might not play by the debt-ceiling rules. They try what Clinton tried; they are astonished to see it fail. And so they try it again. The Washington Democrats will no more acknowledge the possibilities of other tactics than they will abandon Georgetown and move en masse to some burned-out quarter of Baltimore. Instead they deride their liberal critics as impossible dreamers—or as "fucking retarded," in Rahm Emanuel's famous phrase—and try what worked for Clinton yet again. That their own habitual deference to expertise leaves them wide open to the decades-long conservative assault on "elites" never occurs to them. And so do the president's team of Chicago tough guys walk right into the populist buzzsaw—blithely, trustingly, repeatedly.

It is not hard to think of ways that Obama and Company could have stopped the resurgent Right in its tracks, had they wanted to. To begin with the most obvious, Obama and Company could have put themselves at the forefront of populist anger against Wall Street rather than making themselves the embodiment of the cronyism the public despises. They could have captured the outrage of small business by promising to break up the big banks or resuming antitrust enforcement. Another tactic might have built on the well-known facts that Tea Partiers hate NAFTA, and that they're hardly alone: why not announce that it's time to reexamine the nation's disastrous free-trade deals? Still another: As everyone knows, the newest Right has enjoyed amazing success spreading fears that liberal economic moves will automatically erode basic freedoms. Why not undercut this silly idea instead of allowing it to fester? End the Bush administration's domestic wiretapping program. Demand the reregulation of Wall Street *and* the repeal of the Patriot Act.

One reason Democrats didn't do these things, perhaps, is that it's easier to focus on the lunacy of the rejuvenated Right than on the main sources of its ideas. Tea Party leaders are so colorful, and their protest signs are so nutty, that dismissing them is more attractive than engaging them. And so the racist moments in Tea Party history are singled out and obsessively commented upon,* while its vastly more significant free-market streak is either regarded as camouflage for what the libs know to be its *real* payload—some kind of theocratic white supremacy—or else simply ignored.

Unfortunately, the other side wasn't calling for theocratic white supremacy. The threat haunting our time was not some sort of Klan comeback; it was economic disintegration. Bank

---

* This is not to say that some of these moments don't deserve all the commentary they got. For example, there was the idiotic parody letter that the Tea Party leader Mark Williams wrote in July 2010 to "Abraham Lincoln" on behalf of the "NAACP," which had just called on Tea Party chapters to distance themselves from racist commentary. It was so profoundly stupid that I'm not even going to try to summarize it here. Read it for yourself at http://politicalcorrection .org/blog/201007150012.

fraud, bailouts, bonus grabs, BP: these were the burning issues of 2010, and the Democrats pretty much left them to take care of themselves. Instead, they built an enormous Maginot Line on the antilunatic frontier and sat there waiting while the attack came down an entirely different route.

Terminal Niceness

None of these shortcomings should be pinned on President Obama alone, despite his emotional aloofness and his academic background. They are a reflection of the party he leads and the voters for which it increasingly speaks. After all, Barack Obama is not the first Democrat to offer "competence" as the answer to a period of deeply ideological governance; that was Michael Dukakis back in 1988.* And President Obama seems like Demosthenes when his remarks on health care are compared to the town hall disasters presided over by his tongue-tied, detail-dazzled Dems in 2009.

The problem is larger than him; it is a consequence of grander changes in the party's most-favored group of constituents. No one has described the new breed of Democrat better than . . . Barack Obama. "Increasingly I found myself spending time with people of means—law firm partners and investment bankers, hedge fund managers and venture capitalists," reminisced the future president in his 2006 book, *The Audacity of Hope.*

> As a rule, they were smart, interesting people, knowledgeable about public policy, liberal in their politics, expecting nothing more than a hearing of their opinions

---

* Or, arguably, the national security geniuses who got us into the Vietnam War, as immortalized in David Halberstam's 1972 classic, *The Best and the Brightest.*

in exchange for their checks. But they reflected, almost uniformly, the perspectives of their class: the top 1 percent or so of the income scale that can afford to write a $2,000 check to a political candidate. They believed in the free market and an educational meritocracy; they found it hard to imagine that there might be any social ill that could not be cured by a high SAT score. They had no patience with protectionism, found unions troublesome, and were not particularly sympathetic to those whose lives were upended by the movements of global capital. Most were adamantly prochoice and antigun and were vaguely suspicious of deep religious sentiment.[7]

"I know that as a consequence of my fund-raising I became more like the wealthy donors I met," Obama confesses a few paragraphs later.[8] So he has. And so has his party. Modern Democrats don't do things the way Roosevelt and Truman did because their eye is on people who believe, per Obama's description, "in the free market" almost as piously as do Tea Partiers. Class language, on the other hand, feels strange to the new Dems; off-limits. Instead, the party's guiding geniuses like to think of their organization as the vanguard of enlightened professionalism and the shrine of purest globaloney.

As a result of their retreat from populism, Democrats have spent the last several decades systematically extinguishing opportunities to broaden the base of their support. They did little, for example, as their former best friends in organized labor were scythed down by organized money. This was no ordinary misstep, by the way. Labor is one of the last institutional bearers of an ideology capable of countering the market-populist faith; had its voice been strong in 2009, things might have played out very differently. Instead, Obama and Company pretty much sat on their hands as the percentage of unionized workers in the private sector sank lower than at any point in the twentieth century. The fatuity of it all, one would think, has surely become obvious to Democrats: they have permitted nothing less than the decimation of their own grassroots social movement; the silencing of their own ideology. Thanks to this strategy, large parts of America are liberal deserts, places where an economic narrative that might counterbalance the billionaire-pitying wisdom of El Rushbo is never heard and might as well not exist.

The effects of a wrenching recession, on the other hand, aren't likely to touch the new, well-to-do Democrats directly. They know bad things are happening, yes; they express concern and promise to help the suffering, of course; but the urgency of the recession is not something they feel personally. It is not a challenge to their fundamental values. It is, rather, an occasion for charity.

Oh, but a country where everyone listens to experts and gets along—that's a utopia these new Dems regard with prayerful reverence. They dream of bipartisanship and states-that-are-neither-red-nor-blue and some reasonably-arrived-at consensus future where the culture wars cease and everyone improves their SAT scores forevermore under the smiling, beneficent sun of free trade and the knowledge industries.*

Not even from our society's most gifted political critics did we hear anything different (until it was too late). A few

---

* One of the elements distinguishing the two parties these days, Gallup pointed out, is their attitude toward "compromise." In a poll conducted in late 2010, Republican voters, on average, agreed that it was "more important for political leaders to stick to their beliefs even if little gets done." Democratic voters, on the other hand, thought it was "more important for political leaders to compromise in order to get things done." Read more at http://www.gallup.com/poll/144359/Democrats-Republicans-Differ-Views-Compromise.aspx.

days before the 2010 election, for example, Jon Stewart, the perceptive and often ferocious comedian, tried to answer the various Tea Party marches and Glenn Beck rallies with a protest of his own, which he called the "Rally to Restore Sanity," otherwise known as the "million moderate march." It brought a crowd of several hundred thousand to the National Mall in Washington, DC, where they bought "I'm with Reasonable" T-shirts and listened to Stewart's speech about ordinary Americans getting along with their neighbors regardless of political differences.

Now, there was something noble and even Depression-esque about Stewart's invocation of the common man, and I agree with much of what he said on that occasion. But it is more than a little strange to gaze out over a land laid waste by fantastic corporate fraud and declare that partisanship is what ails us and that reasonableness is the cure. Like the national Democrats, Stewart focused on process and expertise and surface etiquette while the real drama was elsewhere: in the mounting unemployment rate, in the still-lingering shock of the bailouts. Conservatives were out in the cul-de-sacs of America following their strategy from the seventies— "organize discontent"—and here were the liberals, on the mall in DC, trying to save the day by organizing civility.

Conclusion: Trample the Weak

In 1944, the Hungarian historian Karl Polanyi told the story of what he called the "utopian" idea of the "self-regulating market"—and of what happened when theorists and dreamers tried to put that utopia into effect. "To allow the market mechanism to be the sole director of the fate of human beings and their natural environment," he wrote, in a celebrated passage, "would result in the demolition of society."

> Robbed of the protective covering of cultural institutions, human beings would perish from the effects of social exposure; they would die as the victims of acute social dislocation through vice, perversion, crime and starvation. Nature would be reduced to its elements, neighborhoods and landscapes defiled, rivers polluted, military safety jeopardized, the power to produce food and raw materials destroyed.[1]

When Polanyi wrote those words, the experience of the Depression had just persuaded the world to forswear any further pursuit of that deadly free-market dream. Society periodically and instinctively tried to defend itself against the depredations of the market, Polanyi wrote, and for decades, the world assumed that this pattern was a natural one. Another economic crisis, and you'd get another New Deal.

But this time around we saw a new pattern develop. After the market vandalized American society along precisely the lines Polanyi described—plus a few bonus ways that neither he nor anybody else saw coming—society fairly begged to be trashed again. Its most influential protest movement demanded that America lace up its running shoes and chase the market utopia even more energetically; that we "trample the weak" instead of coddling them.[2]

It is also true that, beginning in 2011, echoes of the original hard-times song finally became audible. In February, enormous crowds began gathering in Madison, Wisconsin, to protest the war on workplace rights that had been declared by the state's brand-new right-wing government. Phony populism was finally being confronted by the real thing—and sometimes dwarfed by it as well. One snowy weekend, for example, a small delegation of high-ranking conservatives flew into Madison to face down the protesting workers and to remind the world, via the snarling voice of Andrew Breitbart, that the Tea Party was called terrible and unjust names by the mainstream media. Never had the movement's victim complex seemed more risible, more irrelevant.

Then, in September 2011, almost three years to the day after the collapse of Lehman Brothers, enormous crowds began gathering in New York City's Zuccotti Park to "Occupy Wall Street." They remained there for weeks, growing in numbers and finally pushing their way into the consciousness of the nation. There was plenty of silliness associated with these protests, to be sure, but the famous collection of first-person recession narratives, which the protesters collected online under the rubric "I Am the 99 Percent," carried a power and a poignancy that was impossible to deny.

The Occupiers also, and perhaps unintentionally, brought something even more important to the debate: For a time, at least, they broke the monopoly on ostentatious economic protest that the right had enjoyed ever since Rick Santelli first raised his voice to protect the beleaguered trader back in February 2009. Merely by showing up, Occupy problematized the phony, convoluted protest of the last few years and gave the world an idea what the real deal might look like.

The very separate world of the right, meanwhile, spun on as though its inverted take on the subject had become settled wisdom. Tea Party people took jobs on Congressional staffs, and Tea Party organizations became Super PACs, ready to move their missionary work to the airwaves as the election year began.

In the Republican presidential primaries of early 2012, meanwhile, each of the main candidates reiterated the market-populist lessons of the last few years. Rick Santorum told the story of his beaten-down, coal-mining grandfather as a way of introducing his dream of a day when capitalism could go unregulated by the elitist tyrants of Washington. Newt Gingrich ran TV commercials so (superficially) critical of the financial industry that they might have been produced by the CIO in the 1930s. Mitt Romney offered himself up to us: the job creator as national savior, come to restore the blessings of prosperity to a land choked by red tape and over-regulation. And each of them enjoyed the backing of some self-pitying billionaire, freed by the Citizens United Supreme Court decision to express their views with unlimited donations of political cash.

Each of the Republican candidates also took the occasion

of the slump to assail some aspect of the New Deal. Rick Perry growled that Social Security was a "monstrous lie." Ron Paul wanted to go back on the gold standard, which we left—tragically!—in 1933. Rick Santorum, the sentimental champion of the American toiler, insisted that food stamps were unnecessary. Newt Gingrich told us that child labor laws were "stupid"—referring, I suppose, to that infamous violation of the personal freedom of ten-year-olds, the Fair Labor Standards Act of 1938. And every one of the candidates was prepared to take a sledgehammer to the 1935 National Labor Relations Act, if its enforcement meant terminating torrid love matches like the hookup between Boeing and South Carolina.

The Democratic president, meanwhile, triangulated frantically in the direction of Wall Street, talking with populist fire now and then but carefully reserving his signature for such abominations as the deregulatory JOBS Act, by which he no doubt hoped to win Wall Street's favor and divert the cash of those billionaires back toward his own Super PAC. Between Obama's many capitulations and the rise to political preeminence of the billionaire campaign donors, the public was learning an awful lesson: that there was no longer any power capable of confronting the financial industry.

Moneyed interests, for their part, understand this. They know now that with no second FDR, no incorruptible new cop on the financial beat, no return to the rules that once made banking boring but safe, they have nothing to fear from us, and may do as they please. This is the real tragedy of the Great Recession.

And should we continue down this path, it is fairly certain how matters will unfold. Investment banking will eventually recover from its brush with mortality, and it will romp again like an elephant loosed from its cage. As regulatory enforcement diminishes, financial frauds will of course multiply, growing grander and more lucrative in the future just as the subprime fiasco was grander than Enron, and Enron was grander than the financial scandals of the eighties. Anyone else with a viable monopoly strategy will have much to look forward to. The health-care industry, for which patriots shed so many tears in 2009, will hold on to its ability to impose costs, comforted by the knowledge that many Americans would apparently prefer to throw Medicare overboard than do something to rein those tycoons in. Ditto for the megalomaniac schemes of the software industry. The oil barons. The defense contractors. This land is assuredly their land.

But the scenario that should concern us most is what will happen when the new, more ideologically concentrated Right gets their hands on the rest of the machinery of government. They are the same old wrecking crew as their predecessors, naturally, but now there is a swaggering, an in-your-face brazenness to their sabotage. We got a taste of their vision when they reconquered the House of Representatives in 2010—in the name of a nation outraged by economic disaster, remember—and immediately cracked down on the Securities and Exchange Commission, the regulatory agency charged with preventing fraud on Wall Street. They brought the Obama administration's one big populist innovation—the brand-new Consumer Financial Protection Bureau—under a sustained artillery barrage, proposing ingenious ways to cripple the new body or strip away its funding. And during the debt-ceiling crisis of 2011, they came close to bringing on the colossal train wreck that they have always said we deserved.

Given a chance actually to run the government of the most complex economy on earth like a small business, they will slam the brakes on spending and level the regulatory state. Dare we even guess at the consequences? At the levels of desperation the nation will hit when they withdraw federal spending from an economy already starving for demand? At the orgy of deceit into which Wall Street will immediately descend?

This, though, is for certain. As the nation clambers down through the sulfurous fumes into the pit called utopia, the thinking of the market-minded will continue to evolve. Before long they will have discovered that certain once-uncontroversial arms of the state must be amputated immediately. One fine day in the near future, it will dawn on them that the FDIC, for example, just delivers bailouts under another name; that the lazy man down the street should no more get his money back when his bank fails than when the housing market fell apart. What are interstate highways and national parks, they will ask, but wasteful subsidies for leeches who ought to be paying their way? What is disaster relief but a power grab by the losers who can't get themselves out of the path of a hurricane? And though public schools have been under assault for decades on charges of rampant secularism, the time is not far off when the freeloading by poor kids will be the factor that galls our leaders most.

Social Security, of course, will be one of the first institutions to go on the chopping block, as the essential injustice of protecting the weak dawns on them. Why should society pay for the retirement of someone who hasn't been responsible and collected Krugerrands? The older generation had a rendezvous with destiny, their hero FDR used to say, and soon it will occur to America's class-war populists that every slow-moving moocher and senior-parasite needs to make that rendezvous—which is to say, that appointment with the human resources guy at the local big-box store.

Every problem that the editorialists fret about today will get worse, of course: inequality, global warming, financial bubbles. But on America will go, chasing a dream that is more vivid than life itself, on into the seething Arcadia of all against all.

Notes

Introduction

1. As far as I can tell, the first to use a form of this metaphor was Representative Eric Cantor (R-VA), who told the *Washington Independent* reporter Dave Weigel in September of 2009 that the movement was an "awakening in America." "Instapundit" Glenn Reynolds, writing in the *Washington Examiner* on February 7, 2010, was so affected by a Tea Party convention that he upped that description to a "Third Great Awakening." Michael Reagan, son of the former president, made the same point in his syndicated column for September 16 of that year, calling the Tea Party movement "A Great Awakening," while "Signs of a 21st Century Political Awakening" is the subtitle of *Don't Tread on Us*, a coffee-table book of protest placards, published by WND Books in 2010.

2. Dick Armey and Matt Kibbe, *Give Us Liberty: A Tea Party Manifesto* (New York: Harper Collins, 2010), p. 8.

3. See the excerpt from Sidney Blumenthal's book that appeared on Salon.com on April 24, 2008. It is important to remember that Blumenthal, never one to underestimate the dynamism of conservatives, also presciently acknowledged that conservatives had not accepted this verdict and could very well decide to turn farther to the right: "The radicalization of the Republican Party is not at an end, but may only be entering a new phase," he wrote.

> Loss of the Congress in 2006 is not accepted as reproach. Quite the opposite, it is understood by the Republican right as the result of lack of will and nerve, failure of ideological purity, errant immorality by

members of Congress, betrayal by the media, and by moderates within their own party. They may never recover from the election of 2004, when they believed their agenda received majority support and they ecstatically thought they were the "Right Nation."

4. Sean Wilentz: "Conservative Era Is Over," *U.S. News & World Report*, November 24, 2008. Francis Fukuyama: "The Fall of America, Inc.," *Newsweek*, October 4, 2008. *Politico*: Daniel Libit, "'Deregulator,' Our Old Friend," October 1, 2008.

5. Charles Blow: *New York Times*, May 16, 2009. Kathleen Parker: *Washington Post*, November 29, 2009. Stu Rothenberg: see http://rothenbergpoliticalreport.com/news/article/april-madness-can-gop-win-back-the-house-in-2010. Of course, Rothenberg was hardly alone in this prediction; at that stage in the cycle, nearly everyone believed the Republicans' day was done.

6. There have also been several valuable studies of the Right's racial attitudes in recent years. One conducted in 2010 by political scientists at the University of Washington found that "true believers" in the Tea Party movement held less charitable views of blacks than the general population. (You can read about the study at http://depts.washington.edu/uwiser/racepolitics.html.) A study of Tea Party rhetoric from that same year, on the other hand, discovered few instances of overt racism; instead it found that the Tea Party's concerns were overwhelmingly with economic policy. (See "Few Signs at Tea Party Rally Expressed Racially Charged Anti-Obama Themes," *Washington Post*, October 14, 2010.) Most interesting is the 2009 study of the Right by Stanley Greenberg titled *The Very Separate World of Conservative Republicans*. The report concluded: "Instead of focusing on these intense ideological divisions, the press and elites continue to look for a racial element that drives these voters' beliefs—but they need to get over it. . . . We gave these groups of older, white Republican base voters in Georgia full opportunity to bring race into their discussion—but it did not ever become a central element, and indeed, was almost beside the point." Read the full report at http://www.greenbergresearch.com/articles/2398/5488_The Very Separate World of Conservative Republicans 101609.pdf.

7. Amy Gardner, "Gauging the Scope of the Tea Party Movement in America," *Washington Post*, October 24, 2010.

Chapter 1. End Times

1. Christina Romer, "Lessons from the Great Depression for Economic Recovery in 2009," a paper presented at the Brookings Institution, March 9, 2009, p. 2.

2. All of these facts are drawn from chapters 8 and 12 of Irving Bernstein, *The Lean Years: A History of the American Worker, 1920–*

1933 (Chicago: Haymarket Books, 2010 [1969]). The quotes are found on pages 317 and 422.

3. According to Jonathan Alter, *The Defining Moment: FDR's Hundred Days and the Triumph of Hope* (New York: Simon & Schuster, 2006), p. 2.

4. I am relying here on the summary of economic orthodoxy found in Richard Parker's biography of the economist John Kenneth Galbraith, who was studying economics at Harvard at the time. See Richard Parker, *John Kenneth Galbraith: His Life, His Politics, His Economics* (New York: Farrar, Straus and Giroux, 2005), pp. 12, 48, 77.

5. The line comes from *The Green Pastures*, a popular 1930 play by Marc Connelly.

6. Similar statements litter Drucker's first book. In the economic collapse of the thirties, man "can no longer explain or understand his existence as rationally correlated and co-ordinated to the world in which he lives; nor can he coordinate the world and the social reality to his existence. The function of the individual in society has become entirely irrational and senseless." Peter Drucker, *The End of Economic Man: A Study of the New Totalitarianism* (New York: The John Day Company, 1939), p. 55.

7. *Nation's Business*: as quoted in William E. Leuchtenberg, *The FDR Years: On Roosevelt and His Legacy* (New York: Columbia University Press, 1995), p. 6. Another passage that once struck me as overwrought but which now, in the aftermath of 2008, seems bluntly accurate is this summation by the historian Richard Pells in his 1973 book about writers and thinkers in the thirties, *Radical Vision and American Dreams: Culture and Social Thought in the Depression Years* (New York: Harper & Row, 1973):

> The sense of total collapse, of a society in various stages of decomposition, had a profound effect on most Americans—intellectuals as well as ordinary citizens. The depression meant more than simply the failure of business; it was to many people an overwhelming natural catastrophe, much like an earthquake that uprooted and destroyed whatever lay in its path. . . . It gave Americans the feeling that their whole world was literally falling apart, that their traditional expectations and beliefs were absolutely meaningless, that there was no personal escape from the common disaster. It propelled the individual into a void of bewilderment and terror (p. 72).

8. Calvin Coolidge, quoted in Charles A. Andrews, "'I'm All Burned Out,'" *Good Housekeeping*, June 1935, p. 209. Wrote Coolidge's biographer William Allen White of the same period, "The whole world of Calvin Coolidge and his pride in the power of brains and wealth was toppling." White, *A Puritan in Babylon: The Story of Calvin Coolidge* (New York: The Macmillan Company, 1938), p. 432.

9. Warren Susman, *Culture as History: The Transformation of American*

Society in the Twentieth Century (New York: Pantheon, 1984), p. 172. Writers and intellectuals: see Malcolm Cowley, "The 1930s Were An Age of Faith," *New York Times Book Review*, December 13, 1964. Robert McElvaine, *The Great Depression: America, 1929–1941* (New York: Three Rivers Press, 1993), p. 202.

    On the other hand, in *Bowling Alone*, the sociologist Robert Putnam calls the thirties an era of "civic drought," because membership in all manner of professional and civic associations shrank instead of increasing as in the periods before and after.

10. Alan Brinkley, *Voices of Protest: Huey Long, Father Coughlin, and the Great Depression* (New York: Vintage, 1983), p. 22.

11. "But when we wonder what to put in its place, we are extremely perplexed," Keynes continued. John Maynard Keynes, "National Self-Sufficiency," *Yale Review* 22 (1933): 761.

12. Andrew Mellon is quoted in *The Memoirs of Herbert Hoover: The Great Depression, 1929–1941* (New York: Macmillan, 1952), p. 30.

13. One place the idea was tried was in Detroit in February 1933, where the local tycoon Henry Ford refused to join the effort to rescue a large local bank. "'Let the crash come,'" RFC chairman Jesse Jones quotes Ford as saying. Jones continues thusly: "If everything went down the chute there would be a cleaning-up process, [Ford] said, and everybody would then have to get to work. Whatever happened, he said he was sure he could again build up a business, as he still felt young." The result, though, was the catastrophic Michigan bank panic and a "bank holiday" that led to the complete national bank shutdown the next month. Jesse Jones with Edward Angly, *Fifty Billion Dollars: My Thirteen Years with the RFC* (New York: Macmillan, 1951), p. 62.

14. William Randolph Hearst: Arthur M. Schlesinger Jr., *The Politics of Upheaval* (Boston: Houghton Mifflin, 1960), p. 85. The president of the American Liberty League was Jouett Shouse, a former Kansas congressman, but its main backers were the DuPont family, the Koch brothers of their day. The speech in which this passage occurs was called "The New Deal vs. Democracy" and was issued as a pamphlet by the league in 1936.

15. See the account of the American Liberty League in Kim Phillips-Fein's *Invisible Hands: The Making of the Conservative Movement from the New Deal to Reagan* (New York: Norton, 2009), p. 13.

16. Remley J. Glass, "Gentlemen, the Corn Belt!" *Harper's*, July 1933, pp. 199–202.

17. "Virtually impossible": cited in Theodore Saloutos and John D. Hicks, *Twentieth Century Populism: Agricultural Discontent in the Middle West 1900–1939* (Lincoln, NE: University of Nebraska Press, 1951), p. 448. "We pledge ourselves": as quoted in Gilbert Seldes, *The Years of the Locust (America, 1929–1932)* (Boston: Little, Brown, 1933), p. 286.

18. "The days of 1776": Seldes, *The Years of the Locust*, p. 284. "They say blockading the highway's illegal": Mary Heaton Vorse, "Rebellion in the Cornbelt," 1932, reprinted in David Shannon, ed., *The Great Depression* (Englewood Cliffs, NJ: Prentice-Hall, 1960), p. 125. A South Dakota participant in the farm strike told Studs Terkel in 1970 that "it was close in spirit to the American Revolution." *Hard Times: An Oral History of the Great Depression* (New York: Pantheon, 1970), p. 256.

Chapter 2. 1929: The Sequel

1. Joshua Cooper Ramo, "The Three Marketeers," *Time*, February 15, 1999.
2. On financial innovation and its application to real estate, see Simon Johnson and James Kwak, *13 Bankers: The Wall Street Takeover and the Next Financial Meltdown* (New York: Pantheon, 2010), pp. 105–13.
3. These examples are all drawn from the first eighty pages of the *Financial Crisis Inquiry Report: Final Report of the National Commission on the Causes of the Financial and Economic Crisis in the United States* (New York: Public Affairs, 2011).
4. John Lippert, "Friedman Would Be Roiled as Chicago Disciples Rue Repudiation," Bloomberg, December 23, 2008.
5. Gary Becker, quoted in John Cassidy, "After the Blowup," *New Yorker*, January 11, 2010. His colleagues, Becker further confessed, had not fully understood derivatives, deregulation, or the problem of banks that were "too big to fail." Becker also admitted that federal intervention had spared the nation a much greater disaster.
6. Richard Posner, *A Failure of Capitalism: The Crisis of '08 and the Descent into Depression* (Cambridge, MA: Harvard University Press, 2009), p. 306. The crash was the result, Posner wrote, of "innate limitations of the free market—limitations rooted in individuals' incentives, in irresponsible monetary policy adopted and executed by conservative officials inspired by conservative economists . . . and in excessive, ideologically motivated deregulation of banking and finance compounded by lax enforcement of the remaining regulations." See the similar argument made by Jacob Weisberg in "The End of Libertarianism," *Slate*, October 18, 2008.
7. In 2008, Charles Koch wrote that we "could" be facing this "loss of liberty"; in his January 2009 missive, "Perspective," *Discovery, the Quarterly Newsletter of Koch Companies*, January 2009, he announced that "that prediction is coming true."
8. Moe Tkacik, "Waiting for CNBC," *Columbia Journalism Review*, May–June 2009.
9. See Max Abelson, "The New Doom," *New York Observer*, July 13, 2010.

10. "Never underestimate the capacity of angry populism in times of economic stress," Robert Reich told the *New York Times* on March 16, 2009. "A big challenge for President Obama will be to maintain a rational and tactical public discussion in the midst of this severe downturn. The desire for culprits at times like this is strong."

11. See the account in *The Hill* dated January 21, 2010. http://thehill.com/blogs/blog-briefing-room/news/77365-afl-cio-cites-working-class-revolt-in-special-election-aftermath?page=2.

12. The story by Amy Gardner ran in the *Washington Post* on February 18, 2010; the main figure she followed, Representative Rick Boucher of western Virginia, was defeated in November.

13. "57 percent [of whites with no college education] wanted to repeal the health care law—even though they are uninsured at much higher rates than whites with more advanced education." Ronald Brownstein, "White Flight," *National Journal*, January 7, 2011, http://nationaljournal.com/magazine/in-2012-obama-may-need-a-new-coalition-20110105?page=1. See also Brownstein's article "Populists Versus Managers," *National Journal*, December 17, 2010, http://www.nationaljournal.com/magazine/populists-versus-managers-in-the-gop-race-20101217.

Chapter 3. Hold the Note and Change the Key

1. "Simply working people": John M. O'Hara, *A New American Tea Party* (Hoboken, NJ: Wiley, 2010), p. 2. It is worth noting here that John O'Hara, the author of the above sentence, had been an employee of the U.S. Department of Labor during the Bush administration. Surely he would be in a position to know that what workers wanted was to go untroubled by the needs of their neighbors.

2. "Plain-speaking-little-man": Frank Ahrens, "Five Questions for Rick Santelli," November 13, 2008, WashingtonPost.com.

3. The TARP, write Dick Armey and Matt Kibbe in their Tea Party book, is the device that "ignited the firestorm we see today." Dick Armey and Matt Kibbe, *Give Us Liberty*, p. 37.

4. See ibid., p. 68.

5. Ibid., p. 38, my emphasis. See also the appendix to *Give Us Liberty*, in which the value of the home owned by a Tea Party activist plunges, but she doesn't complain. "'We cut our budget and I went back to work. That was my bailout plan,'" she says. "Meanwhile, politicians in Washington were bailing out companies and rewarding people who had made bad investments in homes and mortgage-backed securities," write Armey and Kibbe. "The contrast between her experience and the soft landings for Citigroup, GM, and AIG was galling" (p. 228).

   In his Tea Party book, the radio talker Michael Graham devotes an entire chapter of denunciation ("Honk If I'm Paying Your Mortgage") to the subject of shiftless mortgage borrowers who are now hoping to get off the hook. "Normal Americans," he writes, were going "bonkers" at the bailouts because

> the bailout regime that began under President Bush and blossomed under Obama has repeatedly rewarded those who engaged in bad behavior—and the worse the behavior, the bigger the bailout. The people left holding the bag are those who've sacrificed immediate gratification to do the right thing. They were dumping their change every night into a blue water bottle in the closet of their dumpy apartment, saving for a down payment on their future dream home. Meanwhile, their neighbor was moving into a house he couldn't afford, on a no-money-down, interest-only subprime loan backed by Freddie and Fannie, hoping to ride the real estate bubble and flip it at a profit. (Michael Graham, *That's No Angry Mob, That's My Mom: Team Obama's Assault on Tea-Party, Talk-Radio Americans* [Washington, DC: Regnery, 2010], p. 77.)

6. *Broke* is even the title of one of Beck's 2010 books: *Broke: The Plan to Restore Our Trust, Truth and Treasure* (New York: Threshold Editions, 2010). The "Laws of Nature" are referenced in *Glenn Beck's Common Sense: The Case Against an Out-of-Control Government, Inspired by Thomas Paine* (New York: Threshold Editions, 2009), p. 15.

7. "There's no need to bring progressivism *back* . . . because it never left," writes Glenn Beck in a characteristic passage of *Arguing with Idiots*. The history of the last century, he believes, with the exception of the magical eighties, was merely a gigantic extension of the Progressive era.

> Over the years, it hasn't seemed to matter whether a Republican or Democrat was in office—the government just kept growing and growing. Very few presidents met an agency, department, or program that they didn't want to create or expand and our debates have become less about big vs. small government and more about obscenely large vs. really large government. (*Arguing with Idiots: How to Stop Small Minds and Big Government* [New York: Threshold Editions, 2009], pp. 214, 231.)

A slightly more intellectual example of the same blind view of history can be found in a blogger's review of a 2011 book by former New York governor Eliot Spitzer, who criticized what he saw as the long reign of "libertarianism" in Washington. In response, a libertarian blogger exploded in outrage: "What the hell is he talking about? Spitzer's 'libertarian period' is the most regulated period in the history of the United Sates [*sic*]." The conventional view of the period is upside down, he argued, since the Federal Reserve existed, regulations continued to exist, and true free-marketeers never got to do everything they wanted.

Thirty years of libertarianism? A period when the United States central bank, the Federal Reserve, boosted the money supply from $1.6 trillion to $7.7 trillion. A period during which it became near impossible to start a brokerage firm to compete against the banksters, without spending literally millions to pass through all the regulatory hurdles. A period during which government attempts to regulate every nook and cranny of our lives exploded. This Spitzer tells us was a period of libertarianism.

See http://www.economicpolicyjournal.com/2011/07/eliot-spitzers-outrageous-attack-on.html.

8. Moore's article compared the Paulson scene with scenes from Ayn Rand's *Atlas Shrugged*, in order to establish that book's amazing prescience. Stephen Moore, "'Atlas Shrugged': From Fiction to Fact in 52 Years," *Wall Street Journal*, January 9, 2009.

9. All of these quotations are from Glenn Beck's TV show for March 18, 2009.

10. Beck's populism continued to evolve. In July of 2009, he announced that the government bailed out AIG because Goldman Sachs had an interest in AIG's solvency—in other words, because *government was a puppet of big money*. (See his radio show for July 14, 2009, according to the transcript available at http://www.glennbeck.com/content/articles/article/198/27840/.) A few weeks later, he suggested that the AIG logo, along with some other corporate emblems, should take the place of the stars on the U.S. flag, since government and corporations had been so thoroughly merged. Then, in the novel Beck published in the summer of 2010, *The Overton Window* (New York: Threshold Editions, 2010), the blame for the financial crisis and the bailout was fixed firmly on Wall Street itself, with government and bankers both being steered by the "all-powerful puppetmaster behind it all, Goldman Sachs" (p. 247).

11. Erick Erickson and Lewis K. Uhler, *Red State Uprising: How to Take Back America* (Washington, DC: Regnery, 2010), pp. xv and xvii.

Chapter 4. Nervous System

1. Glenn Beck describes his admiration for Orson Welles on pages 186 and 187 of *The Real America: Messages from the Heart and Heartland* (New York: Pocket Books, 2005). The fact about the *Daily Worker* comes from the historian Michael Denning's account of left culture in the thirties, *The Cultural Front* (New York: Verso, 1996). Given Beck's obsession with the fascist threat, it is interesting to recall Denning's observation that much of Welles's work from that period consisted of "allegories of anti-fascism"; in particular, the 1938 radio show about the Martian invasion was part of a then-familiar genre about fascist atrocities. Denning, *The Cultural Front*, pp. 367, 371, 382.

2. These lines were used, respectively, by Glenn Beck on November 19, 2009; Rush Limbaugh on September 30, 2009; and Jim Quinn on January 5, 2010. All of these and many more panic-screaming accounts were compiled by the good folks at Media Matters for America at http://mediamatters.org/research/201003220034.

3. The full quote goes as follows: "The secular-socialist machine represents as great a threat to America as Nazi Germany or the Soviet Union once did." The book's subtitle identifies the "secular-socialist machine" with the Obama administration. Newt Gingrich, *To Save America: Stopping Obama's Secular-Socialist Machine* (Washington, DC: Regnery, 2010), pp. 4, 5.

4. Erickson and Uhler, *Red State Uprising*, 2010, p. xiv.

5. "Indoctrination": this was a favorite persecution fantasy of September 2009. "The coming insurrection": a French anarchist pamphlet with this title was rescued from obscurity by Glenn Beck in 2009. "Persecution": I am referring to *The Persecution of Sarah Palin* by Matthew Continetti (New York: Sentinel, 2010). "Systematic assault": see David Limbaugh, *Crimes Against Liberty* (Washington, DC: Regnery, 2010), p. 12. "Gulag Bound": read about it at http://gulagbound.com /we-are-gulag-bound-2.

6. Scott Rasmussen and Douglas Schoen, *Mad As Hell: How the Tea Party Movement Is Fundamentally Remaking Our Two-Party System* (New York: Harper, 2010), p. 144.

7. Forbes also says he is going to supply a "Real World Lesson," but then immediately goes into one of those abstract fables economists love about what it would be like if government manufactured pencils, and then starts reminding us that things didn't work well in communist countries. Steve Forbes and Elizabeth Ames, *How Capitalism Will Save Us: Why Free People and Free Markets Are the Best Answer in Today's Economy* (New York: Crown Business, 2011), p. 14.

8. C. Jesse Duke, *Spread* This *Wealth (And Pass* This *Ammunition)* (Amelia Island, FL: Encouraging Word Press, 2009), pp. 69–70. Emphasis added.

9. This is a widely shared view of the newest Right. "Consumers in free markets *uncorrupted by regulatory favoritism* vote untold millions of times a day," write Dick Armey and Matt Kibbe, "punishing irrational behavior, bad actors, and liar loans with equal and swift justice." *Give Us Liberty*, p. 169, emphasis added.

10. Sidney Lens, "The Moral Roots of the New Despair," *Christian Century*, February 26, 1975.

11. Glenn Beck, *Arguing with Idiots: How to Stop Small Minds and Big Government* (New York: Threshold Editions, 2009), pp. 4–5. Beck's emphasis.

12. "It was one of the more extraordinary events in the annals of

American populism," wrote Dana Milbank of the *Washington Post*, "the common man voluntarily giving money to make the rich richer." "The Elite Behind the Tea Party," *Washington Post*, October 20, 2010.

Chapter 5. Making a Business of It

1. See, for example, the op-ed Phil Kerpen published on April 13, 2009, in the *Milwaukee Journal-Sentinel*.
2. Mike Pompeo in a debate found on YouTube, dated September 23, 2010, and available at http://www.youtube.com/watch?v=fXucbt DUl4M&feature=related.
3. Will Bunch, *The Backlash: Right-wing Radicals, High-def Hucksters, and Paranoid Politics in the Age of Obama* (New York: Harper, 2010), p. 209.
4. See http://www.vmionline.com/secrets/slanding.html (accessed December 15, 2010).
5. The first item in this list is described in Alan Crawford's *Thunder on the Right* (New York: Pantheon, 1980); read up on the others in my book *The Wrecking Crew* (New York: Metropolitan Books, 2008).
6. According to Will Bunch, Judson Phillips denounced a group of disgruntled Tea Partiers thusly: "I want you to know that they're socialists." *The Backlash*, p. 212.
7. Chuck Norris, foreword to Mark Karis, *Don't Tread on Us: Signs of a 21st Century Political Awakening* (Los Angeles: WND Books, 2010), n.p.
8. The consultancy is Russo Marsh + Rogers. For more, see Kenneth P. Vogel, "GOP Operatives Crash the Tea Party," *Politico*, April 4, 2010, http://www.politico.com/news/stories/0410/35785.html.
9. "GOOOH stands for 'Get Out of Our House' and is pronounced like the word 'go,'" reads a pamphlet for the group that I picked up at the Liberty XPO in September of 2010. The iCaucus "Big Stick" plan was also outlined in literature distributed there. iCaucus has numerous other plans for reforming Congress, which it outlines on its website. "The Answer We've All Been Waiting for Has Arrived!" is printed on business cards distributed by a group that seems to be called the ReFounders of America! (The exclamation point is part of the name.) In addition to the "Redeclaration of Independence," its website offers a long list of proposed amendments to the Constitution, one of which would outlaw lobbying. We Read the Constitution can be found, obviously, at http://www.wereadtheconstitution.com/.
10. See "Rocking the Town Halls—Best Practices," a memo describing a conservative "action" at a town hall meeting in May 2009. It is available at http://thinkprogress.org/wp-content/uploads/2009/07/townhallactionmemo.pdf.
11. See "Hedrick Urges Social Security Privatization," *Vancouver Colum-*

bian, August 13, 2010: "The Race Is on for a Wide Open U.S. House seat," *Seattle Post-Intelligencer,* April 24, 2010; and "Hedrick Throws His Support to Herrera," *Vancouver Columbian,* August 19, 2010.

Chapter 6. A Mask for Privilege

1. C. Jesse Duke, *Spread* This *Wealth (And Pass This Ammunition)* (Amelia Island, FL: Encouraging Word Press, 2009), p. 19.
2. See *Rolling Stone's* profile of Don Blankenship, "The Dark Lord of Coal Country," in the issue dated November 29, 2010.
3. See the *New York Times'* news story and editorial on the subject, June 29 and 30, 2011, http://www.nytimes.com/2011/07/01/opinion /01fri3.html.
4. "Core competence" of the Tea Party: http://www.michigancapitolcon fidential.com/14194. "Political entrepreneurs": see *Surface Tension: Tea Parties and the Political Establishment,* a report by the Sam Adams Alliance on the Tea Party movement dated October 13, 2010. The term "early adopters" was applied to Tea Partiers in that same firm's much-discussed "market research report" on the movement, *The Next Wave: A Surf Report,* dated August 1, 2010. Read "Surface Tension" at http:// www.samadamsalliance.org/media/17350/surface%20tension.pdf and "The Next Wave" at http://www.samadamsalliance.org/media/13655 /94813%20sam%20adams%20alliance%20-%20next%20wave %20report%20v4%20final.pdf.
5. The work of management theory is *The Starfish and the Spider: The Unstoppable Power of Leaderless Organizations* (New York: Portfolio), a 2006 book by Ori Brafman and Rod Beckstrom. The list of favorite CEOs could be found here as of the summer of 2010: http:// stlouisteaparty.com/brave-ceos/.
6. Don Crist: *What Can I Do?: After the Tea Party* (NP: np, 2009), p. 145. Stephen D. Hanson: *Transcending Time with Thomas Jefferson: Is the Constitution Still Applicable Today?* (New York: iUniverse, 2010), p. 253. DeMint, *Saving Freedom,* pp. 15–17.
7. On Herman Cain and Bill Clinton, see "The Lost Chance," *Newsweek,* September 18, 1994. On Cain and "the real folk," see the *Washington Times* interview with him, July 20, 2011.
8. On Glenn Beck's roots, see chapter 9 of *The Real America: Messages from the Heart and Heartland* (New York: Pocket, 2005). "Spirit of America": according to the official transcript of Beck's program for October 22, 2009.
9. Small Business Bill of Rights: http://www.kirkforsenate.com/?page_ id=1274. Canseco: http://www.cansecoforcongress.com/, accessed April 13, 2011.
10. Robb Mandelbaum, "Meet the New Small Business Owners in Congress," *New York Times,* November 16, 2010, http://boss.blogs

.nytimes.com/2010/11/16/meet-the-new-small-business-owners-in
-congress/?scp=1&sq=small%20business%20congress&st=cse.

11. "The question is, 'Are we going to be living by the same rules that apply to every family, every small business and 49 states, which is, that they cannot spend more money than they have?' " said Senator John Barrasso of Wyoming after the debate ended. See http://www.voanews.com/english/news/Obama-Signs-Debt-Bill-US-Avoids-Default-126600373.html.

12. Nan Hayworth: see the report dated January 28, 2011, in the Westfair Business Publications, http://westfaironline.com/2011/10481-leave-jobs-creation-to-business-says-congresswoman/. Glenn Beck: see the Glenn Beck TV programs for March 5 and October 27, 2009.

13. A particularly painstaking debunking of the myths of small-business job creation and innovation can be found in "What Do Small Businesses Do?," a Brookings Paper on Economic Activity by economists Erik Hurst and Benjamin Wild Pugsley of the University of Chicago, dated August 2011. Another is "Who Creates Jobs? Small vs. Large vs. Young," by economists John Haltiwanger, Ron Jarmin, and Javier Miranda, a National Bureau of Economic Research Working Paper from 2010.

    For a decent journalistic summary of the debunkment, see Steven Pearlstein, "Small Business, Big Fable," *Washington Post*, July 8, 2009. According to Scott Shane, a professor of entrepreneurial studies, the true numbers are just about the reverse of what the propagandists of small business would have us believe. In an article he wrote for the *New York Times* website on August 5, 2009, Shane used Small Business Administration numbers to show that the largest businesses (those with over five hundred employees) created 36 percent of jobs over the period 1992–2008, followed by medium-size businesses (those with between fifty and five hundred employees), which created 30 percent. The smallest businesses created the fewest jobs. Read more at http://boss.blogs.nytimes.com/2009/08/05/are-medium-sized-businesses-the-job-creators/.

14. See http://www.davidrivera.org/issues.html, accessed August 27, 2011.

15. According to the transcript of Ronald Reagan's speech on the website of the "American Presidency Project," http://www.presidency.ucsb.edu/ws/index.php?pid=41324.

16. See Virginia Postrel, "Populist Industrial Policy," *Reason*, January 1994.

17. See, for example, the actual editorial denouncing "socialism" circulated by the Conference of American Small Business Organizations in 1949 and quoted by John H. Bunzel in *The American Small Businessman* (New York: Knopf, 1962), p. 109.

18. According to an item dated November 1, 2010, found on Pat Meehan's website: http://www.meehanforcongress.com/news/heading

-into-election-day-pat-meehan-reiterates-his-commitment-to -improving-economy. This is actually incorrect; the stimulus and the bailout were two separate things.

See Robb Mandelbaum, "Whom Does the N.F.I.B. Represent (Besides Its Members)?," a contribution to the *New York Times*' small-business blog, August 26, 2009. Read it at http://boss.blogs.nytimes .com/2009/08/26/whom-does-the-nfib-represent-besides-its-members/. This is an old story in small-business politics. Richard Lesher's 1996 account of small-business involvement in the Gingrich Revolution, *Meltdown on Main Street* (New York: Dutton, 1996), claims that the famous freshman class of 1994 "[are] all over the lot on volatile social issues such as abortion," but that they speak with one voice "in their outspoken criticism of big government" (p. 11).

19. I am referring to Richard Lesher's 1996 book, *Meltdown on Main Street*, which supplies a seemingly endless tattoo of such tales.

20. Read the interview at http://www.alternet.org/story/148941/?page= entire.

21. See chapter 6 of the FCIR. For a detailed debunking of the myth, see William K. Black's epic smackdown, "Wallison and the Three De's": http://neweconomicperspectives.org/2011/02/wallison-and-three -des-deregulation.html.

22. See Jonathan J. Bean, "Shame of the Cities: Setting Aside Justice for the 'Disadvantaged,'" *Independent Review* 7, no. 1 (Summer 2003). See also Bean's longer essay, "'Burn, Baby, Burn': Small Business in the Urban Riots of the 1960s," *Independent Review* 5, no. 2 (Fall 2000).

23. Richard A. Viguerie, "Bloomberg Vindicates Tea Party Outrage over Favors to Wall Street Aristocracy," an essay posted on Conservative HQ on August 24, 2011. Read it at http://www.conservativehq.com /article/bloomberg-vindicates-tea-party-outrage-over-favors-wall -street-aristocracy

24. NRA was Roosevelt's National Recovery Administration of 1933–35, which wrote "codes" for various industries in cooperation with the big players in each. OPA was the Office of Price Administration, which set price controls during World War II. OPM was the Office of Production Management in that same period. WPB was the War Production Board, which coordinated industry. Bunzel, *The American Small Businessman*, p. 118, emphasis in original.

25. Bunzel notes that one of the "standard works on small business . . . is dedicated simply to 'The American Way of Life'" (ibid., p. 20).

26. This line appears near the beginning of Paul Ryan's essay "Down with Big Business," *Forbes*, December 11, 2009.

27. "Rogues of K Street: Confessions of a Tea Party Consultant," *Playboy*, June 2010, p 102. Italics in original.

28. C. Wright Mills, *White Collar: The American Middle Classes* (New York: Oxford University Press, 1953), pp. 35, 49, 52, 53, 34.

29. Banking deregulation: see "Banking Deregulation Helps Small-Business Owners Stabilize Their Income," a paper published in the *Regional Economist*, a magazine issued by the Saint Louis Fed, in April of 2007, just a month after the first shock of the financial crisis. NAFTA: see the 1993 Heritage Foundation report on NAFTA, *Why the Governors Support the NAFTA (and Washington Doesn't)*, available at http://www.heritage.org/research/reports/1993/06/bg946 nbsp-why-the-governors-support-the-nafta.

30. Dick Armey, for example, stated this unfortunate principle back in 2008 when Mike Huckabee was riding high in Republican primaries. "One of his [i.e., Huckabee's] favorite lines is that he represents the interests of 'Main Street, not Wall Street,'" Armey wrote on the FreedomWorks website. "But this assumes that the interests of the two are not in alignment, that somehow, one group can only gain at the expense of the other—never mind that the jobs and livelihoods of America's workers and small towns are tied inexorably with the larger economy." See http://www.freedomworks.org/news/huckabees -counterproductive-sweet-talk.

31. Phil Gramm, "Reform Will Simplify Banking," *Cleveland Plain Dealer*, September 16, 1999.

32. This particular exchange, which took place on August 12, 2011, must be seen to be believed. One place to watch it is on YouTube: http//www.youtube.com/watch?v=jAWvVTMz5o0&feature=player _embedded#!

33. Dan Eggen, "GOP Freshman Pompeo Turned to Koch," *Washington Post*, March 20, 2011.

34. Ryan, "Down with Big Business."

35. Dan Eggen and T. W. Farnam, "GOP House Leaders See Corporate Donations Surge," *Washington Post*, January 22, 2011.

36. The first quotation comes from Amy Ridenour, president of the National Center for Public Policy Research; it appeared in a blog entry dated October 29, 2010. The second one is by Tom Borelli, director of the NCPPR's Free Enterprise Project. The "opportunistic parasite" phrase first appeared in a press release dated July 28, 2010 (http://www.nationalcenter.org/PR-GE_Jet_072810.html).

37. Numerous right-wingers talked up the idea of a national Tea Party strike; CNN's "political ticker" ran a report on the strike on January 4, 2010. The particular enthusiast I am quoting is one Mike McGowan, who blogged on the subject on January 5, 2010. See http://whenfalls thecoliseum.com/2010/01/05/the-tea-partys-national-day-of-strike/.

Chapter 7. Mimesis

1. Cynicism, protest tactics, guerrilla fandom, mimicking communist tactics: see my book *The Wrecking Crew*, chapters 3 and 6. Weyrich: John S. Saloma III, *Ominous Politics: The New Conservative Labyrinth* (New York: Hill and Wang, 1984), p. 49.
2. For more on this, see my article "The Confessions of Glenn Beck," *Harper's*, March 2011.
3. Another example: in 2009, Glenn Beck professed nearly daily outrage that Barack Obama desired to "fundamentally transform" the country, but by the beginning of 2011, Beck had decided to make that phrase his own; "fundamental transformation" was now "required," he said—provided it followed Beck's own instructions. See Beck's TV program for January 4, 2011. His comments to Newt Gingrich were related to listeners of his radio show on May 17, 2011, according to the transcript on glennbeck.com.
4. David Kahane (Michael A. Walsh), *Rules for Radical Conservatives: Beating the Left at Its Own Game to Take Back America* (New York: Ballantine, 2010), pp. 155, 159.
5. Ibid., pp. 180, 217, 226, 160.
6. Of course, it was no such thing. According to political scientist David Campbell and sociologist Robert Putnam, Tea Party activists tended to be highly partisan Republicans before the Tea Party conquered the headlines in 2009. See Campbell and Putnam, "Crashing the Tea Party," *New York Times*, August 16, 2011.
7. See, for example, http://www.washingtonexaminer.com/opinion/blogs/Examiner-Opinion-Zone/matthew-vadum-The-Lefts-Blueprint-for-perpetual-power-94527604.html.
8. See Naomi Klein, *The Shock Doctrine* (New York: Metropolitan, 2007), pp. 6–7.
9. Glenn Beck, *The Overton Window*, p. 147.
10. Ibid., pp. 74, 276, 286, 296–97, and again on 303–4.
11. FEMA's plans also would have outlawed strikes. See Jack Anderson's column on the subject, September 25, 1984. See also Alfonso Chardy, "Reagan Advisers Ran 'Secret' Government," *Miami Herald*, July 5, 1987.
12. According to the historian David Caute, the act included a measure "providing for camps in times of national emergency, invasion or insurrection to detain without trial anyone who had been a member of the Communist Party since January 1, 1949." Caute, *The Great Fear* (New York: Simon and Schuster, 1978), p. 39. Harry Truman vetoed the McCarran bill, but it was passed anyway; most of it was later struck down by the Supreme Court.
13. Charly Gullett, *Official Tea Party Handbook: A Tactical Playbook for Tea Party Patriots* (Prescott, AZ: Warfield Press, 2009), pp. 39–40. It is

also worth recalling that in 2004, future Tea Party darling Michelle Malkin wrote a book about the roundup of Japanese Americans during World War II that was entitled *In Defense of Internment: The Case for "Racial Profiling" in World War II and the War on Terror.*

14. Michael Graham, *That's No Angry Mob, That's My Mom* (Washington, DC: Regnery 2010), pp. 5–6.

15. Matthew Continetti's "Paranoid Style in Liberal Politics" appeared in the *Weekly Standard* for April 4, 2011. The cover of the magazine depicted the Kochs being burned at the stake. Like Joan of Arc, I guess.

16. David Limbaugh, *Crimes Against Liberty* (Washington, DC: Regnery, 2010), pp. 210, 213, 231, 219, 221, 220, 233.

17. "Beat them at their own game," FreedomWorks reading list: Kate Zernike, *Boiling Mad: Inside Tea Party America* (New York: Times Books, 2010), pp. 47, 38–39, 46. Armey and Kibbe, *Give Us Liberty*, pp. 97, 167, 174. The book on nonviolent protest that inspired FreedomWorks is *A Force More Powerful*, by Peter Ackerman and Jack Duvall. Zernike tells us how it influenced FreedomWorks personnel on page 47 of *Boiling Mad*. See also this April 2009 essay by FreedomWorks campaign director Brendan Steinhauser: http://www.freedomworks.org/blog/bstein80/we-are-all-community-organizers-now.

18. Zernike, *Boiling Mad*, p. 39.

Chapter 8. Say, Don't You Remember

1. *Wizard of Oz* references recur with alarming frequency in the Beck oeuvre. In addition to the political uses I describe here (for an example, see Beck's "Welcome" in *Fusion* magazine for April 2010), he wrote a book of teenage spiritual awakening, *The Christmas Sweater*, in which he uses the familiar plot of the movie to describe the protagonist's moral epiphany. The boy decides to "come home" by walking through a swirling storm, leaving behind an awful monochrome cornfield for a beautiful "Technicolor" landscape. The story ends with the teenager waking up from a deep sleep and realizing that it was all a dream. Glenn Beck, *The Christmas Sweater* (New York: Threshold Editions, 2008).

2. Introduction to *Glenn Beck Special: You Are Not Alone*, March 13, 2009. This was the episode in which Beck introduced his 9/12 Project, named after the day when the country supposedly stood unified in the war on terrorism. Franklin Roosevelt's famous "Forgotten Man" speech of 1932 also looked back to a lost time of unity, the days of 1917 when the nation was preparing for World War I.

3. According to Alexander Zaitchik, *Common Nonsense: Glenn Beck and the Triumph of Ignorance* (Hoboken: Wiley, 2010), p. 88.

4. These were the Beck programs for, respectively, November 17, 2009, and November 30, 2010.

5. These quotations are from the introduction and Beck's opening monologue of his "You Are Not Alone" special introducing the 9/12 Project.

6. These quotations are from the 9/12 page on Beck's website, http://www.glennbeck.com/content/articles/article/198/21018/.

7. *Overton Window*, p. 62. These words are spoken by one of the book's protagonists in an address to a rally modeled after the Tea Party movement. Saint Louis Tea Partier: see "Who Has the Fear," a post for September 22, 2010, on Bill Hennessy's blog: http://hennessysview.com/2010/09/22/who-has-the-fear/?utm_source=feedburner&utm_medium=feed&utm_campaign=Feed%3A+hennessysview%2FXahR+%28Hennessy%27s+View%29.

8. Richard Viguerie's e-mail newsletter, "News from the Front" and later, "Conservative HQ," summarizes journalism that is of interest to conservative activists. Sometimes the phrase "ruling class" would appear in an article the newsletter referenced; sometimes it only appeared in Viguerie's summary. As of January 2011, "Out with the Ruling Class" had its own website: http://www.outwiththerulingclass.com/, the "Conservative Headquarters for Election Victory 2010."

9. I am quoting from the book version of the essay. Angelo Codevilla, *The Ruling Class: How They Corrupted America and What We Can Do About It* (New York: Beaufort Books, 2010), pp. 69, 87, 63.

10. Ibid., p. 31.

11. Ibid., pp. 54, 66.

12. Senator Ron Johnson's affinity for Rand was noted by George Will in his column for May 27, 2010. Paul Ryan gave his thoughts on the novel's prescience in a video posted to his Facebook page in 2009.

13. David Schweikert: see the interview in the *Arizona Republic* for September 28, 2008. Rich Crawford: see his post for February 5, 2010, at http://twitter.com/#%21/rickcrawfish/status/8709825148. Rand Paul: see his 2010 book, *The Tea Party Goes to Washington* (Nashville: Center Street), p. 251.

14. Kendra Marr, "Ayn Rand Goes Mainstream," *Politico*, November 12, 2009.

15. According to Leonard Peikoff's introduction to the 1996 edition of *Atlas Shrugged* (New York: Signet), p. 6.

16. These quotations can be found on pages 536, 925, and 937 of the 1996 Signet edition of *Atlas Shrugged*, in case you care.

17. Ibid., p. 680.

18. Ibid., pp. 534, 685.

19. From a letter dated January 23, 1958, and reprinted in the *Journal of Libertarian Studies*, Winter 2007, p. 11.

20. All these quotations come from http://www.ishrugged.org/, "the web page that promotes shrugging," May 31, 2011.

21. We know that Rand used the Great Northern as one of the models for Dagny Taggart's transcontinental rail empire; that the author greatly admired James J. Hill, the Great Northern's founder; and that the present-day Cascade Tunnel, opened in 1929, is nearly eight miles long, as is the Taggart Tunnel in *Atlas Shrugged*. Like the fictional version, passenger trains passing through the Cascade Tunnel used to be required to switch locomotives, since smoke from a coal-burning engine would have built up inside the tunnel and suffocated the passengers.

The predecessor of today's Cascade Tunnel was opened in 1900. It had the same problem with locomotive smoke as the later tunnel, and in the winter of 1910 it was the scene of one of the nation's worst-ever railroad accidents, in which an avalanche knocked a snowbound passenger train into a ravine, killing ninety-six people. Certain details of that real-life incident are strikingly similar to the plot in *Atlas Shrugged*: a high-priority train was stalled for days at a town named Wellington (in the novel it's "Winston"); desperate passengers pleaded with railroad officials to move the train into the nearby tunnel (for shelter from the feared avalanche); railroad officials refused because of the danger of asphyxiation; as the two sides argued, railroad officials passed the buck and tried to evade responsibility; workers walked off the job in droves; and most of the passengers were killed soon afterward when the avalanche came to pass, sweeping the exposed train over the edge.

When the Wellington disaster was still part of living memory, plenty of people blamed it on Rand's heroes at the Great Northern Railway. The railroad was eventually absolved from charges of negligence by the courts. But Rand tells us in her famous 1961 essay, "America's Persecuted Minority: Big Business," that misdeeds by a corporation are not really something to worry about in the first place: "All the evils, abuses, and iniquities, popularly ascribed to businessmen and to capitalism, were not caused by an unregulated economy or by a free market, but by governmental intervention into the economy." Disasters that people blame on business will usually, upon scrutiny, turn out to be the responsibility of government.

And so Rand seems to rewrite the 1910 disaster in a way that demonstrates this faith. She sets it in the Rockies instead of the Cascades; there is no snow and no avalanche; and she completely reverses the power dynamics among management, government, and customers. In *Atlas Shrugged*, the railroad is always the victim. The reason its special locomotive isn't ready as usual to pull the train through the tunnel is because it's been commandeered by some grandstanding politician. The reason its employees keep melting away is not because they are paid poorly, as in the 1910 reality, but because of insane government rules that have taken all the joy out of life. One of the stranded passengers, meanwhile, possesses great political power; he is able to threaten top railroad officials and have the train proceed into the tunnel of desire just like the flesh-and-blood passengers of 1910 wanted. And then the passengers are suffocated for his insolence. Politics, in short, is what causes train accidents. Government does not protect passengers; it imperils them. If allowed to act on their profit-maximizing own, corporations would never endanger passengers' lives, much as those moochers deserve to be endangered.

For more on the Wellington disaster, see Ruby El Hult, *Northwest Disaster: Avalanche and Fire* (Portland, OR: Binfords and Mort, 1960) and Gary Krist, *The White Cascade: The Great Northern Railway Disaster and America's Deadliest Avalanche* (New York: Henry Holt, 2007). To get up to speed on the history of train wrecks, try Mark Aldrich's *Death Rode the Rails: American Railroad Accidents and Safety, 1828–1965* (Baltimore: Johns Hopkins University Press, 2006).

Chapter 9. He Whom a Dream Hath Possessed Knoweth No More of Doubting

1. The official being quoted is Sir John Gieve. "'Capitalism Is Still the Only Game in Town': Bankers and Regulators See Little Sign of Change," *Guardian Weekly*, August 13, 2010, p. 1.
2. The classic example is a March 19, 2003, *National Review* essay by David Frum, denouncing conservatives who weren't on the Iraq war bandwagon. Among their sins: "The websites of the antiwar conservatives approvingly cite and link to the writings of John Pilger, Robert Fisk, Noam Chomsky, Ted Rall, Gore Vidal, Alexander Cockburn, and other anti-Americans of the far Left." What makes this so striking is that Frum himself was ultimately pretty much expelled from the movement for his independent conservative ways.

   It is important to note that a handful of conservatives themselves, such as the blogger Julian Sanchez, have taken note of this phenomenon, which they mourn as a kind of "epistemic closure." See Patricia Cohen, "'Epistemic Closure'? Those are Fighting Words," *New York Times*, April 27, 2010.
3. Jill Lepore, *Whites of Their Eyes: The Tea Party's Revolution and the Battle over American History* (Princeton, NJ: Princeton University Press, 2010), p. 38.
4. The title for this chapter, "He Whom a Dream Hath Possessed Knoweth No More of Doubting," is the title of a poem by Shaemus O'Sheel; Murray Kempton comments on it at length in *Part of Our Time: Some Ruins and Monuments of the Thirties* (New York: Simon and Schuster, 1955).

5. Kempton, *Part of Our Time*, p. 155.
6. Ibid., p. 159.
7. Harvey Swados, *The American Writer and the Great Depression* (Indianapolis: Bobbs-Merrill, 1966), p. xviii.
8. Malcolm Cowley, *New York Times Book Review*, December 13, 1964, p. 5.
9. Kempton, *Part of Our Time*, p. 11.
10. Jerome Tuccille, *It Usually Begins with Ayn Rand: Revised and Updated* (Kindle edition, 2010), n.p.
11. After the crash, several bloggers compiled lists of economists and government officials who had pooh-poohed the idea of a housing bubble. Two useful lists can be found at http://economicsofcontempt.blogspot.com/2008/07/official-list-of-punditsexperts-who.html and http://bubblemeter.blogspot.com/search/label/Flashback.

    See also the November 2011 remarks of economist Dean Baker, one of the few who got the story right:

    > We have people who have literally been wrong about everything having to do with the economy over the last five years. They totally missed the $8 trillion housing bubble, the largest asset bubble in the history of the world. They were yelling about the budget deficit in 2006 and 2007 as the collapse of the housing bubble was about to explode the economy.
    >
    > Then they underestimated the severity of the downturn, telling us the economy was going to bounce right back. And then they got the interest rate story wrong. They told us that the large budget deficits caused by the downturn would lead the bond vigilantes to send interest rates through the roof. Instead they fell through the floor.
    >
    > So who gets listened to in national debates, those who have been consistently right on all the key points, or those who have gotten things as wrong as you possibly can?

    Read the rest at http://www.nakedcapitalism.com/2011/11/the-end-of-loser-liberalism-an-interview-with-dean-baker-part-ii.html.
12. See Frank Easterbrook and Daniel Fischel, *The Economic Structure of Corporate Law* (Harvard University Press, 1996), p. 283. The best-known advocate of market self-regulation was probably Alan Greenspan; in 1996 he reportedly told Brooksley Born of the Commodity Futures Trading Commission that there was really no need for laws against fraud of the kind she had proposed. (See the profile of Born in the March–April 2009 edition of the Stanford University alumni magazine by Rick Schmitt, "Prophet and Loss.") The *Financial Crisis Inquiry Report* extensively documents the consequences of this faith; see chapter 4 in particular.
13. Jim DeMint, *Saving Freedom: We Can Stop America's Slide into Socialism* (Nashville: Fidelis, 2009), p. 29. "The Siren Song of Socialism" is the name of the chapter in which this sad story is related.

14. Ibid., p. 29.
15. Gilbert Seldes, *Mainland* (New York: Scribner's, 1936), p. 394.
16. Ibid., pp. 394–95.

Chapter 10. The Silence of the Technocrats

1. As Christina Romer put it later in another context, "Policy would be better if we listened to the experts." On the other hand, I do not mean to single out Romer for this criticism. For professional economists to consider only the economic side of political questions is typical and perhaps even unremarkable.

   Romer's 2009 speech is available at http://www.brooking.edu/~ /media/Files/events/2009/0309_lessons/0309_lessons_romer.pdf. She made the comment about experts to the TV host Bill Maher in August 2011. See a recording of it at http://www.realclearpolitics .com/video/2011/08/06/christina_romer_on_credit_downgrade_ were_darned_fked.html.

2. Reviewing the persistent failure by the president to make his ideological case, the psychology professor Drew Westen wrote in 2011 that "Americans needed their president to tell them a story that made sense of what they had just been through, what caused it, and how it was going to end." Telling the story, Westen insisted, was not a detail that had been unfortunately overlooked; it was an essential part of the president's job. Drew Westen, "What Happened to Obama's Passion," *New York Times*, August 7, 2011.

3. See James Stuart Olson, *Herbert Hoover and the Reconstruction Finance Corporation, 1931–1933* (Ames: Iowa State University Press, 1977), pp. 51–60.

4. Quoted in ibid., p. 53.

5. James Stuart Olson, *Saving Capitalism: The Reconstruction Finance Corporation and the New Deal, 1933–1940* (Princeton, NJ: Princeton University Press, 1988), pp. 42, 44, 47. Jesse Jones with Edward Angly, *Fifty Billion Dollars* (New York: Macmillan, 1951), pp. 49, 70, 107, 110, 144.

6. Olson, p. 60.

7. Barack Obama, *The Audacity of Hope* (New York: Crown, 2006), pp. 113–14.

8. Ibid., p. 114.

Conclusion: Trample the Weak

1. Karl Polanyi, *The Great Transformation* (Boston: Beacon, 1957 [1944]), pp. 140, 73.

2. "Trample the Weak" is tea-partying Ted Nugent's summary of his political views. (It was also, apparently, the title for his 2010 tour.) See his editorial, "Trample the Weak, Hurdle the Dead," in the *Washington Times*, June 24, 2010.

Let Us Now Thank Famous Men

I did not take a geographic perspective when I began *Pity the Billionaire*, but looking back over it, I am struck by how many of the episodes I describe took place in Washington State, and how many of the book's characters are sons and daughters of the Pacific Northwest. I have no explanation for this coincidence, but it is probably appropriate that the idea for the book first came to me in the summer of 2009 as I drove down Washington Route 112 to Cape Flattery—the end of the world—listening on the car radio as a town hall meeting somewhere seemed to dissolve into a support group for the chronically suspicious. Later on, I wrote big pieces of the book in the old public library of Port Townsend, a place where I found it easy to get into the 1932 mood.

Several of the passages incorporated in this volume began as columns for the *Wall Street Journal*, and I am much obliged to the editorial team at the *WSJ* op-ed page for their help with the essays I published there. Another heaping of gratitude goes to the editors at *Harper's* magazine, who helped me with the passages that first saw daylight in that publication—also for allowing me to disappear into my book work at crucial moments. Thanks, also, to Lee Froelich at *Playboy*, who first got me thinking about Glenn Beck.

Bill Black and Jamie Galbraith gave valuable assistance as I tried to make my way through a set of economic issues that are, after all, distinguished by their power to confuse. Moe Tkacik helped in this regard as well, as did Kim Phillips-Fein. My research assistant, Annie Swank, was a whiz with the search engines. Chris Lehmann offered excellent editorial advice, as did David Mulcahey and Jim McNeill. Scholars Jacob Hacker and James Olson guided me through certain very particular problems. David Sirota offered a roof when I went to Denver to absorb some vox pop. Alexander Kelly came through with some important research at a crucial moment. And although I don't know anyone there personally, it was uncanny how many times I found myself starting with a clue I gleaned from the collection of right-wing ephemera compiled by Media Matters for America.

My wife, Wendy Edelberg, deserves the greatest appreciation of all for putting up with a solid year of my awful book-writing habits. Joe Spieler looked after my literary affairs with his usual ability. And Sara Bershtel and her colleague Riva Hocherman once again proved themselves the best editors in the business. This book would have been impossible without them. One of these days, I promise, I will write a proper set of acknowledgments and all of you will finally understand the obscure, mumbling gratitude of the scribbler.

Index

abortion, 9, 10n
Abramoff, Jack, 50, 78, 82–83, 114
ACORN, 41
AFL-CIO, 42
Age of Greed (Madrick), 56n
AIG, 32, 57–60, 171, 176
  bonuscs, 39–40, 151
Ailes, Roger, 52n
Alinsky, Saul, 131
American Dream, 96, 132
American Earthquake, The (Wilson),
  14
American Liberty League, 22
American Medical Association
  (AMA), 171
Americans for Prosperity, 78, 113
Americans for Tax Reform, 77
American Small Business League,
  99
American Spectator, 50, 141
"America's Ruling Class"
  (Codevilla), 141
antitrust laws, 101, 182
antiwar movements, 124–25
Appalachia, 42

*Arf! The Life and Hard Times of
  Little Orphan Annie* (Gray),
  146n
Argentina, 121
Arguing with Idiots (Beck), 74–75,
  89n
Armey, Dick, 1, 53, 78, 83, 130–31
Asness, Cliff, 110
Astroturf, 50, 130
Atlas Shrugged (Rand), 143–54, 162
Audacity of Hope, The (Obama),
  183–84
austerity, 180
auto industry, 13, 35, 87, 178n

bailouts, 85, 87, 157. *See also*
  banks; mortgage industry;
  Troubled Asset Relief Fund;
  Wall Street
  alternatives to, 32–34, 177
  conservative attacks on, 7, 38n,
  45, 48–59, 64, 74, 109, 139,
  151
  cronyism and, 176

bailouts *(continued)*
  Democrats and, 39–40, 49, 58,
    171, 174–82, 186
  FDR and, 176
  Wall Street aided by, 32–34, 106,
    169–68, 174–75
Baird, Brian, 86–88
bank holiday of 1933, 14–15
Bank of England, 156
banks. *See also* bailouts; investment
    banks; mortgage industry; Wall
    Street
  crisis of 2008 and, 3
  depositors and, 54
  Depression and, 14–16, 22, 24
  deregulation of, 3, 27, 37, 48,
    103–6, 111
  failure to break up big, 40, 181
  FDIC and, 192
  free market rhetoric of, 55–57
  incentives for bad loans by, 75,
    103, 105–6, 182
  minority lending and, 106
  recast as victims, 57–58, 106, 129
  regulations and, 29, 103, 105
Beale, Howard (fictional character),
    48, 52n, 158
Bear Stearns, 13, 32
Beck, Glenn, 39, 169
  on bailouts, 54–55, 57–59
  on capitalism vs. government,
    70–71, 74–76
  children's literature and, 89n
  on crisis as leftist plot, 63–65,
    122–24
  Depression culture and, 136–40
  doomsday warnings and rise of,
    61–63
  entrepreneurship and, 80–81
  on Europeans, 163–64
  health-care bill and, 66
  Howard Beale and, 52n, 158
  left mimicked by, 117–18
  Meet John Doe and, 139

  MLK and, 117, 131
  small business and, 96, 99
  Stewart protest vs., 186
  targeting by, 95n
Becker, Gary, 36
Beck University, 80n
Belgium, 166
Bernanke, Ben, 56, 178
Bernstein, Irving, 15, 132
Best and the Brightest, The
    (Halberstam), 183n
Bexley, Bruce, 93n
Bible, 85
big business, 99, 103, 108–15, 131,
    141
Big Business Watch, 114
Big Short, The (Lewis), 33n, 37
Bill of Rights, 83
bipartisanship, 176, 185
Black, William K., 71n
Blackwell, Ken, 39
Blankenship, Don, 93–94
Bloomberg news, 39–40
Blow, Charles, 5
Blumenthal, Sidney, 4
Boehner, John, 151
bond traders, 30–31, 45–47, 56, 72,
    93, 157
Bonus Army, 18, 95
bonuses, 29–30, 39, 46, 49, 58, 182
Bork, Robert, 20n
Boston Tea Party, 24–25
BP spill, 103, 107, 174–75, 183
Breitbart, Andrew, 118n, 188
Brinkley, Alan, 19
British Labour Party, 6–7, 164
"Brother, Can You Spare a Dime?"
    (Harburg), 132–34
Brown, Scott, 42
Bryan, William Jennings, 101, 170
budget, balancing, 92, 157
Bunch, Will, 79
Bunzel, John, 107
Burns, Jennifer, 144, 147n

Bush, George W., 3–4, 6, 62, 78, 94,
    119–20, 157
  Beck and, 117, 123
  crisis and bailouts and, 26–27,
    55–56, 171, 179
  regulation and, 103
  tax cuts and, 112
  wiretapping and, 182
business cycle, 167
business leaders. *See also* big
    business; small business
  Atlas Shrugged and, 144, 149–52
  crash of 2008 and, 38–39
  Depression and, 16–17, 19, 22
  as job creators, 98

Cain, Herman, 96
California, 52n
campaign contributions, 98, 113,
    173, 183–84, 189–90
Canseco, Francisco, 97
cap-and-trade proposal, 98
Capitalism (Beck), 71–72
capitalism. *See also* free market
  Atlas Shrugged and, 145–46, 149
  crisis of 2008–9 and, 156
  Depression and, 18
  GOP primaries of 2012 and, 189
  Right's defense of, 10, 82–83
  utopian, 69–76, 101, 104, 108–9,
    113–15, 168–69
capital strike, 145, 148–53
Capra, Frank, 139
card check, 97n
Carender, Keli, 172
Carnegie, Dale, 161
Cato Institute, 27, 77
Cheney, Dick, 5
Chicago, University of, 36
Chicago Board of Trade, 47
child labor laws, 190
children's literature, 89n, 167
Chile, 121

Chomsky, Noam, 118
Chrysler, 13
Churchill, Winston, 164
CIA, 2
Citibank, 56n
Citizens United, 189
Cleaver, Emanuel, 95n
Clinton, Bill, 96, 105, 178–81
Clinton, Hillary, 117
Cloward, Richard, 64n
CNBC, 35, 38, 46–47
coal miners, 93–94, 103, 107,
    152–53
Code Red rally, 91
Codevilla, Angelo, 141–42, 152
collateralized debt obligations, 29,
    76
colleges and universities, 2, 139
Commodity Futures Modernization
    Act, 111
common man, 11, 13, 19, 44, 47,
    72, 76, 92–98, 100, 136, 139,
    139–40, 149, 186. *See also*
    "forgotten man"; social classes
communism, 22, 131, 147n, 159–60
Community Reinvestment Act
    (CRA, 1977), 65, 75, 105–6
Conservative Action Project, 77,
    78n
ConservativeHQ (website), 78
Conservative Political Action
    Conference, 50
conservatives. *See* Right-wing
    revival
construction industry, 13, 15
consumer advocates, 82
Consumer Product Safety
    Commission, 103
Consumer Product Safety
    Improvement Act (2008), 104n
Continetti, Matthew, 128
Contract from America (2009–10),
    9, 69
Contract with America (1994), 2n

Coolidge, Calvin, 16–17, 176
Coughlin, Father Charles, 136
Council of Economic Advisers, 75n,
    174
Cowley, Malcolm, 160
CPAC, 126
credit-card rules, 78
credit default swaps, 10, 29, 48,
    58n, 70
Crimes Against Liberty (Limbaugh),
    129
Crist, Don, 96
cronyism, 108, 113, 176, 181
Culture of Corruption (Malkin),
    119–20
culture wars, 2n, 9–10

Daily Worker, 63
Daley, Bill, 180
Daschle, Tom, 130
"death panels," 67
debt-ceiling debate, 55, 98, 180,
    181, 191
debt securitization, 28
Declaration of Independence, 51n
Dedication and Leadership (Hyde),
    131n
deficit spending, 20, 50, 135n,
    174
DeLay, Tom, 82–83, 117
DeMint, Jim, 96, 165–66
democracy, 69, 150
Democratic Party
    bailouts and, 40, 49, 58, 186
    banks and, 27
    Beck vs., 58–59
    Depression and, 23
    donors and, 175, 183–84
    election losses of 2010, 8
    health-care reform and, 66,
        86–90, 174
    labor unions and, 184–82
    laissez-faire and, 2

Obama and, 35–36
    populist outcry not heeded by,
        170–86
Denning, Michael, 132
deregulation, 2, 4, 10, 27, 29, 34,
    36, 42, 49, 52, 56, 103, 143,
    153, 157, 166
derivatives, 29, 36, 49, 70
disaster relief, 192
DLA Piper firm, 78, 130
Dodd, Chris, 40
Dodd-Frank financial reform bill,
    129
"Don't Tread on Me" flag, 41, 50,
    127
Don't Tread on Us (Karis), 10n
"Down with Big Business" (Ryan),
    108, 110, 113, 180
Drucker, Peter, 16
Dukakis, Michael, 183
Duke, C. Jesse, 69–70, 92

earmarks, 98
economic growth, 132n
economic orthodoxy, 3, 16, 19–22,
    26–27, 163
education, 183, 185
"Effect of Falling Home Prices on
    Small Business Borrowing,
    The" (Schweitzer and Shane),
    102n
elections
    of 1937, 23
    of 2008, 35, 103, 166, 170–68
    of 2010, 5, 8, 10, 42–43, 85n, 94,
        155, 180, 182
    of 2012, 189
electoral system, 120
elites, 7, 78. See also "ruling class"
Emanuel, Rahm, 123, 180–81
End of Economic Man, The
    (Drucker), 16
Enron, 112, 191

entrepreneurship, 79, 91, 95–103,
110–11, 144, 148–49. *See also*
small business
environmentalism, 82, 93, 113, 166
Environmental Protection Agency
(EPA), 102, 113
Erickson, Erick, 67

Failure of Capitalism, A (Posner), 36
Fair Labor Standards Act (1938),
190
Fannie Mae, 32, 58n, 64, 71n, 75
farmers, 23–25, 54, 111
Farmers' Holiday Association, 23, 24
Farm Security Administration, 135n
fascism, 130, 136. *See also* Nazis
Federal Deposit Insurance
Corporation (FDIC), 14, 192
Federal Emergency Management
Agency (FEMA), 124
federal regulatory agencies, 31, 34,
103, 174. *See also* deregulation;
regulation; *and specific*
agencies
Federal Reserve, 29, 32, 36, 58n,
64, 106, 177–75
Fed Up! (Perry), 165
Ferguson, Charles, 167n
Financial Crisis Inquiry Report,
75n, 106
financial crisis of 2008, 3–4, 26, 31,
34–40, 63–65, 105–6, 117,
122–24, 129, 155–56, 163,
169–67, 175, 185. *See also*
bailouts; Wall Street
minority lending and, 103n
populist response to, 35–38, 52
utopian capitalism as response to,
73–76
Flatt, Dickey, 111
food stamps, 190
Forbes, 38, 108, 113
Forbes, Steve, 69–70, 72

"forgotten man," 42, 100, 132,
137–38, 176–74
Forgotten Man, The (Shlaes), 132n
Fox, Justin, 37
Fox News, 39, 52n, 54, 59, 61–62,
77, 88, 123, 159
France, 166
Frank, Barney, 58n
Franklin, Benjamin, 41, 81n, 82
Freddie Mac, 32, 58n, 71n, 75
Freedom Works, 77–78, 130–31
free market, 2–3, 9–12, 27–28,
36–37, 55–56, 92, 94, 108–9,
113, 121–22, 139, 143, 155,
167. *See also* capitalism
Democrats and, 183–84
deification of, 68–76, 78, 108–9,
163–65, 187
effect of unregulated, 187–88
free trade, 2, 27, 110, 182, 185
Frum, David, 5
Fukuyama, Francis, 4
"Fundraising Secrets for Tea Party
Leaders" (DVDs), 81

Galbraith, John Kenneth, 20
Galt, John (fictional character),
148–53
Geithner, Tim, 129, 171, 177–75
General Electric (GE), 114
General Motors, 13, 178n
"Get Back" flag, 91–92
Ghostbusters (film), 103
Gingrich, Newt, 2n, 23, 52n, 66–67,
77, 109, 118, 189–90
Give Us Liberty (Armey and Kibbe),
130
Glass-Steagall Act (1933), 177
Glenn Beck Program, The (TV
show), 85
"God Save the Queen" (Sex Pistols),
133
Gohmert, Louie, 21n

Goldman Sachs, 30, 32, 105, 175
gold standard, 153
GOOOH, 84–85
Graham, Michael, 127
Gramm, Phil, 111
Grapes of Wrath, The (Steinbeck),
    147n
Gray, Harold, 146n
Great Britain, 164
Great Depression, 37–38, 98, 157,
    165, 187–88
    Atlas Shrugged and, 143–54
    attack on "ruling class" and,
        140–43
    Beck and, 136–39
    culture of, mimicked by Right,
        132–37
    hard-times scenario and, 14–18
Great Northern Railway, 154n
Great Recession, 3, 13–14, 165,
    170, 179, 190–91
Greenberg, Stanley, 159
Greenspan, Alan, 27–28, 36, 42
Gregoire, Christine, 88
Guantánamo, 68
Guardian Weekly, 155, 159
Gullett, Charly, 125
Guthrie, Woodie, 146

Halberstam, David, 183n
Hannity, Sean, 88, 93
Hanson, Stephen D., 96
Harburg, Yip, 134, 132
hard-times scenario, 11
    Crash of 2008 and, 34–41
    Depression and, 17–25, 34
    disavowed by Democrats, 179–80
    mimicry of, by Right, 11–12,
        64–65, 98–99, 119, 131, 134,
        135, 147, 165
    Occupy Wall Street and, 188–89
Hard Times (Terkel), 18
Hayek, Friedrich, 164

Hayworth, Nan, 98, 112
health-care industry, 64, 129,
    171–72, 191
health-care reform, 36, 96, 104, 120
    Democrats and, 171–73
    Right attacks on, 64, 66, 129
    town halls and, 86–87
Hearst, William Randolph, 22, 38,
    137
hedge-funds, 29, 31, 110
Hedrick, David W., 86–90
Heritage Foundation, 77
Hill, Napoleon, 161
Hodgson, Godfrey, 2
Home Affordable Modification
    Program (HAMP), 45n
homeowners, 45–46, 102n, 121
Hoover, Herbert, 18, 20, 23, 25, 43,
    145, 176–74
housing bubble, 37, 75n, 76, 163
How Capitalism Will Save Us
    (Forbes), 69
*How to Win Friends and Influence
    People* (Carnegie), 161
Hussein, Saddam, 123
Hyde, Douglas, 131n

iCaucus, 85
IndyMac, 13
inequality, 167. *See also* 99 percent
inheritance tax, 111
Inside Job (documentary), 167n
Insull, Samuel, 135n
insurance industry, 129, 171, 173
intellectuals, 92–94
Internet, 9, 62, 159
internment camps, 124–25
investment banks, 28–29, 37–38,
    41, 70, 177–75, 180, 190–91
Iowa, 23–24
Iran-Contra, 82
Iraq, 121, 123, 157
Italy, 166

Jackson, Andrew, 170
Jarvis, Howard, 52n
Jefferson, Thomas, 41, 100
job creators, 59, 98–100, 112, 130,
    151
Job Creators Caucus, 98
JOBS Act, 179, 190
Joe the Plumber, 50
"John Doe in Post-9/11 America"
    (Malkin), 139n
John Doe Movement, 139n
Johnson, Ron, 144
Jones, Jesse, 177–75
JP Morgan Chase, 32, 105

"Kahane, David" (pseudonym),
    118–19
Kempton, Murray, 159–61
Kennedy, Ted, 42
Kerpen, Phil, 78
Keynes, John Maynard, 16, 19–20,
    37
Kibbe, Matt, 53, 130
King, Martin Luther, Jr., 41, 62,
    117, 130
Kirk, Mark, 97
Klein, Naomi, 121–22
Koch, Charles, 37
Koch brothers, 78, 112–13, 128, 140
Kreuger Ivar, 145
Krugman, Paul, 37
K Street Project, 31, 82

Labor Department, 78
labor unions, 2–3, 18, 41, 73, 82,
    90, 97n, 101, 110, 125, 149,
    168, 184–82, 188–89
laissez-faire, 2, 7, 9–10, 15–16, 20,
    22, 49, 73
Left, 48–49
    fear of, 37, 63–65, 124–25, 136
    mimicry of, by Right, 116–22, 131

Lehman Brothers, 13, 32
Lepore, Jill, 159
"Lessons from the Great Depression"
    (Romer), 132n, 174
"let the failures fail," 20, 49, 52–55,
    68
Lewis, John, 95n
Lewis, Michael, 33n, 37
Liberal Claus, The (Hedrick), 89–90
liberalism, 4, 63–65, 101, 114–15,
    175, 181
libertarians, 28, 37–38, 132, 150
Liberty XPO, 80
Limbaugh, David, 129
Limbaugh, Rush, 5, 66, 141
limited-capitalism model, 74
Lincoln, Abraham, 182n
liquidationists, 20, 25, 53
Little Orphan Annie (comic strip),
    146
lobbyists, 31, 83, 113, 120n, 130
Long, Huey, 19, 136
Lucas, Robert, 36
Ludwig von Mises Institute, 132

"Machine, The" (advertisement), 59
Madrick, Jeff, 2, 56n
Making of GBTV, The (video), 80n
Malkin, Michelle, 50, 119, 139, 143
"Manifesto of Individualism"
    (Rand), 147n
March on Washington (1963), 62,
    117, 131
Marianas Islands sweatshops, 130
Marx, Karl, 72–73, 141
Massey Energy, 93
Matthews, J. B., 159–60
McCain, John, 35
McCarran Act (1950), 125
McCarthyism, 134
McElvaine, Robert, 18, 132
Media Research Center (MRC), 159
Medicare, 180, 191

Meehan, Pat, 102
Meese, Ed, 77, 78n, 125
Meet John Doe (film), 139
Mellon, Andrew, 20, 132n
Mercury Radio Arts, 63, 80n
Mercury Theatre, 63
Merrill Lynch, 13, 35
Michael Moore Is a Big Fat Stupid White Man (Hardy), 120
Milbank, Dana, 62
Mills, C. Wright, 110, 113
Mises, Ludwig von, 150
monopolies, 70, 163, 185
Moore, Stephen, 57
Morgan Stanley, 106–7
mortgage-backed securities, 33n, 58n, 104
mortgage industry
  foreclosures and, 25, 32, 75, 157
  lack of regulation of, 36, 103
  Santelli and, 45–47, 50
  subprime, 28–29, 58, 64, 75n, 105–6, 191
  underwater homeowners and, 45, 101n
Mount Vernon Statement, 78n
MSNBC (cable TV channel), 114
Murdoch, Rupert, 139
Muse (rock band), 163
"My Papa is a Capitalist" (Beck), 89n
Myth of the Rational Market, The (Fox), 37

NAACP, 118n, 182n
Nation, 64
National Aeronautics and Space Administration (NASA), 71n
"National Day of Strike," 114–15
National Economic Council, 40
National Federation of Independent Business (NFIB), 97, 102
National Journal, 43

National Labor Relations Act (1935), 190
National Review, 180
National Review Online, 118
National Tea Party Convention (Nashville, 2010), 79, 82
Nation's Business, 16
Nazis, 65, 87–90
Nazi-Soviet Pact, 160
Nebraska, 23
neoliberalism, 2, 103
net neutrality, 78
Network (film), 48, 52
New Deal, 22–24, 38, 134–35, 165, 167
Newsweek, 4, 5, 38–40, 156
  "socialism" cover, 38–39
New York magazine, 41
New York Times, 5, 62, 97, 151
9/11, 54n
9/12 Project, 81, 138
912 Citizens, Inc., 79
99 percent, 94, 189
Nixon, Richard M., 11, 120
Norquist, Grover, 77, 82, 140
Norris, Chuck, 83
North American Free Trade Agreement (NAFTA), 111, 182
Nugent, Ted, 93

Obama, Barack, 94, 98–99, 132
  Atlas Shrugged and, 143, 152
  bailouts and, 52, 55, 59
  campaign donors and, 40, 183–84
  conservative depictions of, 10n, 46, 52, 55, 59, 66, 89, 118–21, 129, 155, 158, 166
  debt-ceiling debate and, 180
  elections of 2008 and, 4–5, 9, 35–36, 38–39
  elections of 2010 and, 43, 191
  elections of 2012 and, 190

health-care reform and, 65–66, 104, 171–74
Iraq War and, 123
populist outcry not heeded by, 40, 170–71, 174–85
regulation and, 103–4
small business and, 100n
Obama, Michelle, 120n
"Obama's Enemy List," 120
Objectivism, 27–28, 162
Occupational Safety and Health Administration (OSHA), 102
Occupy Wall Street, 41, 188–89
Official Tea Party Handbook (Gullett), 125
O'Hara, John, 78
oil industry, 10, 103, 105, 174–75, 182, 185
oligopolies, 70
one percent, 94
"Out with the Ruling Class" (watch party), 140
Overton Window, The (Beck), 123–24, 140

Paine, Tom, 41
Palin, Sarah, 79–80, 128, 140
Parker, Kathleen, 5
Part of Our Time (Kempton), 159–60
Patman, Wright, 21
Patriot Act, 120, 182
Patriot's Club (website), 89
"Patriots Qualification Cards," 89n
Paul, Rand, 54, 59, 144
Paul, Ron, 190
Paulson, Hank, 32–33, 56–57, 178
Pelosi, Nancy, 87, 120
pension funds, 13, 19
Perry, Rick, 165, 190
Persecution of Sarah Palin, The (Continetti), 128
Phillips, Tim, 140

Piven, Frances Fox, 64n
Pizzella, Patrick, 78
Playboy, 109
Polanyi, Karl, 187–88
Politico, 4, 144
Pompeo, Mike, 79, 112–13, 144
positive thinking, 161
Posner, Richard, 36–37
privatization, 2, 27, 103
Prohibition, 18
proletarian fiction, 146–48
Proposition 13, 52n
public schools, 192
public works, 98, 135n

Quayle, Ben, 120

racism, 8, 130, 182
railroads, 145, 154n, 168, 176–74
"Rallies for America," 123
Rally to Restore Sanity, 186
Rand, Ayn, 27–28, 42, 143–54, 157, 162
ratings agencies, 33n
rattlesnake symbol, 81n
Rauchway, Eric, 132n
Reagan, Ronald, 2, 4, 52n, 56, 77, 100, 103, 124–25, 165
Real America, The (Beck), 63n
Reconstruction Finance Corporation (RFC), 176–74
Redeclaration of Independence, 85
Red State Uprising, 59
regulation, 78, 92–94, 103. *See also* deregulation; and specific agencies
attack on, 3, 7, 37–38, 41–42, 102–8, 139
Depression and, 22, 177
enforcement and, 185
financial crisis and, 29, 31, 58n, 167n

regulation *(continued)*
  Obama and, 35–36
  Rand and, 143, 154n, 162
  utopian capitalism vs., 72–76
Republican Party, 2, 79
  big business and, 110
  elections of 1994 and, 43n, 103
  elections of 2008 and, 35, 39
  elections of 2010 and, 42–43, 88,
    97–98, 113, 155
  expectations of, in 2008, 4–7
  TARP and, 49
  presidential primaries of 2012,
    67, 109, 165, 189–90
  Tea Party and revival of, 42–43
Return of Depression Economics,
  The (Krugman), 37
Rivera, David, 99
Road to Serfdom, The (Hayek), 164
Romer, Christina, 132n, 174–75
Romney, Mitt, 109, 126, 189
Roosevelt, Franklin, 3, 5, 18, 20,
    22–23, 43, 134–35, 145, 157,
    165, 167, 170–71, 185, 192
  Beck and, 137
  "forgotten man" and, 132, 176–77
  Obama and, 36
  RFC and, 176–75
  Ryan and, 180
Rothenberg, Stu, 5
Rubin, Robert, 27
Rules for Radical Conservatives
  ("Kahane"), 118–19
"ruling class," 140–43, 152
Rush Limbaugh Is a Big Fat Idiot
  (Franken), 120
Ryan, Paul, 108–10, 113–14, 130,
    144, 180

same-sex marriage, 9
Samuelson, Robert, 38
Santelli, Rick, 44–51, 52n, 72, 77,
    93, 144, 158, 189

Santorum, Rick, 190
Saving Freedom (DeMint), 165
Schlesinger, Arthur, 134
Schwarzenegger, Arnold, 52n
Schweikert, David, 144
Schweitzer, Mark, 101n
Securities and Exchange Commission
    (SEC), 29, 177, 191
Seldes, Gilbert, 167–68
Sex Pistols, 133
Shane, Scott, 102n
Sherrod, Shirley, 118n
Shlaes, Amity, 132
shock therapy, 121–22
Slouching Towards Gomorrah
    (Bork), 20n
"Small Business Bill of Rights," 97
small business. *See also*
    entrepreneurship
  bailouts and, 103–5
  big business vs., 108–9
  Democrats fail to capture outrage
    of, 181
  failure and, 32
  as front for big business, 110–15
  health reform and, 104
  housing crisis and, 102n
  job creation and, 98–100
  as ordinary Americans, 92–98
  populist heroism and, 100
  regulation and, 102–4
Small Business Week, 100
social classes. *See also* common man;
    Country Class; "Ruling Class"
  class war and, 38–39
  Depression and, 19
  99 vs. one percent and, 94, 189
  obfuscation of, 92–94, 140–43,
    149
social insurance, 98
socialism, 38–39, 56, 66, 68, 82, 101,
    108, 112, 125, 155–56, 165–66
socialist realism, 147n
Social Security, 180, 190, 192

software industry, 185
Soviet Union, 66, 147n, 160, 164
Spread This Wealth (Duke), 69, 92
"Star Spangled Banner," 84
state governments, 29, 40
Steinbeck, John, 147n
Stewart, Jon, 35, 186
stimulus, 35, 98–99, 126, 174–75
Strange Death of Republican
    America, The (Blumenthal), 4
strikes, 18, 125, 145, 148–53
Summers, Larry, 27, 40, 171, 178
SuperPACs, 109, 189, 190
supply-side revolution, 2, 157
Susman, Warren, 18
Swados, Harvey, 160
Sweden, 166

Taibbi, Matt, 104
TARP. See Troubled Asset Relief
    Program
taxes, 2n, 22, 42, 98, 108, 111, 139,
    153, 165
Tea Party, 21n
    anti-Obama rhetoric of, 120–21
    Atlas Shrugged and, 143
    big business and, 109
    confusion over ideology of, 117–15
    conservative institutions and,
        77–78
    costumes and, 84
    health-care reform and, 172
    Kochs and, 112–13
    manifesto of 2009, 68–69
    mimicry of left by, 131
    Network and, 158
    populist anger of, 41–42, 182
    presidential primaries of 2012
        and, 189
    profiteering and, 79–82
    protests of 1930s vs., 25
    rallies by, 41, 49–53, 62, 66
        77–78, 83–84
    ruling class and, 140
    Santelli rant and, 47
    self-segregation by, 159–57
    small business and, 95–96, 104,
        112–15
    social issues and, 102
    victimhood and, 94–95, 126–31
Tea Party Express, 83
"Tea Party Manifesto" (Armey and
    Kibbe), 53
Tea Party Movement, The (Bexley),
    93n
Tea Party Patriots, 9, 89n
Terkel, Studs, 18, 21
terrorists, 21n
Thatcher, Margaret, 6–7, 121
That's No Angry Mob (Graham), 127
Think and Grow Rich (Hill), 161
Thomas, Norman, 38n
Time, 27, 35, 62
"too big to fail," 33, 40
To Renew America (Gingrich), 67
To Save America (Gingrich), 67
Town Hall Summer, 41, 85–90, 130,
    171–69, 183
trade policy, 181–82
Trader Monthly, 30–31, 47
Transcending Time with Thomas
    Jefferson (Hanson), 96
Treasury Department, 32, 57, 106,
    113
Troubled Asset Relief Program
    (TARP), 32, 45, 48–49, 52,
    106n, 113, 126, 178–79
Truman, Harry, 171, 172
Tuccille, Jerome, 162
Twilight of Sovereignty, The
    (Wriston), 56n

Uhler, Lewis, 67
Ukraine famine of 1932, 160
unemployment, 13, 15, 17–19, 32,
    37, 54, 86, 98–99, 186, 132n

U.S. Army, 2
U.S. Chamber of Commerce, 76, 103
U.S. Congress, 32, 35–36, 42–43,
    58n, 66, 90, 94, 96–98, 112–14,
    144, 191
U.S. Constitution, 22, 51, 65, 83,
    85, 87
U.S. House of Representatives, 23,
    36, 42–43, 85, 97, 113, 180, 191
U.S. News & World Report, 4
U.S. Post Office, 2
U.S. Senate, 42
U.S. Supreme Court, 189

Vallee, Rudy, 133
Veblen, Thorstein, 150–51n
Verizon, 112
Vietnam War, 2n, 133, 183n
Viguerie, Richard, 78, 81–82,
    106–7, 140
Virginia Tea Party Convention
    (2010), 84
Voight, Jon, 66

Wachovia bank, 13, 32
"Wallison and the Three De's"
    (Black), 103n
Wall Street (financial industry).
    See also bailouts; banks; bond
    traders; financial crisis of
    2008–9; investment bankers;
    mortgage industry
    bailouts of, 32–34, 39–41, 176–77
    blame shifted from, 40–41,
        44–48, 56–57, 65
    bonuses and, 29–31, 39–40
    compensation levels, 40, 177
    Depression and, 4, 16, 177
    deregulation of, 4, 28–29, 112, 163
    Main Street vs., 112
    Obama and, 40, 171, 178–79,
        181–82, 190

power of, 34, 190–91
    scandals of 1980s and, 185
    self-pity and, 129
    TARP and, 49
    Tea Party as protection for, 42,
        112–10
    truculent attitudes of, 28–31
Wall Street Journal, 143
Walsh, Michael, 118
"War of the Worlds" (radio drama),
    63n
Washington, D.C., September 12,
    2009 rally, 79, 81. See also
    9/12 Project
Washington Mutual, 13
Washington Post, 5, 9, 27, 42, 47,
    62, 78, 113
Weekly Standard, 128
Welles, Orson, 63n
We Read the Constitution
    movement, 85
West Virginia Labor Day rally, 93,
    152
We the Living (Rand), 147n
Weyrich, Paul, 117
What Can I Do? (Crist), 96
Wilentz, Sean, 2, 4
Williams, Mark, 182n
Wilson, Edmund, 14
Wilson, Woodrow, 56, 136, 157
Wisconsin protests of 2011, 188
Wizard of Oz (film), 137
Works Progress Administration
    (WPA), 98, 132
World War I, 18, 136, 181
World War II, 87, 165
Wriston, Walter, 56n

YouTube, 48, 88

Zaitchik, Alexander, 63n
Zuccotti Park, 188–89